Housing and Public Policy

STEWART LANSLEY

CROOM

331-833

BZ43795

©1979 Stewart Lansley
Croom Helm Ltd, 2-10 St John's Road, London SW11

British Library Cataloguing in Publication Data

Lansley, Stewart
    Housing and public policy.
    1. Housing policy – Great Britain
    I. Title
    301.5'4'0941   HD7333.A3

    ISBN 0-7099-0052-X
    ISBN 0-7099-9953-8 Pbk

Printed and bound in Great Britain by
Redwood Burn Limited, Trowbridge & Esher

CONTENTS

TABLES AND FIGURES

Tables

Figures

ACKNOWLEDGEMENTS

Many people have contributed, directly or indirectly, to this book. It would not have been possible to write it without the numerous discussions I have had individually and collectively with friends and colleagues about the housing question and current policy and without the stimulus received from having had access to their work and ideas. I am particularly grateful to Graham Crampton and Martin Smith both of whom read an earlier version of the manuscript and made many helpful suggestions. Guy Fiegehen also made useful comments on Chapters 1 and 3. Any failure to incorporate their ideas reflects the ubiquitous constraint of time as much as any disagreement with their comments. In addition, I have benefited by having seen unpublished papers by Bernard Crofton, David Griffiths, Tony Humphris, Bernard Kilroy and David Webster. I also wish to express my personal thanks to Fiona Metcalfe for her continuous support and encouragement. Finally, I would like to thank Jenny Barten, Francesca Buxton, Nancy Massey, Sheila Stace and Libby Wilson, who between them converted my handwritten and untidy scripts with great care and patience into an accurate typed manuscript. Naturally, all responsibility for the text lies fully with the author.

Stewart Lansley
Centre for Environmental Studies
Winter 1978

INTRODUCTION

Housing has long been an area of central and local government concern and this reflects its vital importance for both individual and social welfare. Since the beginning of direct intervention during the First World War, successive governments have accepted that the state has an important role to play in housing provision, state involvement has grown, and an increasing proportion of public expenditure has been spent on housing. Despite this, housing remains a major problem area of social and economic policy. While housing standards have risen on average, significant sections of the community continue to endure poor housing conditions and prospects.

Throughout the history of intervention, government policy has been the subject of outspoken criticism both from the Right for trying to do too much, and from the Left for doing too little or adopting ineffective policies. Today housing policy remains an area of vigorous political debate. Differences of view abound about both the nature of the current housing situation and the role of government. An increasingly popular view is that major housing problems have been largely solved, that we now enjoy a surplus of houses, that housing problems however severe for some people are mainly residual in nature limited to special circumstances and a relatively small number of areas such as inner cities. In this view, these remaining problems do not require large scale investment in new building, but a combination of locally based policies and better allocation and management of the existing stock. An alternative view is that existing problems are more deep rooted, that shortages exist in many areas, that new needs are arising especially in the form of increasing obsolescence in the private rented stock and in older public housing estates and that housing progress depends upon the maintenance of a high level of state investment in new building and improvement, together with fundamental changes in the structure of housing finance.

Alongside these differing explanations of the current situation, there are major differences in policy outlook. On the one hand there are those who continue to argue for the reinstatement of free market forces by the dismantling of the state housing apparatus, while on the other there are those who advocate greater government control but of a different kind from that which has developed in order to ensure that efficient and just use is made of housing resources. Some have called for

13

cuts in housing subsidies, others for higher subsidies, some for an expansion in public housing investment, others for less public and more private investment. Some have argued for the revival of the private landlord while others have called for the absorption of privately rented property into an expanded public sector; others have called for an increasing role for housing associations and other forms of tenure. There is an increasingly strong voice in favour of the widespread sale of council houses against the opposition of those who support the maintenance and expansion of the role of the local authority sector. In some areas of housing policy, on the other hand, there is greater agreement about the direction of policy such as the need for changes in the management of local authority housing to give tenants more firmly based rights and greater powers of participation. Between the leadership of the two main political parties, though by no means generally accepted, there appears to have emerged a convergence of view that owner-occupation is somehow the 'natural' form of tenure that should be encouraged. This is certainly a view that seems to have been endorsed in the present Labour Government's recent Green Paper on Housing, and some have interpreted this apparent consensus to mean that Labour governments as well as Conservative ones would be prepared to preside over the rundown of the local authority sector to a somewhat residual role.

The emphasis of this book is on the role of public policy in housing. In particular, it examines the case for government intervention in housing markets, describes the problems that such intervention is designed to resolve and presents a critical review of the forms that past intervention has taken. It aims to provide an analysis of the relevance of past and present policies and their alternatives to the nation's housing problems and needs, and considers the main current and future housing issues facing the government and the nation.

While critical throughout of the form that intervention has sometimes taken, its basic theme is that the achievement of housing objectives is dependent upon extensive local and central government involvement, but that such involvement should have taken a different form from that which has evolved. The book therefore makes no claim to political neutrality. In this, it is not different from most other books on the role of government in housing, many of which have adopted the alternative stance of opposition to government intervention. In recent years opposition to the state provision of some goods and services has been gathering force largely as a result of the growing influence of the Institute of Economic Affairs and its stream of output aimed at undermining the role of the 'welfare state' and backing the dismantling of our public services and the reinstatement of market forces. This book aims to provide a counter view to those who argue with increasing frequency that market forces should have freer if not free reins in shaping housing development.

The book also sets out to challenge a number of strands of current conventional wisdom many of which have been reinforced by Labour's housing Green Paper. It argues that housing problems are far from being nearly solved and far from being residual in character. New policies are needed not just to deal with remaining and newly emerging physical problems, but to tackle the many inequalities that pervade our housing provision. Too many of our policies in the past have had the net effect of widening not narrowing inequalities. Such problems depend for their solution on major changes in our housing finance system which is riddled with anomalies and inequities, which reinforces inequalities, and which is wasteful of scarce resources.

The book is not intended to be a textbook on the economics of housing. Nevertheless, since the shaping of policy has too often ignored or been ignorant of underlying economic forces, the importance of economics to an understanding of the nature and significance of housing policy will be emphasised throughout. In particular, considerable attention is given to the role of housing finance because of its critical importance in determining housing provision.

Chapter 1 examines the role of government intervention in housing markets in guaranteeing an adequate supply of housing and its fair allocation. Chapter 2 considers the nature of underlying market forces in housing, how these operate to determine house prices, and the nature of supply and allocation in the local authority rented sector. Chapter 3 presents a brief outline of housing progress since the Second World War, and then provides an appraisal of the current housing situation and the objectives and problems of current housing policy. Chapter 4 summarises the financial arrangements operating in each of the three main housing sectors, and reviews the accounting arrange-ments underlying public expenditure on housing and its trend in recent years. Chapter 5 discusses the impact of our system of housing finance on the level and mix of housing investment and on house prices and the distribution of subsidies between households within and between different sectors. It concludes that the system of housing finance which has developed has been both inefficient and inequitable. Chapter 6 examines the current tenure structure, the future role and development of each of the three main housing sectors, the case against the sale of council housing, and the role of housing associations and alternative forms of tenure. Chapter 7 presents a critical examination of Labour's housing Green Paper, rejects its support for the *status quo* in existing financial arrangements and argues for a series of fundamental reforms in housing finance as a prerequisite for promoting greater equity and efficiency in housing provision. Chapter 8 concludes with an analysis of past and current policy towards housing improvement and the inner cities and argues for a very different emphasis in policy.

1 THE ROLE OF GOVERNMENT

Housing in Britain is subject to a great variety of forms of government intervention and control. This reflects the widespread acceptance of the importance of housing in private and community life and the view that, left to itself, the free operation of the price mechanism would be unable to meet housing objectives. Successive governments in Britain and in most developed nations have taken the view that housing is, up to a point, a social responsibility and should not be left entirely to the free play of market forces. Indeed, over the course of this century, the role of the state in the field of housing has steadily increased. Originally only concerned in the nineteenth century with the public health consequences of bad housing and the laying down of basic standards, intervention has developed since the First World War to cover the regulation of the market through subsidies and through controls of various kinds on building societies and private landlords, and through the direct provision of housing.

Nevertheless, it is easy to exaggerate the extent of government involvement in housing. Even today, after a century of growing intervention, and despite a diversity of planning, social and financial arrangements, the bulk of housing provision remains outside the public sector. Approximately 70 per cent of the housing stock remains privately owned by owner-occupiers or private landlords and at least half of new building and improvement is undertaken as a result of private decisions. This contrasts with other areas of social policy such as education and health where governments have adopted a much more comprehensive and embracing approach. Housing hovers somewhat unhappily between the status of a social service and a private good.

In common with all areas of social and economic policy, the role of government intervention in housing has been and remains a matter of controversy. Different governments have intervened in different ways and have had different views as to the degree of intervention and control that is desirable. Outside of government, views have ranged from those who would support less or even no public intervention, on the one hand, to those who have urged a much more exhaustive role. Because of the importance of the question of the role of government in past and future housing issues, this book begins in this chapter with a discussion of the principles involved in and the objectives underlying housing policy and the place for central and local government in facilitating the achievement of these objectives.

In general, housing policy has been concerned with both the size and quality of the housing stock — the supply objective — and its distribution — the equity objective. The supply objective is concerned with producing an adequate level of investment in housing, while the equity objective relates to the distribution of that investment. One government White Paper, for example, has described the basic aim of housing policy as: 'a decent home for every family at a price within their means, a fairer choice between owning a home and renting one, and fairness between one citizen and another in giving and receiving help towards housing costs'.[1] Governments have therefore been concerned with ensuring that housing of a minimum standard is provided to all households and that housing resources are distributed fairly.

These objectives are, of course, too imprecise as they stand for determining policy. In particular they offer no guidance as to what constitutes 'a decent home', 'a price within their means' or 'fairness between one citizen and another'. Moreover, they leave open the question of the nature and degree of intervention necessary to meet the aims. This chapter considers the question of the importance of government involvement while the questions of standards and housing costs are left to later chapters.

It is possible to identify three broad views about government intervention. First, that housing markets should be allowed to operate freely with little or no intervention. Secondly, that there is a substantial role for both public intervention and the private market, with governments involved in setting standards, in providing subsidies, in exercising control over housing agencies such as building societies, and in the direct provision of housing, with private forces having free rein within these constraints. Thirdly, that there should be a much more comprehensive role for government, with a more extensively controlled and socialised market. Very broadly, Britain's approach to housing policy has tended to fall into the second category.[2]

This chapter looks at the principles underlying government intervention, at the form such intervention can take and at the contrasting views about the need for such intervention. It begins with a brief discussion of the case for a free market in housing. A more detailed description of the way housing markets operate is given in Chapter 2, while the remainder of the book takes up in more detail the form that intervention has taken in the past in Britain, its relevance to housing problems and the future role of government intervention.

A Free Market in Housing

Many would still argue that the supply and distribution of housing
should be left to the price mechanism, with the state playing only a
minimum role, confined, for example, to the encouragement of private
housing provision and possibly slum clearance and subsidising those
who, through lack of income, cannot afford some minimum standard of
housing in the private market. The economic case for the free market in
the production and distribution of a good rests on the argument that
the market provides an efficient way of allocating scarce resources by
directing productive factors into the supply of those goods and services
which are most in demand. Given scarce resources, a society faces three
sets of choices relating to what goods and services should be produced
and in what quantities, how the goods and services should be produced,
and how they should be distributed among consumers. The first two
sets of choices constitute the problem of the allocation of resources,
and the third the problem of distribution. Advocates of the free market
are usually particularly concerned with the efficient allocation of
resources which is said to occur when resources are being used to produce the goods and services most preferred by society and when it is
not possible to reorganise production so that more goods and services
can be produced with the available resources. Proponents of the free
market argue that, under certain conditions, the price mechanism leads
to efficient production in the sense of maximum output for given
resources, to an optimum distribution of resources between outputs and
to an optimum allocation of output between consumers.

A basic proposition of neo-classical welfare economics is that under
conditions of perfect competition, markets distribute resources
between outputs, and outputs between individuals, in such a way as to
maximise social welfare. Under a market system of production and
allocation, for a given distribution of income, individuals demonstrate
their consumption preferences by buying goods up to the point at
which the benefit obtained from purchase of the last unit equals the
price paid. In so doing individuals maximise their own individual
welfare subject to their income or budget constraint. Profit-
maximising producers, on the other hand, will employ factors of
production up to the point where the additional cost of production
is equal to the price they can obtain for the additional unit of
output. The market system brings these two separate and distinctive
groups of consumers and producers together through the price
mechanism, with prices operating as signals or indicators to each group.
An increase in the preferences of consumers for a particular good, for

example, will lead to an increase in demand and so an increase in price which will indicate to producers that it may be worth while to expand output. Similarly, an increase in price resulting from a change in the conditions of production may indicate to consumers that they should adjust their consumption patterns.

In this way, the price mechanism is said to ensure that resources are distributed among productive activities in a way that matches consumers' own preferences. The process is efficient in the sense that output is maximised given available resources. But markets are also seen to satisfy a particular view of equity, because the free market responds to individual consumer choice and emphasises consumer sovereignty; the process is said to be equitable because the efficient bundle of goods produced is allocated in line with the distribution of preferences.[3]

Advocates of a free market in housing claim the same advantages as those outlined above. In particular, they argue that resources would be employed in the production of housing in such a way as to maximise output for given inputs and to ensure that the proportion of a society's total resources devoted to housing as opposed to other goods would correspond with the distribution of society's preferences between housing and other goods, i.e., the market would produce an optimum stock of housing. Equally, because individuals would choose how much to spend on housing, the distribution of the resulting stock would correspond with the structure of preferences among the individuals, i.e., markets produce an equitable allocation. The market in this way is seen as satisfying both the supply and the equity objective. As one proponent of the free market in housing has put it:

> Advantages accrue to consumers when it is possible to organise a competitive market for a commodity. If there are no restrictions on price, consumer choice, or the entry of new producers or sellers, a strongly competitive market will ensure that the size, quantity and quality of houses that are built, and the distribution of the existing stock, will be dictated by the tastes, incomes and preferences of households.[4]

Moreover, supporters of the market, whether in full or in a more limited way, tend also to take the view that housing problems can be traced mainly to the distorting impact of successive government intervention on the working of the market. For example, the theme of one recent book on housing by Stafford, *The Economics of Housing Policy*, is that 'the "housing problem" is very largely the cumulative effect of the damaging and self-defeating policies of successive governments'. Throughout the book, the virtues of the free market are emphasised and the arguments for government intervention sternly dismissed. In Stafford's view, the solution to remaining housing problems requires the 're-creation of housing markets based on consumer preference rather than political predilection and bureaucratic control'.[5]

The Case for Government Intervention

The fundamental case for state intervention in housing is that market forces alone would provide neither an adequate stock nor its fair distribution.[6] There are two basic elements to the case for intervention. First, housing is characterised by a number of distinctive characteristics which means that the market does not work in the smooth functioning way that it is claimed to do for other goods and so would not produce a socially optimal level of output nor an equitable distribution of that output.[7] The basic problem here lies in the presence of a number of market imperfections. Secondly, even if intervention were to correct for such imperfections in order to promote an efficient allocation, the market would still produce an unacceptable distribution of housing resources.

The principle of equity embodied in the market view of the working of the economy — that output is distributed in accordance with consumers' own preferences — has two major weaknesses. In the first place, the distribution of market-expressed preferences depends upon the existing distribution of income. A free market would be unable to provide housing of a socially-acceptable level to those with low incomes because they have insufficient voting power in the market. Secondly, even if the distribution of income could be made less unequal, there are other views of equity than that contained in the consumer-sovereignty outlook which would emphasise the importance of housing resources being distributed less unequally than the ability to pay for them. In this section, these arguments for government intervention are considered in more detail. The characteristics of housing that create imperfections in the market are considered first and then the problems created by income inequalities.

The Characteristics of Housing and Market Imperfections

Housing is characterised by a number of imperfections which impair the efficiency of the pricing mechanism and prevent an optimal allocation of resources. Some of these imperfections arise as a result of the special characteristics of housing which prevent the market from operating in the smooth functioning way that the markets for other goods are generally expected to do. In the first place, housing is a highly hetero-geneous good. Houses differ in age, size, repair, quality, amenities, location and conditions of occupancy. There is therefore no single market for housing but a very large number of separate though related markets.

Another distinctive characteristic of houses is that they are durable and last much longer than ordinary consumer goods and most other consumer durables. Houses last from between 40 and 100 years. Local authorities amortise their housing stock over a period of 60 years, the assumed life of dwellings. As at December 1974, 18.3 per cent of the housing stock in Britain was built before 1890, and 33.4 per cent before 1918.[8] The purchase of a house therefore represents a combina-tion of the purchase of housing services and a way of saving. When a person buying a house on a mortgage has repaid the loan, he becomes the owner of a capital asset which may have many useful years of life left. In contrast, there is no investment element in the rent paid by a tenant.

Further, the cost of housing is very high in relation to income, and houses cannot generally be purchased straight out of income. In 1976 the average new house price of £13,650 represented a ratio of 3.9 of average annual earnings of £3,482. Because houses cannot generally be purchased straight from income, or from accumulated savings, the capital cost of houses has to be financed in other ways, either by direct purchase from money borrowed by the occupiers, or by renting from private or public landlords who finance the capital cost. The operation of the housing market is therefore closely related to the supply and availability of finance and hence to the finance market, changes in which can have a dramatic effect on house prices and the level of building.

Another peculiar feature of housing is its relatively high transaction costs, the buying and selling of houses involving advertising, agents' commission, legal charges, survey fees and moving costs. Further, occupants are subject to powerful subjective ties to their homes. These act as a discouragement to mobility, they slow down the response in market conditions, and encourage under-occupation.

Inelastic Supply. An important characteristic that prevents the housing market from operating like other markets is the low elasticity of supply of housing.[9] The supply of housing responds very slowly to changes in the determinants of supply, and the provision of an adequate quantity of housing would therefore take a long time if left to the market.[10] This is mainly because of the nature of the building process which depends upon a long, complex chain of activities, ranging from the initial decision to build, to the acquisition of land, to the obtaining of planning consent before building begins, as well as the actual construction. These stages can take a considerable time. Supply is also inelastic because of the immobility of homes which cannot move between areas and regions in response to changes in market conditions. A housing surplus in one area can therefore coexist with homelessness and the occupation of inadequate housing in another. Land shortages also operate as a constraint. Because of this sluggishness in supply and the durability of houses, the *stock* of houses is very large in relation to the annual *flow* of new housing. For example, Table 1.1 shows that in 1972, the net addition to the stock of houses (completions less demolitions) in England and Wales of some 220,000 represented only 1.2 per cent of the total stock of 17.2 million, and even in 1967, a peak year with a net gain of 294,000, this only constituted an increase of 1.7 per cent.[11] To increase the stock of housing by 10 per cent would take between seven and eight years at current building rates.

Table 1.1: House Building and Improvement, England and Wales (thousands)

Year	Completions			Slum Clearance	Improvements Grants Approved
	Private Sector	Public[a] Sector	TOTAL		
1967	193 (53%)	170 (47%)	363	69	113
1968	213 (57%)	158 (43%)	372	70	114
1969	173 (54%)	150 (46%)	324	68	109
1970	162 (53%)	145 (47%)	307	60	157
1971	180 (58%)	129 (42%)	310	71	197
1972	185 (64%)	103 (36%)	287	66	319
1973	174 (66%)	90 (34%)	264	64	361
1974	130 (54%)	112 (46%)	241	42	231
1975	140 (50%)	138 (50%)	278	49	127
1976	138 (50%)	140 (50%)	279	48	126

Note: [a]Local authority, new towns, housing associations.
Source: Department of the Environment, *Housing and Construction Statistics*.

Any sudden change in the level of housing demand is therefore likely to be reflected in changes in house prices rather than the supply of housing. The impact on supply of such changes, as discussed in Chapter

2, will only make its effect in the medium or long run, if at all, and we do not have a clear idea of the size or lag in this impact.

Nevertheless, while the total stock of dwellings is fixed, and supply is relatively unresponsive to changes in price in the short term, utilisation of the stock, which is another important aspect of supply, may be more responsive. Thus if house prices and rents rise, a small family living in a large house might decide that it is worthwhile to convert part of their house and sell or lease it. Conversely, if housing is cheap, they may prefer to retain the extra space. Price therefore operates as an allocative device.

In contrast, the demand for housing is much more volatile. Housing demand, as we shall see in Chapter 2, depends in the main on the rate of household formation, and hence on trends in the size and demographic structure of the population, on income levels and the cost of housing, on the availability of house purchase finance and on the level of rents in the public and private rented sector. Any of these factors can change relatively suddenly and fluctuations in demand tend to have their main effect in fluctuations in house prices. The major explanation for the rise in house prices in the period 1971 to 1973 is found, as argued in Chapter 2, in the rise in demand caused by rising incomes, an increase in the rate of household formation and the increased availability of building society mortgages. From 1974 to 1976, house prices fell quite sharply in real terms, largely because of the corresponding fall in demand.

Figure 1.1 shows the impact of an increase in demand from D^0 to D^1. The immediate impact of the increase in demand is a rise in price from P_0 to P_1, given a perfectly inelastic short run supply curve S^s and a static supply of dwellings, N_0. In the longer run, the rise in demand may increase supply. If the long run supply curve is given by S^L, equilibrium will be restored with an increased supply N_1 and a slight fall in prices to P_2 from the immediate rise to P_1. The final impact of the increase in demand is a rise in price to P_2 and in supply to N_1.

In a freely operating market, housing shortages in the economic sense would not persist, because any excess demand that might arise would be met in the short term by a rise in house prices and rents which would choke off the excess demand and restore equality between supply and demand. The market solution to a housing shortage would be to allow prices to rise sufficiently to ration the available stock, encouraging a more intensive use of the existing stock in the short term and an increase in housebuilding only in the long term, if at all. Excess

Figure 1.1: The Impact of an Increase in Demand

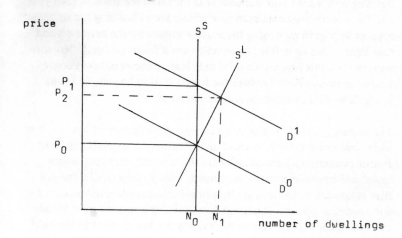

demand would be eliminated but not social need. A serious objection to allowing the market to operate in this way is that it is the least affluent who would suffer from the effect of shortages and be forced into over-crowded conditions paying higher rents than they could afford. More-over, because supply is highly inelastic even a large rise in price may not call forth an increase in supply. Even a small shortage could have the effect of causing a steep rise in prices, provide large gains for existing poperty owners and increase the difficulties of lower-income groups obtaining adequate accommodation.

It is sometimes argued by advocates of the free market that the 'filtering' process whereby houses vacated by households moving to better newly-built accommodation are released to lower-income groups ensures that free market forces would be able to provide housing for the poor. Supporters of filtering claim that building highly-priced houses helps households in need, not because they can afford to move into such dwellings, but because such new building generates a back-ward chain of movements allowing the upward movement of whole groups of households who thereby improve their housing situation. The main weakness of the filtering process is that at the best it works very slowly and many of the vacancy chains are broken before the poor benefit to any significant degree. We have already seen that new building only adds 1 to 2 per cent at the most to the stock in each year and there is evidence that such new private sector building has its greatest impact in improving the space occupied by the better-off and that little of the benefit is passed on to less affluent groups.[12] Moreover, unmitigated, this process would simply lead to the permanent concentration of poorer households in the lowest quality housing and thus has 'indefensible distributional consequences'.[13]

The Impact of Bad Housing. Another important feature of housing is its wider impact upon other areas of an individual's and community's life. Housing conditions have an influence upon health, attitudes, educational and employment opportunities and the quality of life. Inequalities in housing conditions are in turn reflected in educational, cultural and economic opportunities, and poor housing is restricting to social and individual welfare. Moreover, housing is a key element in the total environment, affecting regional planning and the attractiveness of our cities and countryside. Housing therefore concerns not merely the individual but society at large.

This aspect of housing is part of the wider phenomenon of externalities. Externalities in economics arise whenever there is a divergence between private and social costs or benefits. In general, because free market forces only respond to private costs and benefits, the free market would not lead to an optimal allocation of resources in a situation where a private activity imposes social costs or generates social benefits.[14] In such circumstances, government intervention is justified on purely economic grounds to ensure that resources are allocated in an optimal way.

Externalities in housing arise in various ways. First, in the context of urban decay. Individual housing neglect can affect neighbours and the immediate community by imposing social costs on other local residents. The urban decay to which this can give rise can be a cumulative process that escalates once properties in a particular neighbourhood begin to deteriorate, causing better-off inhabitants to move out and poorer households to move in. These processes are only too evident in many inner city areas. In general, the private market will not be able to deal with this problem and public action is required. The combination of uncertainty and interdependence in decision-making are at the roots of such urban decline. If a neighbourhood is suffering from blight, property owners have a choice of maintaining their property or allowing it to deteriorate. Since the value of property is partly determined by the condition of the surrounding area, the owner's choice is influenced by what he thinks other owners will do. If all, or a high proportion of properties in the area are rehabilitated, then property values would rise by more than enough to compensate each owner for his maintenance expenditure. If only one or a few owners invest, however, the neighbourhood would not be sufficiently upgraded to ensure a large enough rise in values to compensate for the outgoings. Individual owners are therefore unlikely to undertake improvement unless they are confident that other owners will do the same, and, once begun, area deterioration is unlikely to be arrested by private decision. The problem is only soluble through co-operation to remove the element of uncertainty.[15] It is also a problem which is compounded by the typically limited resources of households in such areas and their limited access to capital. These constitute further barriers to neighbourhood improvement.

To reverse such neighbourhood decline, therefore, public intervention is required to reduce this uncertainty by encouraging and stimulating improvement activity. This is the underlying justification for improvement grants and loans, the provision of local athority powers of compulsory improvement and purchase, and area improvement strategies in the form of general improvement and housing action areas. Urban renewal policies of these kinds aim to overcome local uncertainty, create greater confidence and improve resource allocation by reducing social costs and improving the quality of neighbourhoods.

While private residential renewal is not in general a feasible one, there have been examples of where semi-independent private forces have started to arrest and reverse such area decline through the process that has become known as 'gentrification'. This is the process whereby relatively low-income households such as manual workers and their families previously living in relatively cheap albeit substandard or deficient property either owner-occupied or privately rented, have been displaced by better-off households moving into the area. Such processes have led to improvement in local housing conditions in areas that may have previously been rundown but at the social cost of the eviction of some existing residents and the general restriction of the housing opportunities of lower-income groups. Studies undertaken for the Milner Holland Committee on *Housing in Greater London*, for example, showed that in the early 1960s private renewal — whether wholesale redevelopment or rehabilitation — generally led to a

remarkable rise in prices; the progressive transfer of housing stock from renting to owner-occupancy; the reduction in net occupancy rate and density as individual households replace multiple occupation; and the alteration in socio-economic structure as the population changes from mainly working class to mainly upper middle class.[16]

During the early 1970s such processes became more widespread especially in the more fashionable parts of inner London, such as Kensington, Islington and Clapham, partly as the result of the availability of higher improvement grants and the General Improvement Area policies introduced in the 1969 Housing Act and partly as the result of the boom in property values at that time which made it increasingly profitable for landlords to obtain vacant possession and sell. Property values in such areas increased dramatically and there was evidence of 'increasing pressure and near harassment of existing tenants in order to secure vacant possession [causing] great insecurity even among unfurnished tenants'.[17] The supply of cheap accommodation to let in such inner city areas was further eroded adding to the difficulties of the lowest-income groups in obtaining access to the housing market in the centre of cities.

Another source of externality arises from the impact of housing conditions on wider aspects of family and community life and well-being. At the roots of public involvement in housing is the recognition of the importance of housing in human welfare and that housing constitutes more than just shelter. As Rasmussen has stated, 'Basic needs must be satisfied before people desire higher order needs . . . If the need for safety and security is clearly related to the quality of living environment, good housing is a prerequisite for realizing one's full potential.'[18] Traditionally, concern about housing conditions has centred around the effect of poor housing on physical and mental health and safety — on the incidence of disease, illness and accidents. Gradually, such concern has extended to the relationship between inadequate housing and educational and job opportunities, delinquency and crime and other aspects of social and personal life such as family stability and self-respect and recreational opportunities. Bad housing conditions in this context refer not just to deficiencies in individual dwellings such as inadequate sanitary facilities, lack of space, bad ventilation and dampness, but also to the whole neighbourhood which may be characterised by high densities, lack of amenities and excessive traffic.

The view that poor housing is an important cause of ill-health, educational and occupational disadvantage and crime has long been at the basis of the justification for government intervention to raise the level of housing provision above its natural private level especially for lower-income groups. Nevertheless, such relationships are extremely complex and, while there has been no lack of analysis and study of the social and personal consequences of substandard dwellings and neighbourhoods, and there is extensive documentation by social and community workers, environmental health officers and doctors about such relationships, it is sometimes argued that such evidence as does exist is somewhat inconclusive.

Numerous studies have been undertaken.[19] One longitudinal study based its findings on the effect of the transfer of slum dwellers to a large public housing project in Baltimore. The results indicated the existence of a positive association between better housing and improved social and psychological activity in the case of some social disorders such as child morbidity rates, but not for others such as children's school performance.[20] The problem with such longitudinal studies is that they tend to measure not just the effect of improved dwelling conditions but also the effect of a new situation including such factors as unfamiliar surroundings, possible segregation and other elements connected with moving to new housing estates. A review in 1964 of existing studies pointed to the numerous correlations indicating positive associations between poor housing and individual and social disorder, and concluded that while 'the connecting links between poor housing and poor health are well understood', the role of housing in delinquency, mental illness and illegitimacy is less clear.[21] It has also been argued that poor housing is an important cause of poverty in the longer term, or at least helps to maintain poverty, via its effect on health, pessimism and passivity, poor household management and inability to handle stress.[22] In Britain, evidence to the Milner Holland Committee on *Housing in Greater London* by the Medical Officer of Health for Kensington and Chelsea pointed to the relationship between mental and physical health — bronchitis, pneumonia, persistent severe colds and mental stress — and bad housing.[23] Other evidence from the National Children's Bureau's report *From Birth to Seven* (1972) suggests that overcrowding in a child's home has the effect of retarding reading age by nine months at the age of seven.[24]

Such studies have been criticised because they pinpont statistical associations and not real explanations; correlation does not necessarily imply causality.[25] Nevertheless, despite the lack of firm evidence, few researchers would actually deny that there is a relationship between bad housing and individual and social ills. As Rothenberg has argued, 'the external social costs allegedly generated by slums probably exist but it is extremely difficult to find out even roughly how important they are.'[26]

To the extent that ill health, crime and lack of opportunity are associated with poor housing, together with the effect on the household concerned, poor housing imposes indirect costs on society at large in the form of greater public spending on, for example, medical services' and crime prevention. There is widespread evidence that urban renewal tends to reduce the demands on medical, police and fire services. Intervention is therefore justified purely on the grounds of the wider savings to society from housing improvements. This emphasises the interdependence between different forms of social policy in meeting social objectives. As one commentator has put it,

> housing can be seen as an in-put into the other social services. Good housing conditions can, arguably, contribute as much to improving health or education as more doctors or teachers. Providing tailor-made flats for the elderly and disabled . . . can help to sustain these vulnerable groups as self-supporting members of the community, instead of dependent users of residential accommodation. From another point of view housing can be seen as a generator of demands on other forms of public expenditure. High-rise flats, for example, may add to the cost of maintaining law and order.[27]

Finally, it is important to emphasise the relative nature of housing standards. In defining poor housing, society takes as its yardstick the average housing conditions found in that society. Equally, a family's own perception of their housing situation is closely determined by the typical housing conditions enjoyed by the majority. As a result, those living in relatively substandard housing will be vulnerable to feelings of demoralisation, anger, despair and lack of self-respect. It has long been accepted that poverty is in essence a relative concept, that minimum acceptable living standards should be determined in the light of those applying within a particular society at a particular point in time. The Royal Commission on the Distribution of Income and Wealth, for example, has pointed to the evidence received that a poverty standard 'is now generally accepted as a standard which changes with the general standard of living of society; and therefore the fixing of minimum needs cannot be absolute or immutable.'[28] Equally, minimum acceptable housing standards need to be based on prevailing housing conditions. Because the expectations of households are determined by the housing standards enjoyed by others, major inequalities in housing provision can cause social stigma and shame among the poorly housed.

These considerations — the importance of good housing to the health, attitudes, opportunities and quality of life of individuals and communities — imply that housing has special characteristics which mean that its consumption should be encouraged. To the extent that consumer ignorance or lack of information about these external benefits will prevent consumers from making well informed decisions about the desirable level of housing consumption, government intervention is required, say, in the form of a general subsidy, to prevent under-consumption.

A third form of externality is associated with the type and location of housing. Left to themselves, free market forces might lead to unacceptable design and location of residential dwellings, quite unrelated to access to amenities, jobs and transport, and to environmental considerations such as density levels, congestion and nearness to factories or major roads which may be unsightly or noisy. To ensure adequate location and design, numerous planning regulations have been introduced.

Housing and Income Inequality

A second important argument for government action arises from the need to compensate for poverty and inequality in the distribution of income. In a free market, the extent to which housing need will be met depends upon the population's capacity to pay and its preferences, and hence the relationship between the level and distribution of income and the cost of housing. The high cost of housing and the unequal distribution of income has meant that significant sections of the population would have been unable, without assistance, to afford the full economic price of decent accommodation. In 1961, for example, assuming a maximum expenditure on housing of 25 per cent of income, Needleman estimated that two-thirds of households could still not afford to pay the economic rent of a new house and something like 90 per cent could not afford to buy a new house.[29]

The consequence of this inequality and the inability of the poor to exercise effective housing demand is that the private market, left to itself, would produce a very unequal distribution of housing resources. Housing space would be allocated according to the distribution of income and individual preferences. For a given set of preferences, income inequality would mean that in a housing shortage the rich can always outbid the poor for the available supply. Given 96 houses of equal quality and 100 families, for example, and each family wanting a house, the most likely market outcome would be about 92 families with the highest incomes with one house each, leaving the poorest 8 families to share 4 houses. Alternatively, with variations in quality, the poor would end up living in dwellings of the lowest quality. In a market situation, the distribution of houses would tend to match the distribution of ability to pay — housing inequality would reflect income inequality. Even advocates of the free market such as Friedman and Stigler have recognised that 'under free market conditions, the better quarters will go to those who pay more, either because they have larger incomes or more wealth, or because they prefer better housing to, say, better automobiles'.[30]

The housing problems that would be faced by lower income groups in the absence of government intervention are well illustrated by the actual working of the relatively free housing market in nineteenth-century London. It has been argued, for example, that

> The housing problem in Britain in the nineteenth century provides a clear example of the inability of a capitalist free market in housing to provide satisfactorily, if at all, for those at the bottom of the pile in income and occupational terms.[31]

During the nineteenth century, London and other major industrial centres evolved from essentially residential to commercial and industrial areas resulting in widespread demolition, homelessness and overcrowding. The various solutions applied to this problem at the time, ranging from the clearance of poor housing, the building of model dwellings by philanthropic organisations such as the Peabody and Guinness Trusts, the introduction of sanitary legislation to check overcrowding and the housing schemes of Octavia Hill aimed at encouraging self-help and thriftiness among the poor, all proved ineffective.[32] The basic problem remained that the cost of adequate housing was too high in relation to wage levels at the time. As one commentator has noted:

> With the wages artisans and labourers were earning, the basic economic factors were clearly at the root of the overcrowding situation. Yet contemporaries were slow to awaken to the fact that the housing problem was part of a greater poverty problem . . . the will to believe in the efficacy of free market capitalism to solve most social problems was still immensely strong.[33]

Because of the important social and economic consequences of poor housing, and the implications of major inequalities in housing provision, housing policy has aimed to ensure a minimum level of housing provision for all, independently of income, and that high rent and housing costs are not a cause of poverty. Since the free market would be unable to provide decent housing for low-income households, governments have intervened in a variety of ways with the object of ensuring that such households enjoy better accommodation than they would otherwise have been able to afford. Such intervention is an acknowledgement that the social need for housing differs markedly from economic demand based on ability to pay to which market forces respond. If the level of housing provision is to be determined on the basis of meeting need, of course, some method of defining minimum standards is required. In attempting to respond to need other than demand, governments have therefore had to take a view about the standard of housing to be provided and at what price. Need, however, is not a concept entirely independent of the conventional economic concept of demand. Housing demand depends on the average level of affluence and the price of housing, and the adoption of a relative measure in determining minimum standards means that average housing conditions influence the social concept of need. The various conventions that have been developed about such standards are discussed in Chapter 3 where the success of governments in meeting need is examined more closely.

Governments have used a variety of methods to try and improve the housing situation of lower income groups. Policies have included rent control, the provision of public sector housing at subsidised rents, and rent rebates and allowances. In consequence, the association between poverty and bad housing has been partly broken. The poor are less concentrated in the poorer end of the housing market than might otherwise have been the case and high rent is no longer a major cause of poverty. Nevertheless, as we shall see in Chapter 3, the link has by no means been completely broken; there is evidence that the poor, on average, live in inferior accommodation – that those with the lowest incomes are also often those with the worst housing. We still have two nations in housing. Governments have been more successful in expanding the supply of housing than in reducing inequalities. Indeed, the policies adopted by governments, as we shall argue in Chapters 3 and 5, have often contributed to and accentuated such inequalities.

What Forms Can Intervention Take?

A free market in housing would therefore provide neither an adequate stock of housing nor its equitable distribution. But there remains the question of the form that public intervention should take. The aims of housing policy underlying government intervention are to ensure an adequate supply of housing of some minimum quality, at a cost that lower income groups can afford; and to ensure equity in housing provision between tenures and between households in each tenure, in order to produce a genuinely fair choice in housing. There are a number of forms that intervention could take in order to meet these objectives.

Subsidies to Demand

First, there are subsidies to demand. These can be rent or interest subsidies and have the aim of shifting the demand curve for housing by encouraging higher housing expenditure. They can take the form of a 'general' subsidy to all households or more selective subsidies to particular households by income or tenure. A 'general' subsidy might take the form of a housing allowance or voucher which could be used to help pay for accommodation.[34] They can be introduced in the context of other controls on the housing market, or allow a free market to operate in all other respects. Most advocates of such schemes assume a free market otherwise, with rents and house prices determined by supply and demand conditions, and justify them on the grounds of externalities or income deficiency, and that such subsidies interfere least with market processes.

The main disadvantage of demand subsidies aimed at reducing individual housing costs and stimulating supply is that, in the absence of wider controls, the effect and the beneficiaries of such subsidies will be determined by the prevailing conditions of supply and demand. The actual incidence of the subsidy may in consequence differ from what is intended. Given the inelastic supply of housing, such that house prices and rents are largely demand determined, subsidies will increase prices before they affect output and will therefore be of main benefit to existing home owners, landlords and land owners. Even in the longer run, higher house prices may have only a marginal impact on new construction if the main beneficiaries have been landlords rather than builders. Demand subsidies to owner-occupiers raise the price of owner-occupied dwellings above open market prices unless the long run supply of owner-occupied housing is perfectly price elastic, which is most unlikely. Such schemes on their own may therefore be partially if not wholly self-defeating.

Alternatively, subsidies may take more specific forms, by being directed to particular households only, by tenure or income. Giving subsidies to houses or households of a particular tenure can only be justified on the grounds of the particular benefit offered by that sector. Providing subsidies to households by income level in order to overcome the problem of income inequality raises the question of whether guaranteeing some minimum level of housing to low-income groups can be best achieved by general policies of income maintenance, by specific income-related subsidies, or by the direct public provision of subsidised housing. Those who favour a free market system in housing usually support general income subsidies. Indeed, it can be shown, theoretically, that rent or interest subsidies are less efficient than income subsidies in terms of consumer welfare, though specific housing subsidies, via their influence on relative prices, do generate greater housing consumption than income subsidies.[35] The practical disadvantages of using income subsidies to encourage housing consumption by the poor are considerable, however. Clearly, a more effective anti-poverty policy that also reduced inequalities in income would enable the less well-off to consume a more equal share of housing resources and reduce the additional help needed specifically for housing. Nevertheless, the extent of redistribution effected through general policies of income support has never been and is never likely to be sufficient on its own to create an effective demand for housing of a good quality by low-income households. Indeed, it has been shown that, over the 20-year period 1953 to 1973, there was little change in the distribution of household income, and little change in the extent of relative poverty.[36] Moreover, low-income households would still be likely to consume less housing than is desirable on the grounds of externalities and the beneficial characteristics of good housing. This is partly because there is no guarantee that households will spend sufficient of the additional income on housing. How much they would spend depends on their preferences which are expressed in the income elasticity of demand for housing and this may be less than that of higher-income households.[37] Even if their income elasticity is in the region of unity, an increased demand for housing, in the absence of additional controls, may simply result in a transfer of income to landlords or house owners, as argued above.

Specific assistance for housing would therefore be required even in the context of more effective income support programmes. General ways of relieving poverty cannot deal with wide variations in housing costs, and lower-income households with higher costs, for example, would continue to require assistance if their overall living standard is not to suffer. Improving the purchasing power of the poor does not necessarily improve their ability to secure decent housing.

Subsidies to Supply

Alternatively, financial aid can take the form of subsidies to supply. Direct subsidies to builders, public or private, involve subsidising the house rather than the household, and the intention is to reduce the house price to the buyer or the rent to the tenant and expand output by shifting the supply curve to the right. This approach has the effect of expanding supply directly and so does not suffer from the weakness of general demand subsidies which may increase prices rather than output. Nevertheless, the effect of the subsidy depends on the elasticities of demand and supply. Since short-run supply is relatively inelastic, the subsidy may lead to only a small reduction in price and a small increase in output and may therefore be of main benefit to builders or landowners. Another objection to supply subsidies is that by subsidising the house rather than the household, aid is not directly related to household income and this can lead to inequity between tenants in different financial circumstances. The main beneficiary of the subsidy is the household who lives in the house and pays less than the market price, irrespective of its need or income.

The justification for the direct provision of houses by public authorities is that this is more effective in providing for need than the use of subsidies to promote demand or encourage private supply. The advantage of the direct public provision of housing is that it guarantees a supply of housing that might otherwise not have been provided and poses less of a problem with respect to the incidence of subsidies. Such housing can also be allocated on the basis of need rather than ability to pay and rents set at levels which it is felt that tenants can afford. By by-passing normal market processes, access to decent housing at reasonable cost is improved. As we shall see in Chapter 3, the provision of public housing has been the main factor by which the association between poverty and bad housing has been weakened in Britain. In the past, public housebuilding has tended to be particularly encouraged at times when it was felt that the private market would be unable to meet housing shortages or would divert housing resources away from those most needing help, such as in the periods following the First and Second World Wars. At other times, the role of council housing has been a matter of greater controversy and in general, the share of public sector completions in total building has been greater under Labour governments and local authorities than Conservative ones.

Subsidies in Britain

The existing system of housing finance is considered in detail in
Chapter 4 and only a summary is presented here. In Britain, there have
been a variety of subsidies both to demand and supply. It could be
argued that VAT and purchase tax exemption and also domestic rate
relief have constituted forms of general subsidy to all households. Since
before the Second World War, local authorities have provided housing
at rents subsidised by the central government and by local rates, and in
1972, the Housing Finance Act introduced a national scheme of rent
rebates such that local authority tenants are now subsidised somewhat
indiscriminately by the taxpayer and ratepayer in general subsidies and
less indiscriminately through rent rebates. Subsidies have also been
provided to owner-occupiers, though what precisely constitutes their
subsidy has been a matter of controversy. These subsidies have represented a direct boost to demand for owner-occupation and it is arguable
that while the impetus to demand has led to an increase in new
building, part of the effect has also been felt in higher prices, in an
increase in under-occupation and in the decline of the private rented
sector. The private tenant has never been the recipient of a direct
subsidy from the state except recently in the form of rent allowances.
Landlords have been treated unfavourably for tax purposes in
comparison with owner-occupiers, who have been exempt from
Schedule A taxation since 1963 and are exempt from capital gains tax.
The main remaining form of subsidy has been to landlords and owner-
occupiers in the form of improvement grants designed to maintain an
adequate level of modernisation and improvement.

Another form of intervention used has been rent control. The main
objective of rent control has been to protect tenants from the high rents
that would result from shortages in rented accommodation. Rent
control operates by specifying a maximum rent that landlords can
charge for a dwelling. Provided the maximum rent is less than the
market rent, rent controls involve a direct subsidy from the landlord
to the tenant, equal to the difference between the market rent and the
controlled rent. To the extent that rent control causes excess demand,
some rationing device other than price is needed to allocate the available supply of dwellings, and an entry price in the form of 'key money'
has sometimes developed. Moreover, in the longer run, the reduction in
rents, while helping low-income tenants, may discourage the supply of
homes for renting. Rent control over privately rented houses was first
introduced as a temporary measure during the First World War and has
remained in one form or another ever since. The precise impact of these

various forms of control is the subject of controversy and is considered in more detail in Chapter 4.

Planning Policy

A further instrument used by public bodies has been planning policy. In this way, governments and local authorities can control housing developments in the interests of public health and safety, to guarantee minimum standards of design and workmanship, and to ensure adequate densities and amenities. Such intervention can be justified on the basis of controlling the externalities associated with development and the problem of lack of information. Further, planning policies can provide public bodies with active powers to initiate and undertake development of various kinds, perhaps in partnership with private developers, particularly when such schemes provide social benefits and which would not otherwise be undertaken. Such schemes can cover large-scale projects such as shopping centres to smaller-scale environmental improvement such as landscaping and tree planting.

Public policy which has the effect of regulating or limiting individual freedom by planning restrictions on development, encouragement of Green Belts and conservation, is justified on the grounds that it benefits the community as a whole. The main problem of planning controls is that, given a largely free market in other areas, the benefits and costs of such controls may well be unevenly borne. Private and public developers, owners of land and owners of houses can all be closely affected by planning decisions. One of the unintended effects of controls on office building in central London by the Labour Government of 1964, for example, was to make millionaires of those who already owned office buildings or who had already obtained planning permission.[38]

Similarly, one of the consequences of policies which have the effect of limiting the supply of land is to increase land values and so benefit landowners at the expense of private and public developers of land and those on to whom they pass the costs. This is one of the explanations for the fact that land prices have generally risen faster than other elements of the cost of building houses, though planning controls are not the only cause of high land prices.[39] Land prices are determined like the prices of other goods by the supply and demand for land, and an increase in the demand for property, such as during the boom period of the early 1970s, leads to additional demand for land and so bids up its price. The price of land is therefore a reflection of the demand for its use. The price a developer will pay for land is the difference between the cost of building and the price he expects for his property on the open market — the residual valuation. This is not to argue against the need for planning controls but to emphasise that given a mixture of government control and free enterprise the consequences of such controls can be very complex and original objectives can sometimes be thwarted or other policies affected.

Summary

In summary, the main planks of government housing policy since the Second World War have been the encouragement of owner-occupation through a variety of aids and concessions, varying forms of rent control and protection in the privately rented sector, and the promotion of local authority building through various subsidies. Within these broad areas the strategies of individual governments have differed in emphasis and approach. Labour governments generally favoured a greater degree of state involvement and Conservatives less. The Conservatives' 1957 Rent Act, for example, introduced widespread decontrol in an attempt to revive the role of the private rented sector. In 1965, the Labour Government reintroduced rent control in the form of rent regulation, instituting the concept of the 'fair' rent designed to give landlords a reasonable rate of return from letting. The 1970 to 1974 Conservative Government had a clear intent to reduce the role of the state and cut public spending on housing. The 1972 Housing Finance Act sought a fundamental change in the financial basis of public sector housing by raising rents to 'fair' rent levels and introducing a national scheme of rent rebates, while the rate of public sector building fell substantially. Since 1974, the Labour Government has restored public spending on housing to pre-1970 levels, repealed the Housing Finance Act of 1972 and generally moved towards greater public involvement.

Nevertheless, as regards the overall degree of public intervention, there has never been a significant departure from the prevailing view that housing falls somewhere between an ordinary consumer good that should be provided predominantly through the mechanism of the private market and a social service such as education or health that should be provided predominantly through state machinery. The provision of housing has been characterised by a mixture of unfettered free enterprise, free enterprise subject to controls and public enterprise, with slight shifts of emphasis at different times.

Different Views About Government Intervention

Having considered the special features of the housing market and the importance and nature of government intervention, it is now useful to summarise in broad terms the various views that have evolved about the relevance and effectiveness of the instruments adopted by successive governments. Throughout the post-war period government policy towards housing has been the subject of criticism from various quarters. Criticism has been directed at a number of aspects of policy, but has centred on the financial nature of housing support from the indiscriminate nature of rent control to the inequity and inefficiency of subsidies to owner-occupiers and council tenants, and the lack of a coherent and consistent national housing strategy. These criticisms are considered in more detail in Chapters 4 and 5. Many of them are not so surprising in view of the persistence of many problems, despite over 20 years of extensive central and local government action. Nevertheless, the solutions advocated by critics are very different. Steady progress has been made, as will be seen in Chapter 3, but the question remains as to whether progress would have been quicker with less government intervention, or whether some alternative set of measures or greater intervention would have been more effective.

While views vary widely and any categorisation will inevitably involve simplification, it is possible to identify two broadly distinctive schools of thought about the role of government. First, there are those supporters of the free market in general who argue that housing is not so different from other goods that government intervention is required, except in very limited ways. This is a view that is expounded most forcefully by writers of the Institute of Economic Affairs who tend to reject the various arguments in favour of intervention as being wrong or unimportant.[40]

Of course, under this broad heading, there are a variety of views, but their common thread is that of the need for less central control. Some writers would accept the need for slum clearance policies and incentives for improvement on the grounds of externalities. Most would also accept the need to boost the demand of lower-income groups, either by general policies of income maintenance, through, for example, a negative income-tax scheme, and which leaves individuals free to choose how to spend their extra income, or through some kind of housing voucher or allowance to households which has to be spent on housing. To their advocates, the advantage of this approach is seen to lie in the fact that the demand and supply of housing is left in the hands of market forces. The role of government is limited purely to encouraging the market supply of housing and to dealing with the problem of urban decay. Direct public sector provision would be limited to the residual role of providing a sort of safety net for those unable to obtain housing through the market. A voucher or negative income-tax system would 'replace the unwieldy, complex and frequently inequitable structure of public housing and other social services'.[41] How far such writers are prepared to go in pressing their views is not altogether clear. In general, they would argue for the removal of the existing system of subsidies to owner-occupiers and public tenants, the dismantling of the role of local authorities by the gradual disposal of the council stock until such authorities only cater for certain social groups such as the elderly, the disabled and the poor, the removal of rent control and security of tenure in the private sector and the introduction of some form of universal or means-tested housing voucher or allowance to households, independently of tenure. This is seen as a way of promoting greater freedom of enterprise in the supply and allocation of housing and in the exercise of individual choice. Apart from the economic consequences of such a policy, which are a matter of dispute, such a strategy would encounter severe political constraints, not least the difficulties associated with raising individual housing costs and the effect on the private rented sector, but these are generally ignored.

Nevertheless this approach is not entirely academic. Much of it is reflected in the outlook of some Conservative politicians. The 1972 Housing Finance Act, for example, with its attempt to move towards higher rents in the public sector, along with the introduction of means-tested assistance to tenants on a large scale, and the implicit stimulus to the private rented sector and owner-occupation, can be seen as a partial expression of this outlook. More recently, Conservatives at the level of central and local government have adopted policies attempting to sell council houses on a widespread scale aimed at the disposal of the council stock and the lessening of the local authority's housing role. They also support measures to resuscitate the private rented sector.

The contrasting view comes from those who see housing as an integral part of our social services and who emphasise the importance of the public role in limiting and controlling the anarchy of the market. This view holds that housing of a good quality is a basic social right that governments should therefore take responsibility for providing. It is founded on the importance of housing to all other areas of community and individual well-being, and the inability of the market to ensure that decent housing of a good quality is provided to all households and that housing resources are distributed equally and fairly on the basis of need and independently of income. It holds that the private market left to itself would produce a very unacceptable distribution of housing resources and sees the historical dominance of the private sector as largely responsible for many of our continuing housing problems. A guarantee of an adequate level of housebuilding and its fair allocation requires wider assessment of housing need, an overall planning of the housing programme and comprehensive involvement by central and local government including direct public sector construction.

While Britain has never adopted a complete social service outlook, housing policy has been marked by varying degrees of a social service philosophy which emphasises at least the partial responsibility of government for the housing conditions of its citizens. This is in contrast to most other Western countries where the emphasis on the social service element has been weaker. The scope of the responsibilities implied by this approach is, of course, quite wide. Some have interpreted it to mean purely the need for a public housing sector whose construction, management and allocation is in the hands of local authorities. Others have urged a much more comprehensive involvement.

Within this group there are therefore wide differences of view with the common ground being the importance of extensive public involvement and the relegation of the private market. One view is that, with some modification, present policies are about right and in particular that the existing system of subsidies does not require any overhaul. Perhaps not surprisingly, the main exponent of this view is the present Labour Government. The recent Green Paper on housing, for example, the result of a two-year review of housing finance by the Department of the Environment, has argued, as discussed in Chapter 7, very broadly in defence of the existing system of finance.[42]

Others have argued for fairly extensive reform of housing finance, while maintaining and strengthening the role of the public sector. What is required, it is maintained, is a set of reforms which approximately maintains existing levels of subsidy but redirects them in a more efficient and coherent manner. In *Labour's Programme for Britain 1976* and their *Evidence to the Review of Housing Finance,* for example, the Labour Party have argued for a greater degree of public control along with reforms in the existing forms of intervention.[43] Their policy recommendations have included a national housing plan, the strengthening of the role of local authorities through an expansion of building, improvement and municipalisation programmes, greater control of the building societies and reforms in finance which would include the limitation of tax relief on mortgage interest to the standard rate of income tax. Others have called for greater public intervention such as the nationalisation of the building societies and a greater role for direct labour building and more extensive financial reforms involving, for example, greater restrictions on mortgage interest tax relief and a system of national pooling in the public rented sector. These reforms will be discussed in more detail in Chapter 7.

Notes

1. *Fair Deal for Housing* (HMSO, Cmnd 4728, 1971), para. 5, p. 1.
2. See, for example, B. Headey, *Housing Policy in the Developed Economy* (London, Croom Helm, 1978).
3. This discussion provides only a highly simplified outline of the way a free market would operate, ignores a number of the underlying assumptions, and is designed simply to identify the basic advantages of efficiency and perhaps equity claimed for the price mechanism. Because it is so simplified, it may be misleading. Those unfamiliar with the elementary theory of the price mechanism can turn to a great number of economic textbooks which describe the workings of markets, such as B.J. McCormick, *Introducing Economics* (London, Penguin, 1977). D. Collard, *Prices, Markets and Welfare* (London, Faber and Faber, 1972), provides a useful and critical account of the workings of free markets.
4. F.G. Pennance and H. Gray, *Choice in Housing* (London, Institute of Economic Affairs, 1968), pp. 9-10. See also, F.G. Pennance, *Housing Market Analysis and Policy* (London, Institute of Economic Affairs, Hobart Paper 48, 1969).
5. D.C. Stafford, *The Economics of Housing Policy* (London, Croom Helm, 1978), the Preface. See also, D.C. Stafford, 'Government and the Housing Situation', *Westminster Bank Review* (November 1976).
6. See, for example, John Greve, *The Housing Problem*, Fabian Research Series 224 (Fabian Society, 1961); L. Needleman, *The Economics of Housing* (Staples Press, 1965), pp. 177 and 191; D. Collard, *The New Right: A Critique*, Fabian Tract 387 (Fabian Society, 1968); J. Le Grand and R. Robinson, *The Economics of Social Problems* (London, Macmillan, 1976), chapter 4.
7. For a discussion of the extent to which the market will achieve the objectives of efficiency and equity, see Le Grand and Robinson, *The Economics of Social Problems*, and Collard, *Prices, Markets and Welfare*.
8. Department of the Environment, *Housing and Construction Statistics*, no. 13 (1st quarter 1975) (London, HMSO, 1976) supplementary table XII.
9. The elasticity of supply measures the ratio of a proportional change in supply to a given proportional change in price.
10. J. Tobin, 'On Limiting the Domain of Inequality', *Journal of Law and Economics*, vol. 13, no. 2 (1970), pp. 263-77.
11. These net figures relate to completions less demolitions. Adding in the small gain through conversions plus the number of improved dwellings through grants gives figures of 2.3 per cent in 1967 and 3.0 per cent in 1972, the latter year being one of a high level of improvement.
12. See, for example, *Chains of Sales in Private Housing* (Building Statistical Services, 14 Great College Street, London, 1973), a study commissioned jointly by the Department of the Environment and the Housing Research Foundation.
13. H.J. Aaron, *Shelter and Subsidies: Who benefits from Federal Housing Policies?* (Washington DC, The Brooking Institution, 1972), p. 165. For a

summary of the evidence on the effect of 'filtering', see A. Murie, P. Niner and C. Watson, *Housing Policy and the Housing System* (London, Allen and Unwin, 1976), pp. 69-75 and 256-7.

14. For a more detailed discussion of the economic consequences for resource allocation of externalities, see Collard, *Prices, Markets and Welfare*, ch. 7.

15. This is an example of the 'prisoner's dilemma', the application of a non-zero sum game to urban renewal and rehabilitation decisions. See, for example, D.W. Rasmussen, *Urban Economics* (New York, Harper and Row, 1974), ch. 6.

16. *Report of the Committee on Housing in Greater London* (The Milner Holland Report), (HMSO, Cmnd 2605, 1965), appendix VI 'Redevelopment and Rehabilitation: Three Case Studies'.

17. Tenth Report of the Expenditure Committee, Minutes of Evidence taken before the Expenditure Committee, *House Improvement Grants* (HMSO, 1973), para. 13, p. 58.

18. Rasmussen, *Urban Economics*, p. 83.

19. For summaries, see A.D. Wilner (*et al.*), *The Housing Environment and Family Life* (Baltimore, Md: Johns Hopkins Press, 1962); A.L. Schorr, *Slums and Social Insecurity* (Washington DC, US Department of Health, Education and Welfare, Social Security Administration, 1963); J. Rothenberg, *Economic Evaluation of Urban Renewal* (Washington DC, The Brookings Institute, 1967).

20. Wilner, *The Housing Environment and Family Life*.

21. Schorr, *Slums and Social Insecurity*, p. 142.

22. A.L. Schorr, 'Housing Policy and Poverty', in P. Townsend (ed.), *The Concept of Poverty* (London, Heinemann, 1970), p. 123.

23. *Report of the Committee on Housing in Greater London* (Milner Holland Report).

24. Quoted in C. Holmes, 'The Cost to the Community', *Housing Review* (September to October 1974).

25. See, for example, L.S. Burns and L. Grebler, *The Housing of Nations* (London, Macmillan, 1977), ch. 6. For a more refined attempt to identify causality, see A.E. Martin, 'Environment, Housing and Health', *Urban Studies*, vol. 4, no. 1 (February 1967).

26. Rothenberg, *Economic Evaluation of Urban Renewal*, p. 174.

27. R. Klein (*et al.*), *Social Policy and Public Expenditure, 1974* (London, Centre for Studies in Social Policy, 1974), p. 53.

28. Royal Commission on the Distribution of Income and Wealth, *Report No. 6 Lower Incomes* (HMSO, Cmnd 7175, May 1978), para. 1.11, p. 3.

29. L. Needleman, 'A Long Term View of Housing', *National Institute Economic Review*, no. 18 (November 1961), p. 27; while such estimates are subject to a number of qualifications – see Needleman, *The Economics of Housing*, p. 160 – they still indicate that the great majority of families could not afford to buy or pay the full cost rent for a new house.

30. M. Friedman and G. Stigler, 'Roofs and Ceilings? The Current Housing Problem', in *Popular Essays on Current Problems*, vol. 1, no. 2 (1946), reprinted in *Verdict on Rent Control* (London, Institute of Economic Affairs, 1972), p. 21.

31. C. Hamnett, *Inequality within Nations: Inequality in Housing* (The Open University, 1976), p. 39.

32. G. Steadman-Jones, *Outcast London* (Oxford University Press, 1971).

33. A.S. Wohl, 'The Housing of the Working Class in London 1815-1914', in S.D. Chapman, *A History of Working Class Housing* (David and Charles, 1971), p. 37.

34. See, for example, Pennance and Gray, *Choice in Housing*.

35. See, for example, H.W. Richardson, *Regional and Urban Economics* (London, Penguin, 1978), p. 352.

36. G.C. Fiegehen, P.S. Lansley and A.D. Smith, *Poverty and Progress in*

Britain, 1953-1973 (London, Cambridge University Press, 1977), ch. 3.

37. Though R. Uhler, 'The Demand for Housing: An Inverse Probability Approach', *The Review of Economics and Statistics*, no. 50 (1968), found evidence of a decreasing income elasticity as incomes rise.

38. P. Ambrose and B. Colenutt, *The Property Machine* (London, Penguin, 1975), p. 24.

39. See, for example, Klein, *Social Policy and Public Expenditure, 1974*, pp. 54-6.

40. See, for example, R. Harris and A. Seldon, *Not from Benevolence . . .* (London, Institute of Economic Affairs, 1977); Pennance and Gray, *Choice in Housing*; Pennance, *Housing Market Analysis and Policy*. See, also, Stafford, *The Economics of Housing Policy*. For a critique of these views, see Collard, *The New Right: A Critique*.

41. Pennance and Gray, *Choice in Housing*, p. 70.

42. Department of the Environment, *Housing Policy: A Consultative Document* (HMSO, Cmnd 6851, 1977).

43. The Labour Party, *Labour's Programme for Britain, 1976* (1976), ch. 7, p. 61; and The Labour Party, *Labour Party Evidence to the Review of Housing Finance* (1976).

2 THE OPERATION OF THE HOUSING MARKET

In Chapter 1 it was seen that successive governments in Britain have not been prepared to leave the provision and allocation of housing entirely to the free play of market forces. Nevertheless, housing is not and has never been a social service available to all. As one commentator has argued, housing is a 'microcosm of the mixed economy' with the co-existence of private and public housing.[1] Approximately 70 per cent of the housing stock remains privately owned while 30 per cent is owned by local authorities or new towns, and each year around 50 per cent of additions to the housing stock are in the private sector, the design, building and allocation of which are determined by predominantly private decisions. While some of these private activities are constrained or encouraged in various ways by public intervention in the form of planning controls or subsidies, it remains the case that in contrast to other areas of public spending and other 'social services', housing remains dominated by the private market. An understanding of the working of private forces in the housing market is therefore of importance. Indeed the shaping of policy in the past has too often ignored or been ignorant of underlying economic forces.

In this chapter, we look at the way the housing market works and the forces that shape demand and supply and determine house prices. An understanding of the way in which market forces operate in the housing field is crucial to an understanding of the extent to which the various controls and measures that have been used by governments have been successful or not in promoting the achievement of housing objectives. Further, many areas of government activity outside of housing, such as in the field of demand management and control of the economy, have important implications for housing and the building industry. As one commentator has put it,

> the market for housing is, like all markets, subject to the forces of supply and demand. To say this is not to say that the authorities must never intervene but, rather, that any intervention must take account of the forces of supply and demand.[2]

The Owner-Occupied Sector and the Determination of House Prices

As we saw in Chapter 1, housing has a number of special features which distinguish it from other markets, is characterised by a great variety of government aids, concessions and controls, and has a large public sector which accounts for approximately one-third of the housing stock. As a result, the housing market is imperfect and highly complex. It consists of three separate but interdependent sectors, the owner-occupied, public and private rented sectors, and the latter can be further sub-divided. While the laws of supply and demand operate in housing, as in other markets, the factors that determine them in each sector are very different. Moreover, there are close interactions. Thus a change in the conditions affecting one sector such as rent control or the average level of council rents will have repercussions in the other sectors.

The Demand for Housing

Chapter 3 considers the nature of housing need in the social sense of the volume and type of housing required to provide all households with a house of some minimum standard suited to their needs. An approximate tentative estimate of the scale of outstanding housing need on this basis is then made. The actual demand for housing as expressed in the market is very different from housing need in this sense, and is important because the demand for housing determines the extent to which needs will be met through the market and in turn the scale of activity in the building industry. Various forecasts of demand for housing have been made from time to time.[3] Effective demand for housing depends on how much households are able and willing to pay for housing and their preferences between tenures, and these are determined by a large number of factors. Housing is demanded for both consumption and investment reasons, both of which are affected by largely independent developments in macroeconomic conditions, especially changes in incomes, prices and interest rates. Government policy with respect to tax relief, subsidies and rent regulation are also important. In the medium to long term, demand is also crucially dependent upon demographic factors.

Because of the sheer complexity of the housing market, accurate forecasts of demand are difficult to make. Generally they begin with the market for owner-occupation where house prices are determined by the forces of supply and demand, though these forces are influenced by government policy. The demand for houses to buy comes from newly formed households, from existing home owners moving to another owner-occupied dwelling, from households transferring from other markets, from immigration and from purchases of second houses. In 1971, 47 per cent of purchases were by existing owner-occupiers, and

53 per cent by first-time buyers.[4] First-time purchasers are predominantly newly formed households (mainly couples but also one-person
households) and former private or public tenants.[5] The change in net
household formation (the difference between new and dissolved households) depends in turn on the size, age and sex composition of the
population, and hence on birth and death rates and the number of
marriages, divorces, and headship rates.[6] In turn, headship rates, and so
the rate of new household formation is not a purely independent factor
but depends not only on income but also on the availability of
housing.[7]

The supply of dwellings for purchase comes from existing second-
hand houses, conversions and new dwellings. Within the second-hand
market, supply comes from houses sold by households purchasing
another house, from household dissolution mainly through death, from
houses vacated by moves to other tenures and by transfers of
dwellings from the rented sector.

It is sometimes argued that moves by owner-occupier to owner-
occupier do not, in general, alter the balance of demand and supply
very significantly, since the purchase of a house involves the simultaneous release of another. While the majority of such moves are
sideways or to more expensive dwellings, this is compensated for, to
some extent, by those released through death or emigration which tend
to be 'up-market'. In essence, therefore, the change in the balance of
supply and demand depends in the main on net household formation,
the transfer of households and properties from the rented sector and
new house building.[8]

What determines the demand for houses to buy? Given the rate of
household formation, which sector *new* households move into and
hence the effective demand for owner-occupation from this source,
depends largely upon economic factors. Tenure preference will depend
upon initial (and anticipated) mortgage outgoings — and hence house
prices and the cost of credit — in relation to local authority and private
rents, expectations of changes in house prices, and the ease of entry
into renting. The ability to satisfy tenure preference will depend on the
ease of entry into owner-occupation, and hence income and ease of
borrowing, and into other sectors. Similarly, the rate of transfer from
the rented sector depends on the relative current and future cost of
house purchase, and income and ease of borrowing.

Households moving from one owner-occupied dwelling to another
can be distinguished by moves related to work, moves related to the
family cycle, moves to better housing by people below retirement age

and moves by retired people. The mobility of existing owners therefore depends mainly on employment factors, the rate of retirement and preference for moving, and the willingness to take out larger commitments in relation to income and expected income levels. It has been estimated that of the 410,000 moves by existing owners in 1971, about 20 per cent were for employment reasons, 17 per cent were by retired people, 41 per cent were 'up-market' and 22 per cent were for miscellaneous reasons.[9]

The effective demand for housing for owner-occupation therefore depends, in the main, on demographic and economic factors which determine household formation and dissolution, the level of house prices in relation to rents and other prices, the level of real income and the cost and ease of borrowing, and the ease of entry into other sectors. Income is important both because it determines the ability of a household to spend, and because of the institutional rules imposed by building societies as to the relationship between income and the sum lent which act as a constraint on borrowing. The rate of change of incomes depends upon a number of independent economic factors. A number of studies have examined the relationship between income and the demand for housing.[10] One would expect demand to rise as incomes rise. Increases in income enable renting households who may have been previously prevented from buying because of lack of income to move to owner-occupation, enable existing owner-occupiers to move to more expensive homes or buy second homes, and may increase the rate of household formation. Estimates suggest that the income elasticity of demand for owner-occupation lies within the range of 0.6 to 1.0,[11] which suggests that an annual rise in real income of the order of 2 per cent can be expected to increase the effective demand for owner-occupation by the order of 1.2 per cent to 2.0 per cent a year, *ceteris paribus*. The size of the income elasticity for housing is particularly important since it is a major factor determining the rate of growth of demand for housing.

The cost of buying in terms of outgoings depends on house prices and mortgage interest rates. The rate of change of house prices depends on changes in the demand and supply of housing. In general, one would expect an inverse relationship between the level of house prices and demand, though it should be remembered that it is the cost of financing the purchase which is the important factor. For first-time buyers, higher prices would be expected to reduce demand, though if there is a widespread expectation of a continuing rise in prices, demand may rise initially. For moving owner-occupiers, price is less important, since rising prices offset the price at which the owner sells his own house as well as the one being purchased. The level of mortgage interest rates depends mainly on independent factors determining the supply and demand for credit, though they may also be influenced by the demand for mortgages. The effect of the cost of purchase on demand is given by the price elasticity of demand. For the above reasons, this would, in general, be expected to be low, though there have been few estimates. In his forecasts of the future demand for housing, Holmans used a figure of -0.3 for the house price elasticity of demand.[12]

Demand will also be determined by the price of substitutes. An increase in the level of rents in relation to mortgage outgoings will increase the demand for owner-occupation. Other factors of importance are the availability of credit and the amount building societies are prepared to lend in relation to income, a factor which is particularly important in determining short term demand. Ease of entry into other sectors may also be important and this depends on the availability of accommodation in the private and public rented sector. Preference for renting may be frustrated by the inability to secure accommodation. Finally, special factors sometimes operate. Thus the price inflation of 1972 stimulated a purely inflationary demand for purchase, and the demand for purchase was also boosted by the intention of the 1972 Housing Finance Act to increase council house rents.

In the short term, demand for housing can be highly volatile. This is partly because household formation, and households' choices and income can change quite abruptly but also because the availability of mortgage finance which is the factor converting underlying demand into effective demand is subject to considerable fluctuation.

The Finance of Owner-Occupation. The most important factor determining effective, rather than underlying, demand in the short run is the availability of mortgage finance. Houses are unique among consumer goods in their high cost in relation to income and in how long they last, and housing services therefore have to be obtained either through renting or through purchase with the aid of long term credit. There are six main sources of funds for the purchase of homes, building societies, local authorities, insurance companies, bank loans and ready money. The great majority of house purchases are financed by loans rather than outright purchase, and building societies are the dominant source of funds. Table 2.1 shows that in 1973, 71 per cent of first-time purchasers in England and Wales borrowed from building societies, 12 per cent from local authorities and 6 per cent with ready money. 63 per cent of moving owner-occupiers financed their move by a loan from a building society and 24 per cent with ready cash.

Table 2.1: Source of Funds: House Purchasers in England and Wales, 1973 (percentages)

Source of Funds	First-Time Buyers	Owner-Occupiers Moving
Building Society	71	63
Local authority	12	2
Insurance company, bank	7	10
Private loan	3	2
Ready money (proceeds of previous sale or money available)	6	24
Total	100	100
Average price paid	£7,405	£11,500

Source: Department of the Environment, *Housing Policy Technical Volume II*, table VII.1, p. 83, based on Department of the Environment, National Movers Survey.

The relative shares of the financial institutions providing house purchase finance have fluctuated considerably in the 1970s. While the share of insurance companies has been relatively stable, the share provided by local authorities increased quite sharply over the period 1973 to 1975, after providing only about 6 per cent of advances throughout the 1960s. During the 'mortgage famine' of 1974, for example, the building society share fell to 65 per cent while the local authority share increased to 20 per cent, in part as a result of deliberate government stimulus to offset the fall in building society lending. Since 1975, the share of lending from local authorities has declined considerably, while the share provided by buildings societies has correspondingly increased. The government has tried to compensate for this deliberate cutback in local authority lending by the introduction of the support lending scheme whereby local authorities nominate prospective borrowers to building societies, but this scheme has not been entirely successful (see Chapter 6).

Building societies are by far the most important source of funds. Over the course of the century, their total assets have expanded dramatically from £60m in 1900 to £34,00m in 1977, while the actual number of societies has declined from 2,286 in 1900 to 339 in 1977 (Table 2.2). As the building society movement has developed, it has also become heavily concentrated with the 5 largest building societies now accounting for more than 50 per cent of total assets, and the largest 20

Table 2.2: The Development of Building Societies, 1900 to 1977

	Number of Societies	Total Assets £m	Number of Share Accounts ('000s)	Number of Borrowers ('000s)	Mortgage Advances £m
1900	2286	60	585	–	25
1920	1271	87	748	–	25
1940	952	756	2,088	1,503	21
1960	726	3,166	3,910	2,349	560
1977	339	34,200	22,536	4,836	6,721

Source: Building Societies Association, *Facts and Figures*, no. 15 (July 1978).

for approximately 85 per cent. In turn, the building societies have taken an increasing share of the savings market, holding 47 per cent of total savings in 1977 compared with only 9 per cent in 1950.[13]

Building societies finance their loans partly from the repayment of principle from earlier loans, but mainly from the attraction of savings. In competing for savings, the societies have a slight advantage over other savings institutions from the special arrangement they have with the Inland Revenue for paying savers' taxes; under this arrangement, the 'composite' rate paid on behalf of investors was 27.75 per cent in 1976/7 when the standard rate of income tax was 35 per cent.[14] In attempting to attract savings, building societies must compete with other savings outlets, and their receipts from investors – especially those in larger amounts – have proved very sensitive to changes in building society rates relative to those offered by competitors. In the last few years especially, these competing rates have been subject to large fluctuations, but the rates offered by building societies have tended to change only slowly with a long lag, and not by as much. In consequence, as Table 2.3 shows, the net receipts of building societies have fluctuated considerably; for example, from an average of £202 million a month in the second quarter of 1973 to –£7 million a month in the first quarter of 1974. Between 1970 and 1972 when other interest rates fell, the building societies, whose gross rates on deposit shares remained constant, enjoyed a substantial increase in net receipts, a situation that was reversed in 1973 and 1974 when the rates offered by building societies lagged behind competitors, and net receipts fell. The number and amount of advances made by building societies has therefore fluctuated, as shown in Table 2.4.

Building societies are private non-profit making bodies, and are subject to certain government regulations. They are required to satisfy two basic ratios in their portfolio structure, the most important of

Table 2.3: Short Term Variations in Building Societies' Net Receipts, 1972 to 1973, United Kingdom (£ million a month)

Period	Amount	Indicator of Changes in Competitive- ness[a]	Period	Amount	Indicator of Changes in Competitive- ness[a]
1972 Q1	168	+ 2.90	1975 Q1	243	− 0.30
2	158	+ 2.68	2	304	+ 1.37
3	120	+ 0.06	3	261	+ 0.48
4	155	+ 0.58	4	255	− 0.62
1973 Q1	109	− 1.18	1976 Q1	348	+ 1.33
2	202	+ 0.19	2	229	+ 0.03
3	109	− 2.13	3	176	− 1.46
4	84	− 3.48	4	64	− 3.40
1974 Q1	− 7	− 4.96	1977 Q1	164	− 0.13
2	86	− 2.18			
3	129	− 1.59			
4	180	− 1.19			

Note: [a]'Indicator of changes in competitiveness' is the Building Societies Association's recommended share rate grossed up at the standard or basic rate of income tax, *minus* the local authority 3-month deposit rate.

Source: Department of the Environment, *Housing Policy, A Consultative Document*, table 15.

Table 2.4: Building Societies' Receipts, Repayments of Principal and Advances, United Kingdom

	Advances		Net[a] Receipts	Repayments of Principal
	Number	Amount £m	£m	£m
1968	498,000	1,587	594	
1969	460,000	1,556	674	774
1970	540,000	2,021	1,213	933
1971	653,000	2,758	1,700	1,158
1972	681,000	3,649	1,801	1,434
1973	545,000	3,540	1,512	1,541
1974	433,000	2,950	1,165	1,460
1975	651,000	4,965	3,191	2,197
1976	715,000	6,117	2,278	2,487
1977	754,000	6,721	4,431	2,961

Note: [a]Receipts less withdrawals.

Source: Building Societies Association, *Facts and Figures*.

which is the minimum liquidity ratio of 7½ per cent liquid assets to total assets. This minimum liquidity ratio is necessary to cover withdrawals of deposits, to act as a cushion for increases in advances and to cover seasonal variations in the inflow and outflow of funds. The reason why the minimum liquidity ratio imposed on building societies is relatively low is that the societies lend money only against the security of freehold and leasehold estates, are circumscribed in the way in which liquid funds can be invested − in a narrow range of government and government-backed securities − and adopt very cautious lending policies. The risk of loss is therefore very small. In practice, building societies operate liquidity ratios which are greatly in excess of this minimum, and these have varied in recent years from a combined average of 16.2 per cent in 1974 to 21.1 per cent in 1975.

Building societies have adopted a number of rules and guidelines in granting mortgages, though these do vary widely between societies and local branches. They generally only lend to shareholders who have been saving with the society for some minimum, short period of time. The size of loan granted depends on both the characteristics, especially the 'credit-worthiness', of the borrower and the nature and collateral value of the property. The maximum mortgage granted is usually based on some multiple between 2½ and 3 times income, and some elements of income such as overtime earnings are often excluded, and societies will only lend up to some maximum figure. Loans are given up to a percentage of the society's own valuation of the property which may be less than the market price, particularly in the case of older properties. Such percentages may be up to 95 per cent for new property but are much lower, usually around 70 per cent for older property. On average, around 30 to 40 per cent of the cost of purchase is met from sources other than the building society, though this figure includes loans made to existing owner-occupiers who are moving. About 75 per cent of first-time buyers obtain an advance for 80 per cent or more of valuation. These rules mean that owner-occupation is difficult to achieve for those with lower incomes and first-time buyers, especially new households.

This difficulty is also compounded by the fact that the majority of mortgages advanced are of the annuity type under which equal payments are made throughout the term, mostly 25 years, each payment consisting partly of interest on the outstanding loan and partly of capital repayment. In the early years, most of the repayment is interest and the capital owed declines only slowly. Since tax relief is given on interest payments only, the net money cost to the borrower rises slowly through time as the interest element in the repayment falls. With inflation, however, repayments fixed in money terms decline substantially in real terms over the life of the loan. This type of mortgage therefore has the effect of placing the heaviest burden on the borrower in the early years of a mortgage, thus adding to the difficulties faced by lower income and younger households in buying a home. Alternative forms of low-start mortgages have been advocated which involve lower repayments initially and higher repayments later, thereby taking into account future rises in personal incomes and prices, but these have not been widely adopted.[15]

There are very distinctive differences between the lending behaviour of building societies and local authorities as shown by Table 2.5. Local authorities generally lend on cheaper and older property and to those with lower incomes who would be unlikely to obtain a mortgage from a building society. Local authorities also give considerably more 100 per cent loans. In 1976, the average advance by building societies to first-time buyers of £8,073 represented 79 per cent of the average purchase

Table 2.5: Differences in Building Society and Local Authority Lending, 1976[a]

	Building Societies	Local Authorities
Average price paid (£)	10,181	6,190
Average advance (£)	8,073	5,640
Average income (£)	4,285	3,400
Average ratio of advance to price	79%	91%
Average ratio of advance to income	1.88	1.66
Proportion of first time purchaser	49%*	92%*
Proportion of mortgages of 100 per cent of valuation	negligible	37%*
Proportion of option mortgages	15%*	48%*
Proportion of pre-1919 properties	23%*	74%*
Proportion of purchases under age 25	34%*	43%*
Proportion of low-start mortgages	NA	3%*

Note: [a]First-time purchasers only, except for the proportions marked (*), which are of all purchasers.
NA Not available.

Source: The Labour Party, *News Release: Statement on Local Authority Mortgage Lending* (22 March 1978).

price, while the average by local authorities was about £5,650 or 91 per cent of average purchase price. Nevertheless, as we have said, the proportion of all advances made by local authorities has fluctuated widely and is small in comparison with other institutions. Total lending by local authorities rose from £284m in 1972/3 to £786m in 1974/5 but has since slumped to £157m in 1977/8.[16]

The Supply of Housing

This represents the demand side of the market for owner-occupation. But while demand is likely to be variable in the short run, supply, as we have seen, is relatively fixed. Supply in the short run comes from new dwellings and conversions, from houses vacated by owner-occupiers moving to another owner-occupied dwelling, from household dissolution or emigration, from houses vacated by moves to other tenures and by transfers of dwellings from the rented sector. In 1971, new building accounted for 21 per cent of the total of houses purchased, houses sold by households buying another for 46 per cent, household dissolution for 16 per cent, transfers to other tenures for 8 per cent, and transfers from private renting for 7 per cent.[17] Supply is therefore dominated by turnover in the existing stock. There are also some losses through demolition, closing or purchase by local authorities, but these are insignificant.

The number of dwellings vacated by owners moving to another owner-occupied house depends, as we have seen, on the ability of such households to move, and this source of move is unlikely to alter the balance of demand and supply to any great significance. The increase in demand generated by owning households moving up market is at least partly counterbalanced by the addition to supply from household dissolution and which is predominantly up market. The supply resulting from the vacation of homes through household dissolution or emigration depends largely on demographic factors. Transfers from the public sector can be treated as unimportant, partly because the number is insignificant but also because the household and dwelling move together. It may be a reasonable working assumption, therefore, that the balance of supply and demand depends *in the main* on net household formation and the transfer of households from the privately rented sector, on the demand side, and on new housebuilding and the transfer of property from the rented sector, on the supply side.

The number of new completions is fixed in the short term, determined by past decisions. In the longer term, supply depends on the rate of building starts and the rate at which the work is completed. The number of starts at a particular point in time depends on a variety of factors but especially on expected profitability, on the availability of credit to builders, and on the profitability of other construction work. Anticipated profits depend on the expected price that builders can get on completion in relation to the cost of building from the purchase of land, construction and labour costs. The price of new houses is determined by the conditions of supply and demand prevailing at the date of completion, and since the housing market is dominated by transactions in the second-hand market, that price is largely independent of the individual builder's output and costs. The cost of land will depend upon local conditions of supply and demand, and others costs — materials, wages, interest rates — will also be largely independent of the selling price that can be got.

Because of this dependence on expectations of the state of the market over the future, the construction industry with its multiplicity of small firms, is characterised by considerable uncertainty. Builders generally react with considerable caution when the market is weak because of the long production period. Because of the lags involved in the construction process, the building industry is also dependent upon the availability and cost of credit. It is therefore difficult for builders to plan their land purchases and house construction in the knowledge that there will be a continuous and sufficient supply of credit to enable their property to sell at prices which will guarantee them a profit. Only the largest building firms which are involved in many different sectors of the construction industry can deflect the threat of bankruptcy by moving into more profitable activity. A period of rising interest rates can be particularly difficult for construction firms, since this may result in higher mortgage rates or the rationing of building society lending, which may reduce the demand for housing at a time when houses are approaching completion, such that builders may face falling prices and unsold houses, alongside higher interest charges on land and credit. Conversely a period of boom is not necessarily beneficial to house construction. Increases in house and land prices occasioned by, say, plentiful mortgage funds, as in the early 1970s, may lead to high profits but this may not generate additional construction activity. The profitability of other construction work is also important in determining the volume of residential construction. Because of the nature of the construction industry, housebuilding is particularly vulnerable to cyclical movements of the economy, as is clear from Table 2.7.

The Determination of House Prices — The 1970s Experience

Since the market for home ownership is a largely free market, house prices are determined by the forces of demand and supply. Demand for houses to buy depends, as we have seen, on demographic factors, incomes, prices, rents and the availability of credit. Supply comes from the second-hand market and new building which depends predominantly upon expected future house prices and costs, the availability of credit and the profitability of non-residential construction. Because the supply of new houses is relatively fixed in the short term and unresponsive to changes in house prices, house prices in the short term are largely demand determined.

It is now possible to examine the circumstances underlying the acceleration and subsequent slump in house prices which has taken place in the 1970s. Table 2.6 shows that new house prices rose dramatically and at a much faster pace than other prices between 1970 and 1973. Thus house prices rose by 106 per cent over this period, while retail prices rose by 27 per cent on average. Since 1973, the rate of increase has slowed considerably and house prices have fallen in real terms. Between 1973 and 1976 new house prices rose by 28 per cent compared with a 68 per cent increase in the index of retail prices.

The house price boom between 1971 and 1973 was unprecedented. Second-hand house prices rose by 47 per cent between the second half of 1971 and the second half of 1972, while the price of new houses rose by 30 per cent; between the second half of 1972 and the second half of 1973, new house prices rose by 32 per cent and second-hand house prices by 27 per cent.[18] These compare with an average annual rate of increase for new houses of 6.8 per cent between 1964 and 1970. Surprisingly, there has been little detailed economic analysis of this phenomenon.[19] Nevertheless, it is generally agreed that the boom was demand led.

For effective demand to increase, there needs to be both an increase in underlying demand and the means to convert this into effective demand. In the period 1971 to 1973 both factors seem to have been operating. Certainly, there were a number of special factors working to stimulate the latent demand to buy. First, there was the demographic impact of the post-war baby boom which increased the number of first marriages, peaking in 1970, and which increased the number of potential first-time buyers. This high number of marriages was also accompanied by a sharp fall in the rate of net emigration. Secondly, there may have been some impetus to the demand to buy from households in rented accommodation because, as Table 2.6 shows, the ratio of initial mortgage repayments to council rents was relatively low in the period 1968 to 1972, and the Conservative Government at the time had indicated its intention in the White Paper *Fair Deal for Housing* of July 1971 to make substantial increases in council house rents through the 1972 Housing Finance Act. Nevertheless, this factor

Table 2.6: Housing Costs and Prices

	Average new House Prices[a]		Average Unrebated Council Rent[b]		Index Retail Prices	Average Earnings[d]		Gross Mortgage Repayments as Ratio Council Rents[e]	House Price/ I.R.P. Ratio	House Price/ Earnings Ratio
	£	Index 1970=100	£ p.a.	Index 1970=100	Index[c]	£ p.a.	Index 1970=100			
1968	4640	89	94	81	89.0	1196	82	3.3	100	3.9
1969	4880	94	106	91	94.2	1290	88	3.5	100	3.8
1970	5180	100	116	100	100.0	1459	100	3.4	100	3.6
1971	5970	115	129	111	109.0	1610	110	3.4	105	3.7
1972	7850	152	143	123	116.7	1863	128	3.6	130	4.2
1973	10690	206	179	154	127.4	2128	146	4.8	162	5.0
1974	11340	219	197	170	147.9	2528	173	5.4	148	4.5
1975	12400	239	216	186	183.8	3098	212	5.4	130	4.0
1976	13650	264	247	213	214.1	3482	239	5.1	123	3.9

Sources:
a Building Societies Association, *Facts and Figures.*
b Department of the Environment, *Housing and Construction Statistics.*
c Department of Employment *Gazette.*
d Average earnings of male manual workers over 21, October, Department of Employment, *Gazette.*
e Average initial gross mortgage repayments relate to an 80 per cent advance on an average priced new house, taken from Building Societies Association, *Facts and Figures,* no. 7.

is unlikely to have been of major importance. In 1971, for example, while 41 per cent of first-time purchasers (who accounted for 53 per cent of all purchasers) were previously tenants of private landlords, only 16 per cent were tenants of a local authority or new town, and this latter proportion fell slightly over the period 1971 to 1976.[20]

Another contributory factor was the large increase in real and money incomes in 1971 and 1972 which we will consider in more detail later. An important explanation of the self-sustaining nature of the boom, if not its initiator, was the rising rate of inflation and the expectation of its continuing rise in the future since this made the attraction of early purchase particularly strong. Indeed, the expectation of rising prices boosted the investment demand for housing.

While these factors were all important in adding to the latent demand for house purchase, demand is only made effective by access to mortgage funds. Of particular significance in this period, therefore, was the increased availability of mortgage funds since it is this which converts latent into effective demand. Between 1970 and 1972 the Conservative Government was operating a highly expansionary monetary policy which led to a general fall in short-term interest rates. As a result, building societies, who maintained their deposit rates, offered highly competitive rates and enjoyed a substantial increase in net receipts in 1971 and 1972. Table 2.4 shows that the value of mortgage advances increased by 80 per cent between 1970 and 1972, but that this provided an increase of only 27 per cent in the number of advances, though some of the increase in the average size of advance would have been a response to the increase in house prices.

While the boom was largely demand led in this way, the response of supply is of particular interest. The increase in demand came at a time of a very low level of building activity. The number of private sector completions was the lowest for many years as was the number of public sector dwellings. There was an increase of 18,000 in the number of private completions in 1971, as Table 1.1 showed, but only 5,000 in 1972, and a fall of 10,000 in 1973. The boom in prices appeared to have surprisingly little impact on the rate of private building starts, as shown in Table 2.7. While starts jumped by about 40,000 in 1971 following the very poor year of 1970, they only increased by 20,000 in 1972 and fell by 14,000 in 1973. This contrasts with the earlier periods in 1962 to 1964 and 1967 to 1968 when there were noticeable increases in building society lending, though not of the same magnitude or duration as in 1971 to 1972. These earlier expansions in lending were not accompanied by discernible increases in house prices, partly because the supply of new dwellings was higher and the supply response was more favourable. The reason for the poor response from the building industry in the early 1970s is not clear, since in 1972 house building was very profitable and builders could get finance very easily. It would seem that the optimism indicated by the higher level of starts in 1972 was not sustained.[21]

Table 2.7: Annual Housing Starts, England and Wales (thousands, percentages in brackets)

	Private Sector		Local Authority including New Towns		Housing Associations and Government Departments		Total
1967	225	(56%)	167	(41%)	11	(3%)	404
1968	190	(54%)	149	(43%)	11	(3%)	350
1969	158	(52%)	134	(44%)	11	(4%)	304
1970	157	(56%)	115	(40%)	11	(4%)	282
1971	196	(63%)	102	(33%)	13	(4%)	310
1972	214	(67%)	91	(29%)	12	(4%)	317
1973	200	(68%)	84	(28%)	12	(4%)	296
1974	96	(43%)	111	(51%(	12	(6%)	220
1975	137	(47%)	134	(46%)	20	(7%)	291
1976	138	(47%)	127	(43%)	30	(10%)	295

Source: Department of the Environment, *Housing and Construction Statistics.*

A factor we have mentioned as being of importance was the large increase in real and money incomes. As Table 2.6 shows, the earnings of manual men rose by about 16 per cent between October 1971 and 1972 while the index of retail prices rose by 7 per cent. Nevertheless, income does not appear to be of major importance in the determination of house prices in the short run, since its role is outweighed by the greater significance of other factors. Indeed, the relationship between house prices and incomes and their rates of change shows no clear pattern on a year to year basis. In the long run, however, there appears a much more stable connection between incomes and house prices. Between 1960 and 1976, for example, house prices rose at a slightly faster rate than average earnings.[22] Over shorter periods there is no such consistency. Over the period 1970 to 1973, as Table 2.6 shows, house prices rose at a much faster rate than earnings, but this proved to be a temporary phenomenon, and the long run relatively stable pattern has been restored. It is not entirely clear why this long run stability should persist, nor is it particularly desirable since a consequence of the tendency for house prices to rise at least as fast as incomes is that the proportion of households that can afford to buy, given the institutional rules affecting building society lending behaviour, will show no tendency to increase over time. One factor underlying the relationship is that building societies ration mortgage advances largely on the basis of income. Otherwise, the relationship between house prices and income will depend on the income elasticity of demand and the slope of the supply curve for new housing, which depends in turn on building and land costs.

A qualification to Table 2.6 is that it only shows the relationship with earnings, and not net disposable income, after the deduction of tax and national insurance contributions. In general, net incomes have risen more slowly than gross incomes because of the increasing impact of taxation. Between 1971 and 1975, for example, real median gross income rose by 19.1 per cent, while real median net income rose by 11.9 per cent, such that house prices will have risen somewhat faster than net incomes.[23]

Finally, Table 2.6 shows the relationship between house prices and the index of retail prices. House prices have shown a tendency to rise at a somewhat faster pace than other prices, on average. Between 1969 and 1976 house prices rose 24 per cent more quickly than other prices. A similar relationship is observed over longer periods.[24] One explanation for this is the increase in the quality of houses, but it is unlikely that the increase in quality is sufficient to account for the full relative increase in house prices. Other explanations lie in the slower rate of increase in productivity in housebuilding than in the economy as a whole, limitations in the supply of land, and because new house prices are determined largely by prices of second-hand houses, by the extent of excess demand.

Since the boom, house prices have tumbled in real terms. Between 1973 and 1976 new house prices rose by only 28 per cent while the index of retail prices rose 68 per cent. While house prices rose much more quickly than earnings between 1970 and 1973, the long run stability between house prices and earnings had been largely restored by the end of 1976. The explanation for this slump is to be found in the same factors working largely in the opposite direction to reduce demand for owner-occupation. Since 1971, there have been fewer first marriages and the household formation rate has fallen while net emigration has risen. The initial gross cost of house purchase has been high in relation to local authority rents, as a result of both the increase in house prices and the rise in nominal mortgage interest rates since 1973. The house price/earnings ratio in 1973 and 1974 was historically very high. Real incomes have risen only slightly since 1973, and actually fell between 1975 and 1976. Building society net receipts collapsed in the second half of 1973 and first half of 1974 following the erosion of their competitive position as other interest rates rose. Lending therefore fell sharply in 1974, and while it increased rapidly in 1975, this was almost matched by the increase in the *number* of advances.

The Public Rented Sector

An important feature of the housing market is that about a third of the housing stock is owned by local authorities, the supply and allocation of which is not determined, at least directly, by market forces. Conditions of demand and supply are very different in the public sector. Demand is only a semi-demand concept because houses are not available on the open market, households cannot outbid each other for the available supply, and houses are allocated on the basis of the local authority's perception of need, not ability to pay. Supply is not responsive to market pressure but administrative decisions. Rents are not set at market clearing levels or at levels which yield a profit, but at levels which reflect a mixture of political, social and economic factors. Nevertheless, while market forces do not operate directly in this sector, they do have an indirect influence through their determination of land and house prices, and in turn, the price and availability of public housing does affect demand and hence supply in the owner-occupied and private rental sectors. The separate sub-markets within housing are, indeed, highly interdependent. An increase in public sector rents for example, would increase the demand for owner-occupied and private houses to rent, while an increase in supply of local authority dwellings might reduce demand in these sectors to the extent that such demand is a partial expression of the inability to obtain council housing. The public housing sector therefore has an important role in determining the supply and demand and prices of dwellings in the private sector.

The main purpose of public sector housing has been to cater for needs which would otherwise not be met. In general, however, the statutory responsibilities for housing provision are ill-defined, local authorities being required to consider the need for additional accommodation arising from the housing situation in the area, and to provide relief for overcrowding and the rehousing of persons displaced by clearance, redevelopment or other public action. Nevertheless, the responsibility for direct provision to meet these needs is limited, in general terms, to situations where alternative accommodation is unavailable. Moreover, within this framework, authorities have considerable autonomy, adopting their own criteria for assessing need, building, allocation and rents, though in practice, such discretion is somewhat limited, especially on rents, standards and financial matters.

The Supply of Local Authority Dwellings

The supply of accommodation in the public sector consists of relets and new additions. The volume of relets depends on the size of the local stock and tenant mobility. The supply of new dwellings depends in the main on a local authority's assessment of local needs, its willingness to undertake building, the cost of provision, the level of government subsidy, the availability of land, and the capacity of the local building industry. A number of factors can be used to determine the extent of local housing need such as the existence of a crude shortage of dwellings over households, the quality of the housing stock, the local tenure structure, and expected population or household growth. The level of homelessness and overcrowding and the size of the waiting list are sometimes used as guides to the extent of local needs. In general, local authorities vary widely in the methods used to assess such need and in their response to such assessment. While in the past few authorities would have been in a situation of a local housing surplus, the increasing likelihood of such surpluses means that such assessment will be especially important in the future.

The ability of local authorities to meet assessed needs depends crucially upon the costs involved in the provision of new housing. Local authorities finance new building by 60-year loans borrowed from the open market and the Public Works Loan Board. The cost to the local authority depends upon the cost of building, the cost of financing the loan over 60 years, and the level of central government subsidy received. The cost after subsidy is met by a combination of rent and rates, and the financial situation of local authority housing relating to these revenues and costs is shown in the housing revenue account. This is discussed in more detail in Chapter 4.

The Role of Subsidies

In order to encourage local authorities to build houses, successive central governments have provided subsidies to help meet the loan charges arising from borrowing. Subsidies of this kind were first introduced in the Housing and Town Planning Act of 1919, the act designed to encourage the building of 'homes fit for heroes'. The act was necessitated by the then inability of private enterprise to provide homes at appropriate rents or in sufficient numbers to meet the post-war housing shortage.[25] This is the act which marks the birth of council housing in Britain. Subsidies of one kind or another remained until 1933 when they were discontinued mainly in order to discourage public sector building in favour of private building. Subsidies of a general nature were reintroduced in the 1946 Housing Act along with extensive controls over private building in order to concentrate the building effort where it was felt to be most needed, and then reduced and eventually eliminated in the 1956 Housing Subsidies Act. They were reintroduced again in 1961 and subsidies of varying kinds have remained ever since.

Subsidy policy has therefore been characterised by substantial changes, reflecting changing views about the desirabilityof encouraging private or public building, and within the public sector, changes in emphasis in the importance of slum clearance or meeting special rather than general needs.[26] The very large fluctuations in the rate of public housebuilding both before and after the Second World War are associated particularly with these changes in subsidy policy, though other factors of importance include the capacity of the building industry, the availability and cost of land and interest rate levels. These latter factors are of special relevance in accounting for variations in the level of building between different authorities.

Central Government Control

While local authorities have considerable discretion to undertake building programmes, subject to the constraints of cost, and the availability of land, materials and labour already mentioned, they are not completely free of central government intervention. Central governments exercise control in three main ways. (They have also exercised control over local authority rent levels from time to time as discussed in Chapter 4.) First, all building schemes have to be submitted to the Department of the Environment for loan sanction approval. While such approval has usually been given, there have been occasions when restrictions have been imposed, particularly for wider macro-economic reasons. In 1976, for example, as part of the then government's policy of containing public spending, restrictions were placed on the building programmes of a number of designated 'non-stress' authorities.

Secondly, throughout the history of council house building, minimum standards have been enforced as a condition of approval for loan sanction and subsidy. Currently such standards are based on the recommendations of the Parker Morris Committee which reported in 1966, and were embodied in the 1967 Housing Subsidies Act which made subsidies dependent on the adoption of the Parker Morris standards for all public sector housing built after 1968. These standards cover space and heating requirements in addition to room sizes as under previous standards, and lay down the minimum floor space necessary for households of different size, minimum storage space needs, and capacity for heating installations. As perceived by the Committee, these were devised as minimum standards and it was intended that they should be gradually raised. However, the standard has increasingly become a maximum, a reflection of the increased cost of building and the use of the housing cost yardstick.

Thirdly, through cost control. Before the 1967 Act, Exchequer subsidies had been unit cost subsidies, a fixed amount per dwelling which did not vary with the cost of provision and new housing schemes were vetted according to value for money. The 1967 Act meant that subsidies were now related directly to the cost of new schemes, and it was felt necessary to introduce some new kind of control to limit what might otherwise have been an open-ended subsidy. The housing cost yardstick was therefore introduced designed to reflect the cost of pro-viding dwellings to Parker Morris standards, and eligibility for subsidy was dependent on the programme falling within the yardstick. It was originally intended that the allowable costs would be regularly reviewed to ensure that they were a realistic reflection of tender prices, but while the yardstick has been increased from time to time and includes an element for tolerance, it has rarely kept pace with increases in building costs and this has led to difficulties for local authorities in obtaining tenders within the yardstick, and led to delays in the start of schemes and so sometimes had the perverse effect of increasing costs, particularly in periods of severe inflation. The system has as a result been the subject of widespread criticism. Indeed, the recent Green Paper on housing recognised that 'the present "housing cost yardstick" involves too much detailed and time-consuming work for both central and local government', and suggested the need for a simpler system, based on 'a fixed level of costs per house eligible for subsidy combined with monitoring of overall cost trends [which] could provide local authorities with greater incentives to seek value for money in their building schemes'.[27]

Despite these various controls, there have been few attempts by central government to influence the allocation of resources between areas in relation to variations in need. Nor has the subsidy system been designed to impose a particular allocation of subsidy though recent subsidy systems have included an additional high cost element to assist areas such as the inner city authorities with specially high costs. An attempt was made by the 1964 Labour Government to concentrate building effort in areas of greatest need by establishing the Greater London Council and 130 other local authorities as 'priority areas' which were to receive special treatment.[28] More recently, in 1976, Peter Shore announced that only designated stress areas would be eligible for loan sanction for new building, though this move was motivated more by the government's aim to reduce public spending than by any distributive objective.

Allocations Policy

The allocation of local authority houses to individual tenants is made not through price, but on the basis of housing need through locally determined administrative procedures. Households indicate their demand by joining the waiting list. Entry to such lists is sometimes made dependent on a residence qualification. A survey of the allocation schemes of English housing authorities in early 1978 has shown that only 17 per cent of all authorities maintained an open list with no restrictions, while a further 42 per cent operated unrestricted access for both residents and employees in the area, and a further 18 per cent unrestricted access for residents but not employees. While 23 per cent of councils required a specific period of residence before an applicant could be accepted on to the waiting list, 35 per cent required a period of residence before rehousing could be considered.[29]

In addition to residence qualifications, 8 per cent of local authorities either excluded single people below retirement age from their waiting lists or would not consider them for rehousing. A further 13 per cent operated an age cut-off below which applicants are not accepted, the most frequently mentioned age being 25. It has long been argued that there should be no restrictions on access to waiting lists, since this conflicts with the principle of allocation on the basis of housing need and restricts labour mobility. The view of the Cullingworth Committee that it is 'fundamental that no one should be precluded from applying for, or being considered for, a council tenancy on any ground whatsoever'[30] was endorsed by the government in the housing Green Paper.[31]

In addition to housing those on the waiting list, authorities also have a statutory obligation to rehouse those displaced by clearance and rehabilitation schemes, those living in overcrowded and insanitary conditions and certain categories of the homeless. Allocation systems therefore have to allow some ordering of priority between those on the waiting list, clearance cases, the homeless and those on transfer lists wishing to move from one council dwelling to another. The actual allocation schemes adopted vary widely between authorities. There are three basic types of scheme: date order schemes, merit schemes and point schemes. With date order schemes, dwellings are simply allocated according to the date order in which applications are received. In those areas where there is only a small waiting list and no real housing shortage, such 'first come first served' schemes provide a fair and simple method of allocation. Under merit schemes, allocations are made by local officers or a committee according to the merit of the case. Point schemes work by awarding points on the basis of such factors as household size, age, health, housing conditions and sometimes length of residence, though the methods used for allocating points vary widely between authorities. In 1978, 66 per cent of local authorities in England used points schemes, 24 per cent date order, and 10 per cent merit schemes.[32] In general, point schemes are more likely to produce rehousing on the basis of greatest need, and have the advantage that they can be published. Merit schemes cannot be published and are less likely to be consistent and impartial. In recent years, the procedures used by some local authorities to determine priorities have come under considerable criticism, and it is now widely accepted that local authorities should have a statutory obligation to publish their allocation schemes as well as ease the qualifications for registration.

Notes

1. E. Craven, 'Housing' in R. Klein (ed.), *Social Policy and Public Expenditure* (London, Centre for Studies in Social Policy, 1975).

2. R. Harrington, 'Housing – Supply and Demand', *National Westminster Bank Review* (May 1972), p. 53.

3. See, for example, L. Needleman, 'A Long Term View of Housing', *National Institute Economic Review*, no. 18 (November 1961); D.C. Paige, 'Housing', in W. Beckerman (ed.) *The British Economy in 1975* (London, Cambridge University Press, 1965), ch. XII; H.W. Richardson, 'Housing in the 1970s', *Lloyds Bank Review* (April 1970); A.E. Holmans, 'A Forecast of Effective Demand for Housing in Great Britain in the 1970s', *Social Trends No. 1* (HMSO, 1970); Department of the Environment, *Housing Policy Technical Volume 1* (HMSO, 1977), ch. 3. For a detailed discussion of the determinants of demand, see C. Whitehead, *The UK Housing Market* (London, Saxon House, 1974).

4. Purchases of second dwellings accounted for about 0.5 per cent of all sales; Department of the Environment, *Housing Policy Technical Volume 1*, p. 122.

5. In 1971, 39 per cent of first time purchasers were new hoseholds, 16 per cent former tenants of local authorities and new towns, 41 per cent former tenants of private landlords, and about 4 per cent households from outside Great Britain and 'successor households from divorce'. Department of Environment, *Housing Policy Technical Volume 1*, table III.II, p. 126.

6. Headship rates are the proportion of persons in each age, sex, marital status group who are heads of households.

7. Department of the Environment 1974 based household projections predict an increase in the number of households (Census definition) in England and Wales from 17,574,000 in 1976 to 18,929,000 in 1986, a rise of 8 per cent over the decade. The estimated net increase for 1976 was projected at 150,000 and in 1981, 135,000; Department of the Environment, *Housing Policy Technical Volume 1*, table III.2.

8. In this sense, the demand for new buildings can be looked on as a residual, or that part of the total demand for owner-occupation that cannot be met from the second-hand market. The effective demand for new homes for owner-occupation can then be built up from forecasts of the individual items of demand and supply. For a more detailed discussion of these forces, see Department of the Environment, *Housing Policy Technical Volume 1*, ch. 3.

9. Department of the Environment, *Housing Policy Technical Volume 1*, table II.42, p. 95.

10. See, for example, C. Clark and J.T. Jones, *The Demand for Housing* (Centre for Environmental Studies, 1971); I.C.R. Byatt, A.G. Holmans and D.E. W. Laidler, 'Income and the Demand for Housing' in M. Parkin and A.R. Nobay (eds.), *Essays in Modern Economics* (London, Longman, 1973); R.K. Wilkinson, 'The Income Elasticity of Demand for Housing', *Oxford Economic Papers* (1973); D. Stanton, 'Income and the Demand for Housing: Further Evidence in the UK', Department of the Environment *Economic and Statistical Notes*, no. 16 (HMSO, 1973).

11. An income elasticity measures the ratio of a proportional change in demand to a given proportional change in income.

12. Holmans, 'A Forecast of the Effective Demand for Housing in Great Britain', p. 39.

13. Building Societies Association, *Building Society Affairs* (October 1978).

14. See, for example, J. Foster, 'The Redistributive Effects of the Composite Income Tax Arrangements', *Manchester School*, vol. 43 (1975).

15. See, for example, J. Black, 'New Systems for Mortgages', *Lloyds Bank Review*, no. 111 (1974); National Economic Development Office, *Low Start Mortgage Scheme* (1972).

16. See Table 4.6, Ch. 4.

17. Department of the Environment, *Housing Policy Technical Volume I*, table 111.10, p. 122.

18. Ibid., p. 171.

19. With the main exceptions of H.L.I. Newburger and B.M. Nichol, *The Recent Course of Land and Property Prices and the Factors Underlying It* (Department of the Environment Research Report, 4, 1976); C.M.E. Whitehead, 'Inflation and the New Housing Market', *Oxford Bulletin of Economics and Statistics* (1973), and *The UK Housing Market*; R.K. Wilkinson and C. Archer, 'Uncertainty, Prices and the Supply of Housing', *Policy and Politics*, 5 (1976).

20. Department of the Environment, *Housing Policy Technical Volume II*, table VI.5, p. 32.

21. Though see Department of the Environment, *Housing Policy Technical Volume I*, p. 173.

22. Department of the Environment, *Housing Policy Technical Volume II*, table VI.19, p. 49.

23. S. Lansley, 'Changes in the Inequality of Household Incomes in the UK, 1971-1975', *University of Reading Discussion Paper in Economics, Series A*, no. 98 (1977).

24. Department of the Environment, *Housing Policy Technical Volume II*,

table VI.19, p. 49.

25. Marian Bowley, *Housing and the State 1919-1945* (London, Allen and Unwin, 1945), p. 9.

26. See, for example, A. Murie, P. Niner and C. Watson, *Housing Policy and the Housing System* (London, Allen and Unwin, 1976), pp. 92-101.

27. Department of the Environment, *Housing Policy – A Consultative Document* (HMSO, Cmnd 6851, 1977), para 9.11, p. 77.

28. See Fourth Report of the Estimates Committee, *Housing Subsidies*, vol. 1, para 24 (October 1969).

29. S. Winyard, 'Points to a good policy', *Roof* (Shelter, July 1978).

30. *Council Housing: Purposes, Procedures and Priorities* (Ninth Report of the Housing Management Sub-Committee of the Central Housing Advisory Committee, HMSO, 1969), para. 169.

31. Department of the Environment, *Housing Policy – A Consultative Document*, para. 9.20 to 9.21, p. 79.

32. S. Winyard, 'Points to a good policy'.

3 PAST PROGRESS AND CURRENT PROBLEMS

Few other areas of our lives affect us in the way that housing does. Housing conditions have a major influence on the health, attitudes, opportunities and quality of life of individuals and communities and, in consequence, housing has long been an area of local and central government concern and activity. Despite this, housing remains a major problem area of social and economic policy.

There is no single housing problem. Housing problems arise from a variety of circumstances and poor housing conditions affect people in different ways. For those living in unfit and substandard conditions in the decaying houses and tenement blocks of some of our industrial towns or in the ugly and neglected estates and tower blocks of our inner cities, the housing problem is only too visible. For others, the homeless and overcrowded, those familes forced to share with friends or relatives and those facing housing payments they can barely meet, the housing situation may be no less serious, but less conspicuous. These represent the most serious forms of housing stress. But other households may also find their housing situation repressive and intolerable because of the unpleasantness of the neighbourhood, because of inhibiting petty restrictions, because their housing is totally unsuited to their needs or because of difficulties of moving to another area or tenure.

Past Progress

This is not to deny that the great majority of the population now enjoy good housing conditions that are high by historical and international standards. Indeed considerable progress has been made. For most of the population housing standards have risen since the Second World War, and on almost any definition, we are now much better housed, *on average*, than in the past. We have more homes. Table 3.1 shows that the total housing stock in England and Wales increased by about 5½ million dwellings or 44 per cent over the 25 years from 1951 to 1976. This increase in the housing stock outstripped the increase in the number of households of 4.3 million, a rise of 32 per cent. A crude deficit of 800,000 dwellings in 1951 has therefore been turned into a crude surplus of 500,000 dwellings in 1976.

We have better houses. The average quality of the housing stock has also risen. Table 3.3 shows a steady decline in the number of house-

Table 3.1: National Balance of Dwellings and Households, 1951 to 1976, England and Wales (millions)

	1951	1956	1961	1966	1971	1976
Dwellings[a]	12.5	13.7	14.6	15.8	17.0	18.1
Households[b]	13.3	14.0	14.7	15.9	16.8	17.6
Balance	- 0.8	- 0.3	- 0.1	- 0.1	+ 0.2	+ 0.5

Notes:
[a] A 'dwelling' is 'a building, or part of a building which provides structurally separate living accommodation'. For further details of the definition of a dwelling, see Central Statistical Office, *Social Trends*, no. 6 (1975), p. 250.
[b] A 'household' is defined as 'two or more persons living together with common housekeeping or a person living alone who is responsible for providing his or her own meals'.
Source: Department of the Environment, *Housing Policy: A Consultative Document*, annex B, table 3.

holds living in unfit or substandard dwellings from 7.5 million in 1951 to 1.65 million in 1976. In the 10 years before the 1969 Housing Act, about 100,000 dwellings a year were improved with the aid of a public grant and between 1969 and 1975 an annual average of 250,000. As well as the new stock, at least 3 million homes have been improved since 1960. Between 1951 and 1971, the percentage of households that did not have sole or shared use of a fixed bath fell from 37.6 per cent to 9.1 per cent and of a water closet from 7.7 per cent to 1.1 per cent.[1] We have less overcrowding and sharing. Table 3.3 shows that the number of overcrowded households fell from 664,000 in 1951 to 150,000 in 1976 and the number of households sharing or concealed fell from 2.8 million to about 1 million over the period.

There has also been a major redistribution of property rights in the last 60 years which have transformed the lives of most households. In the nineteenth century the allocation of land was determined by its most profitable use. The consequence of this free rein of economic forces was that the great majority of the population had no long-term rights in property, and they legally occupied property only from moment to moment while their rents were determined by market forces.[2] Since then the importance of the territorial needs and ambitions of households and of rights of occupation have been recognised by planning legislation of various kinds and by the granting of security of tenure. The reduction in insecurity through legislation first took place after the First World War but since then, such security has sometimes been removed and modified by Conservative governments because of its inevitable conflict with the free market use of land.

Nevertheless, the current situation is one where the great majority of households enjoy legal or effective security of tenure, a reflection of the steady transfer of property rights from property owners to tenants since 1918.

International comparisons, too, show that, on the basis of simple indicators of basic amenities and overcrowding, Britain has better housing than most other countries, even those with higher *per capita* income. Thus, Table 3.2 shows that, in 1971, 91 per cent of dwellings

Table 3.2: International Housing Comparisons

		Average Number of Persons per Room	Proportion of Dwellings with Bath or Shower (per cent)	Proportion of Dwellings with Flush Toilet (per cent)
Austria	(1970)	1.1	55[a]	NA
Canada	(1971)	0.6	90[b]	94
Denmark	(1970)	0.8	63[c]	96
France	(1968)	0.9	49	52
Germany				
(Federal Republic)	(1972)	0.7	83	94
Italy	(1971)	0.9	29[d]	79
Norway	(1970)	0.8	45[e]	72
New Zealand	(1971)	0.7	98[f]	97
United States	(1970)	0.6	95	96
Japan	(1970)	1.0	66[g]	NA
Great Britain	(1971)	0.6	91	99

Notes: [a]1970; [b]1967; [c]1965; [d]1961; [e]1960; [f]1966; [g]1968.
     NA: Not available.
Source: Department of the Environment, *Housing Policy: A Consultative Document*, annex B, table 1 (a).

in Great Britain had a bath or shower compared with 83 per cent in Germany and 49 per cent in France, while 99 per cent had a flush toilet compared with 94 per cent in Germany and 52 per cent in France. In terms of the average number of persons per room, Britain enjoyed the highest standards in Europe, though this may be partly explained by our smaller household size. Nevertheless, since 1970, our building rate has been strikingly poorer than most other European countries, an average of 5.9 dwellings per thousand inhabitants between 1970 and 1974 compared with about 8.0 dwellings in the EEC as a whole.[3] By the end of the decade, our standards may not look so favourable.

The progress made since the Second World War should not therefore be understated. It could be argued that we are sometimes too critical of housing achievements since the turn of the century. As Della Nevitt has argued,

> it may be thought that British housing policies have been operating
> in an environment in which failure was certain . . . This seems not
> only an unduly pessimistic view, but also an inaccurate one . . . The
> move from an almost totally unprotected market condition to the
> current situation has occurred since 1918; this is a remarkable
> achievement which has involved a massive transfer of property rights
> from the few to the many, and has taken much of the anxiety from
> the lives of both working- and middle-class people.[4]

Nevertheless, this achievement also needs to be seen in the context of
general improvements in living standards on all fronts. In the quarter-
century since 1960, real income per head in the UK rose by an unprecedented 85 to 90 per cent. Yes, we are better housed but we are also
better fed, better clothed and have longer life expectations. Housing
deprivation, like poverty, is now accepted to be a relative phenomenon.
Acceptable housing standards should be defined in terms of average
housing conditions and the housing situation analysed in the context of
current standards and expectations, not those of a generation ago.
Quoting George Orwell in his *The Road to Wigan Pier*, talking once
with a miner . . . [I] asked him when the housing shortage first became
acute in his district; he answered, "when we were told about it" '
David Donnison noted, for example, that this meant 'that until recently
people's standards were so low that they took almost any degree of
overcrowding for granted'.[5] Without in any way denying the serious
nature of housing conditions before the Second World War, it is clear
that contemporary aspirations are higher while perceptions are sharper.

Moreover, this past achievement is inevitably tempered by the continuation of many housing problems. While housing standards for the
majority have been improving and will go on improving, significant
sections of the community have continued to endure poor housing
conditions. Not everybody has shared in the progress that has been
made and, as a result, the gap between the well and the badly housed
has widened. As the recent Green Paper on Housing Policy has observed,
'the continuing improvement in national housing conditions is no
consolation to people who remain in poor conditions. On the contrary,
their problems are thrown into sharp relief.'[6] The fact that homelessness is widespread and rising, and that 15 per cent of households live in
unfit, substandard or overcrowded accommodation or share unwillingly,
can be viewed as a measure of the failure of housing policy over the

last two and a half decades, just as much as the fact that 80 per cent are well housed by current standards is a measure of its success. The remainder of this chapter examines the nature and extent of current housing problems.

Current Housing Problems

Identifying housing problems depends on having a clear set of objectives. The basic housing objective remains that of meeting remaining housing need by ensuring that everyone has a decent home at a price they can afford. According to the housing Green Paper, 'The traditional aim of a decent home for all families at a price within their means must remain our primary objective.'[7] As will be seen in this chapter, much remains to be done to meet even this basic objective. In addition, public policy should aim for equitable treatment of households in different tenures and of households in the same tenure. A further objective is to widen choice in housing by making both private and public housing accessible to a wider range of people than at present. These objectives give rise, in turn, to the need for changes in our system of housing finance and in the administration of our housing stock, and they raise a number of related issues such as the access to housing of special groups such as the elderly and the mentally ill, the future of our tenure structure and what to do about variations in housing costs to the individual. All these issues are the concern of public policy and many of them will be raised in the course of this book. Throughout, there will be an emphasis on inequality — in physical housing conditions, in access to housing and in the cost of housing. The reduction of inequality in housing should be a major thrust of all housing policy.

Before turning to current housing problems, it is important to emphasise that these aims are by no means complementary. Within a given resource total, they can easily conflict. There is, for example, the question of whether to go for quality or quantity. The higher the standard of new housing, the fewer households can be rehoused; the better the quality of rehabilitation, the fewer houses can be improved. Opting for quality means larger benefits for a smaller number. In the past 20 years, policy makers seem to have gone for quality, at least in the public sector. By way of example, it has been estimated that the provision of housing to Parker Morris standards resulted in a loss of over 94,600 houses over the period 1964 to 1969, or about 10 per cent of the total number of local authority dwellings built in this period.[8] While the adoption of high standards means a lower rate of obsolescence, it may be one reason why we continue to suffer from a housing shortage. Another conflict relates to the choice between housing costs and housing standards: the adoption of high standards means higher rents (or higher rates and taxes). It is perhaps ironic that the sweeping away of substandard and slum dwellings in the redevelopment programmes of the last two decades also involved the replacement of cheap houses with expensive ones, and the gradual erosion of low-priced accommodation, especially privately rented. The objectives as stated above are therefore too imprecise for operational purposes and need to be spelt out clearly. A housing programme aimed at meeting these aims must also face up to the constraint of limited resources and the competing demands of other consumer and welfare services. Difficult choices have to be made between the conflicting aims of a larger stock, higher standards and keeping costs down.

Substandard Housing

Given these objectives, there are a number of current housing problems which policy needs to tackle. In the first place, much of our existing housing stock remains substandard in some way — unfit, lacking in amenities, in a poor state of repair or environmentally oppressive. Table 3.3 shows that in 1976 the House Condition Survey found approxi-

Table 3.3: Households in Physically Poor Houses, Overcrowded or Sharing, 1951 to 1976, England and Wales (thousands)

	1951	1961	1971	1976[a]
Multi-persons households sharing	1,442	582	380	275
One-person households sharing	430	448	440	375
Concealed households[b]	935	702	426	360
Crowded households[c]	664	415	226	150
Households in unfit or substandard dwellings	7,500	4,700	2,850	1,650
TOTAL (rounded)	11,000	6,800	4,300	2,800
TOTAL (free of duplication)[d]	9,700	6,400	4,100	2,700
Unduplicated total as percentage of all households plus concealed households	69%	42%	24%	15%

Notes:
[a]Estimates.
[b]Married couples or one-parent families living as part of another household.
[c]At densities above 1½ persons per room.
[d]Duplication in sharing households who are crowded; and sharing households in unfit or substandard dwellings.
Source: Department of the Environment, *Housing Policy, A Consultative Document*, annex B, table 4.

mately 700,000 households (about 4 per cent of all households) living in unfit houses, and a further 950,000 (5.4 per cent of all households) in substandard houses — houses not unfit but lacking one or more of the five basic amenities. The table also shows comparable figures for earlier years. These figures understate the extent of the problem of poor quality housing, since they do not include those houses neither unfit nor substandard but which are in disrepair. The 1976 House Condition Survey found 1.1 million dwellings needing repairs costing more than £2,350, a sizeable increase over the finding of the 1971 House Condition Survey. They also exclude those local authority estates which, though structurally sound and containing basic amenities, have severe environmental disadvantages.

Apart from the physical quality of accommodation, some households are living in overcrowded conditions, some are sharing a house with other households and some are concealed households living as part of other households.[9] Table 3.3 shows that, in 1976, an estimated 150,000 households were living in overcrowded[10] conditions, some 650,000 sharing, and 360,000 concealed. In total, there were approximately 2.7 million households living in unfit or overcrowded conditions or sharing in 1976. These figures still take no account of families living in housing of a good standard but unsuited to their needs, such as families with small children in high-rise flats and elderly or disabled people living in houses ill-suited to their special needs. No estimate is available on the extent of this need. Indeed unsatisfactory housing is a problem much more diverse than unfitness and lack of amenities, and also embraces problems connected with system-built houses and flats and with location, design and layout.

Homelessness

In addition to the problem of the physical inadequacy of the housing stock, there is a continuing problem of homlessness. Table 3.4 shows the number of families accepted as homeless since 1970. It is difficult to identify trends in homelessness with any accuracy because of variations in definitions and changes in the method of collecting statistics. Nevertheless, it is clear that there has been a sizeable rise since the early 1960s when concern was first expressed that the number of homeless families in welfare accommodation in London had risen above 1,000.[11] In 1976, approximately 50,000 households approached local authorities for help and some 34,000 were accepted as homeless. Moreover, these figures exclude the single homeless, a group which remains inadequately protected by the 1977 Homeless Persons Act. The main reason

Table 3.4: Homelessness[a]

	Greater London	Rest of England and Wales	Total
1970	3,193	3,351	6,544
1973	3,446	5,106	8,552
1974	11,360	NA	NA
1975	12,610	21,100	33,710
1976	12,400	21,280	33,680

Note: [a]The jump in the figures between 1973 and 1974 is explained by a change in the method of collection instituted in 1974.
NA: Not available.
Source: Central Statistical Office, *Social Trends*, no. 5 (HMSO, 1974) and no. 8 (HMSO, 1977).

for homelessness among those helped by local authorities in 1976 was domestic disputes which accounted for 38 per cent. Other reasons included repossession by landlord (17 per cent), rent arrears (7 per cent) and illegal letting (5 per cent).[12] The statistics also show that homelessness is concentrated in the inner areas of major conurbations, especially London, that the great majority of homeless people are not newly arrived in an area and that homelessness is a special risk for one-parent families. While the extent of homelessness is not large in relation to the total population, it remains a serious and special problem. The growth in homelessness since the early 1960s also emphasises that while the housing situation has improved for many groups it has deteriorated for others.

Inequalities in Housing

Inequalities in housing provision are reflected in variations in physical quality, in housing payments, in the allocation of subsidies and in access. It has already been seen that some 2.7 million households, 15 per cent of all households, are living in substandard housing conditions of one kind or another. There are also very wide variations in the size and quality of accommodation that can be obtained for a given amount spent, a situation which, as shown in Chapters 4 and 5, is accentuated by the existing capricious distribution of housing subsidies. Many of these inequalities are closely associated with our tenure structure. Housing sectors differ very widely in their physical condition, in the legal and financial previleges they offer and in their degree of access. In general, the quality of housing in terms of size, space, amenities and design, as shown in Chapter 6, is much higher in the owner-occupied and local authority rented sectors than in the privately rented sector.

Table 6.3 shows how in 1976 poor housing is concentrated in the privately rented sector, as is overcrowding. In contrast, privately rented accommodation offers less security than owner-occupation and public renting, and is characterised by very wide variations in rents. Between the owner-occupied sector and publicly rented sector as a whole there are major differences which make owner-occupation, in general, a more attractive form of tenure. If housing policy is concerned with greater equity, measures are needed which aim at evening out these differences in finance, conditions and access.

Housing and Deprivation. Before looking at the nature of variations in costs and access, it is important to consider the extent to which problems associated with poor housing are equally shared by different groups in society or whether such inequalities are associated with variations in income and socio-economic status.

In Chapter 1, it was argued that a basic objective of housing policy has been to break the link that would otherwise exist between bad housing and poverty by ensuring that low-income groups are not excluded from decent housing by lack of income. Governments have used a number of measures including rent control, the direct provision of local authority housing and rent rebates and allowances, in an attempt to improve the housing standards of lower-income groups and prevent families falling into poverty because of high housing costs. How far have these policies been successful? While it is difficult to provide a definitive answer to this question, there are a number of sources of evidence for the association between low income and housing conditions.

Some evidence is provided by small-scale surveys. The Lambeth Inner Area Study, for example, found an almost complete lack of correlation between low income and housing deprivation in a survey of households in the Stockwell area of Lambeth.[13] While some families in the survey were found to be poor and also living in rundown houses lacking amenities, and although many of those in bad housing were certainly not affluent, the general picture to emerge was that a particular household's difficulties were 'primarily housing' or 'primarily income'. Within the area of Lambeth covered, those with higher income were not necessarily better housed than those with lower incomes. Another survey by the Institute of Community Studies in Bethnal Green similarly found that 'very few of the income poor were particularly badly off for housing'.[14] A subsequent survey in Camden, however, did find that there 'the connection between poverty and bad housing had

not been removed'.[15] Similar evidence of some association between low
income and bad housing was also found in a social survey in Small
Heath, Birmingham.[16] The main reason for the lack of correlation in
Lambeth and Bethnal Green seems to be the impact of local authority
housing. Both areas had a relatively high proportion of such housing —
about a half in Lambeth, compared with a third in Camden and under a
quarter in Small Heath. It would seem, therefore, that the provision of
local authority housing in these areas has assisted in breaking the link
between income and housing quality. This is especially so in those areas
of our inner cities where local authorities have engaged in large-scale
redevelopment, clearing large areas of older houses and slums and
replacing them with new housing estates. To the extent that these older
areas of housing contained a high proportion of poor households, this
process of slum clearance will have led to the transfer of poorer families
into local authority housing.

Nevertheless, these results should be used cautiously before con-
cluding that the poor are not concentrated in poor housing and that bad
housing is not mainly occupied by lower-income groups. In the first
place, these surveys are confined to areas of relatively low income and a
relatively low proportion of owner-occupation, and national studies
would be more likely to identify a closer association between low
income and poor housing. Secondly, some of the estates found in these
inner city areas, while adequate in terms of the provision of internal
amenities, do suffer from a number of environmental deficiencies such
as high densities, inadequate social amenities and a rundown and
depressing environment. Thirdly, there is evidence that, within local
authority housing, low income and disadvantaged groups are sometimes
concentrated in poorer quality dwellings. The Inner Area Study in
Lambeth, for example, found that black families were more often in
the older and less desirable council property.[17] Other studies have
suggested that higher-income tenants tend to live in dwellings with the
highest gross values.

National evidence about the relationship between housing quality
and income is provided by the General Household Survey. Table 3.5
shows the proportion of households with given levels of household
income without certain basic amenities — a sole use of a bath or shower,
a sole use of an inside WC and central heating. This demonstrates that
those without such amenities also tend to be those with the lowest
incomes. This does not necessarily mean that low income is the main
cause of bad housing, though low income inevitably contributes to the
difficulty of obtaining decent accommodation. Poor housing is also

Table 3.5: Gross Weekly Income of Head of Household by Amenities, Great Britain, 1976 (percentages)

Income (£)	Without Sole Use of Bath or Shower	Without Sole Use of a WC. Inside Accommodation	Without Central Heating
< 15	19	20	72
15 – 20	15	15	68
20 – 40	9	10	62
40 – 80	5	5	48
80 – 100	2	3	28
>100	1	1	12
All	8	8	52

Source: Office of Population Censuses and Surveys, *The General Household Survey, 1976* (London, HMSO, 1978), table 5.31, p. 143.

sometimes occupied by the better-off and those with moderate to high incomes may find it more difficult to obtain decent housing in areas where shortages still exist such as London than those with lower incomes in areas with an adequate supply of housing. Table 3.6, however, confirms the general tendency for housing problems to be borne disproportionately by unskilled and semi-skilled manual groups. Thus 14 per cent of unskilled manual households lived in accommodation in 1976 without sole use of a bath or shower, compared with only 3 per cent of households with a professional head; 12 per cent of unskilled households lived in privately unfurnished accommodation compared with 4 per cent of professionals; in contrast, 72 per cent of unskilled households lacked central heating compared with 28 per cent of professionals while 5 per cent of the unskilled lived in detached houses compared with 39 per cent of professionals. The chances of lower-income and unskilled manual groups living in housing lacking basic amenities, or lacking central heating, or living in privately rented accommodation or accommodation below the bedroom standard are much higher than for higher-income and professional groups.

Comparisons between poverty and tenure also show that the poor are heavily over-represented in the private rented sector which offers the least attractive and most insecure accommodation, while the better-off are concentrated in the owner-occupied sector. As Chapter 6 shows, trends in housing are towards an increasing segregation of households by income between owner-occupation, on the one hand, and renting, public and private, on the other. Table 3.7 shows that in 1971, 45 per cent of poor households lived in the local authority sector compared with 31 per cent of all households; 28 per cent in the privately rented

Table 3.6: Housing Amenities by Socio-Economic Group of Head of Household, Great Britain, 1976 (percentages)

	Professional Employees and Managers	Intermediate and Junior Non-manual	Skilled Manual	Semi-skilled Manual	Unskilled Manual	All
Without sole use of bath or shower	3	7	7	12	14	8
Without sole use of inside WC	3	8	9	14	15	8
Without central heating	28	47	57	66	72	52
Renting privately furnished	2	4	1	2	2	2
Renting privately unfurnished	4	9	8	11	12	9
In accommodation below the bedroom standard	3	4	5	7	5	4
In detached house	39	17	10	8	5	16

Source: Office of Population Censuses and Surveys, *The General Household Survey, 1976*, tables 5.6, 5.20 and 5.32.

Table 3.7: The Distribution of Poor Households by Tenure Groups, 1971 (percentages)

	All Households	Poor Households[a]
Local authority rented	31	45
Other unfurnished rented	15	23
Furnished rented	4	5
Rent free	3	2
Owned with mortgage	27	4
Owned outright	20	22
All groups	100	100

Note: [a]Households with net income less than the official supplementary benefit level. Poor households in each tenure group as a proportion of all households in poverty.
Source: G.C. Fiegehen, P.S. Lansley, A.D. Smith, *Poverty and Progress in Britain 1953-73* (Cambridge University Press, London, 1977), table 6.10, p. 87.

sector compared with 19 per cent of all households; 4 per cent in houses owned with a mortgage compared with 27 per cent of all households; and 22 per cent in houses owned outright compared with 20 per cent of all households.

Housing Choice and Access. The reason for the broad associations between income, tenure and housing conditions observed above is that we have not achieved equality of access to housing whereby households, independently of their income, have a relatively free choice about the housing type and tenure they chose to live in. Housing choices remain heavily restricted for many families, partly for institutional reasons, partly because of inadequate income. Some households are also very immobile. Once having obtained accommodation, they may be effectively trapped in it for a long period of time because of difficulties in finding alternative housing. Problems of access and mobility are not evenly shared among different types of household. Groups who tend to face particular difficulties of access include low-income households, one-parent families, battered women, the disabled, the mobile and single people, though, of course, many people in most of these groups will not be especially restricted.

Barriers to access are institutional as well as financial. Access to owner-occupation depends on income, access to loan finance and a number of market factors influencing ability to pay. Building societies impose income rules governing the size of income needed to get a mortgage, but also take into account income stability, occupation and status. Entry to owner-occupation is constrained by these income conditions and the ability to meet mortgage repayments but also by the policies of building societies which tend to discriminate against certain groups such as manual employees with more irregular earning patterns and less employment and income stability.[18] There is also evidence of discrimination against black households.[19] Building societies tend to selectively apply their own income conditions to the benefit of professional and white-collar groups partly because of the assumed salary growth of such groups, while in the case of manual workers even stable or guaranteed overtime earnings are often ignored and these groups do not enjoy incremental salary scales. The chances of low-income manual worker households and also households with heads aged above about 45 becoming owner-occupiers are therefore limited. These barriers to access are the main reasons for the strong relationship between owner-occupation, income and social class. In 1976, the General Household Survey has shown that some 91 per cent of households with professional heads and 82 per cent of households with employer or managerial heads were owner-occupiers, either outright owners or mortgagors, compared with only 33 per cent of semi-skilled manual households and 21 per cent of unskilled manual.[20]

Lower-income groups are therefore, in general, forced to rent their homes, either in the public sector or from a private landlord. The better-off who can afford to buy a home but live in rented accommodation either live in luxury rented accommodation or choose renting to avoid the responsibility of home ownership or because of their need for mobility. Our system of housing tenure therefore continues to reflect established income inequalities.

Within the rented sector, it is generally the case that households would prefer local authority housing to private renting. Access to dwellings of different size and type in the publicly rented sector depends on a variety of local grading, transfer and allocation policies. As seen in Chapter 2, local authority dwellings are allocated on the basis of need, as defined by the authority. In general, such housing in the past has tended to be allocated to certain categories of household, especially lower-income households, young families and elderly households, groups which have traditionally been defined as those particularly in need. Certain groups have tended to be low in local authority housing priorities such as the young, the childless and the 'undeserving poor'.[21] There is evidence that some authorities have adopted the practice of 'grading' tenants and properties. The 1969 Central Housing Advisory Committee Report on *Council Housing: Purposes, Procedures and Priorities*, for example, was of the view that

there is a danger that applicants are graded according to an inter-
pretation of their desert; . . . the underlying philosophy seemed to
be that council tenancies were to be given only to those who
'deserved' them, and that the 'most deserving' should get the best
houses. Thus, unmarried mothers, cohabitees, 'dirty' families and
'transients' tended to be grouped together as 'undesirables'. Moral
rectitude, social conformity, clean living and a 'clean' rent book on
occasion seemed to be essential qualifications for eligibility — at least
for new houses.[22]

It is also clear that in the past black households have suffered discrimination in the selection and allocation proecedures operated by some local
authorities.[23] The extent to which current allocation policies operate
in these discriminatory ways is less clear, though there must be little
doubt that they still exist.

Whatever the limitations of access to local authority housing
experienced by these particular groups, it is clear that council housing
has tended to cater for lower-income households and particular socio-
economic groups. In 1976, only 2 per cent of professional households
and 11 per cent of employer and managerial houeholds were local
authority tenants compared with 53 per cent of semi-skilled and 65 per
cent of unskilled workers.[24] Table 3.7 shows that 45 per cent of poor
households live in the local authority rented sector compared with 31
per cent of all households.

The Cost of Housing. Housing costs have a number of special characteristics and are a major source of inequality in housing. After food (and
taxation), housing represents the largest item in the budgets of most
households. Moreover, because housing choice and mobility are
heavily restricted, housing costs are largely inflexible at least in the
short run. The main problems with housing costs are that some households continue to face housing payments they can ill afford, that there
is a wide variation in the standard of housing given levels of expenditure
will buy and that, even at particular income levels, there are wide
variations in housing payments.

High costs are found most often in the privately rented sector,
especially in furnished accommodation. Surveys in the 1960s and early
1970s have shown that households often paid exceptionally high rents
for what was often inferior accommodation, especially tenants of
furnished dwellings. For example, the Francis Committee found that in
Greater London in 1970 median rent as a percentage of median take-

home pay of heads of furnished tenant households – who were typically low earners – was as high as 33 per cent and that 53 per cent of these households were paying more than 30 per cent of their take-home pay as rent.[25] A study of housing costs in North Islington in 1970 found that tenants of privately rented furnished accommodation paid £2.55 in rent per room, privately rented unfurnished, uncontrolled tenants paid £1.36 per room, privately rented unfurnished controlled tenants paid £0.55 per room and local authority tenants paid £0.95 per room.[26] That furnished tenants paid a much higher proportion of their income in rent was also confirmed in a survey of Liverpool.[27]

On average, therefore, low-income groups in the furnished sector were paying a relatively high proportion of their income for generally poor quality accommodation in the 1960s and early 1970s. Moreover, despite the introduction of rent allowances for furnished tenants in 1973 and the provision of security of tenure for such tenants through the 1974 Rent Act, there is good reason to believe that such tenants continue to pay high rents. While the 1974 Act was designed to remove the problem of insecurity which was very much at the root of the high rents being charged for furnished dwellings, there is evidence that land-lords are exploiting various loopholes in the act such that it is not being fully implemented.[28] Again, the take-up rate for furnished allowances was estimated at only 10 per cent in 1974/5.[29] High rent is also not a problem that is confined to the privately rented sector. Rents vary widely in the public sector and, on average, are higher than privately rented unfurnished rents though lower than privately-rented furnished rents.[30] The take-up of rent rebates is higher in the local authority sector but still only estimated to be 70 to 75 per cent in 1975.[31] Despite policies of rent control, public housing subsidies, the provision of security of tenure and rebates and allowances, high rents may well remain a cause of poverty and low disposable income for many families.

Another problem with housing costs is that there is little correlation between housing payments and the quality of accommodation purchased, and households can pay very different sums for a similar standard of accommodation. Among tenants costs very between the public and private, furnished and unfurnished sectors for other similar accommodation and within these sectors according to a variety of regional, legal and historical differences, and whether or not the tenant is entitled to, and in receipt of, a rebate or allowance. In the owner-occupied sector, mortgage payments at a given moment in time reflect not so much 'quality' as the date of purchase, interest rates and the (variable) amount of tax relief.

A further problem concerns the relationship between housing costs and income. On average, housing payments fall proportionately as income rises — low-income groups pay a higher proportion of their income in housing costs than the better-off. In 1976, for example, the Family Expenditure Survey shows that households with gross incomes less than £25 a week spent 22 per cent of their total expenditure on housing compared with only 12 per cent by households with incomes of more than £200 a week.[32] Moreover, within income levels, housing payments can vary sharply. Table 3.8 shows the dispersion of 'net rent' paid by individuals receiving supplementary benefits. This is the sum taken into account in the practice of adding 'reasonable' housing costs to other entitlements when calculating supplementary benefits, a recognition of the high variability of housing costs and the difficulties of making adjustments in such costs.

Table 3.8: 'Net Rent'[a] Paid by Individuals Receiving Supplementary Benefit, November 1975

| | Number of Individuals (000's) | Average 'net rent' (£ per week) | Proportion of mean paid by | |
			10th percentile (%)	90th percentile (%)
Public tenants	1,297	5.79	70.0	134.7
Private tenants	573	4.26	30.5	185.4
Owner-Occupiers	391	3.05	36.0	223.0

Note: [a]Includes rent, rates and mortgage interest, less income from subtenants and rent and rate rebates.
Source: Department of Health and Social Security, *Social Security Statistics, 1976* (HMSO, London, 1977).

Housing payments therefore vary widely between and within tenures, between and within income groups, and often bear little relationship to the quality of accommodation purchased. These differences reflect regional variations, variations in pricing arrangements between tenures and unco-ordinated and haphazard subsidy policies. The financial arrangements underlying these differences are considered in more detail in Chapter 4. As well as improving the physical housing conditions of those who are currently poorly housed, improving housing mobility and finding ways of limiting and relieving homelessness, housing policy should also aim at evening out these differences in costs so that payments are more closely related to housing quality and ability to pay.

Future Policy

Physical inadequacy, homelessness and inequalities in choice, access and housing costs therefore represent the main housing problems for housing policy. Solving these problems requires policies which increase the output of new dwellings and the rate of improvement, and which reduce current inequalities, and this means action on both the supply and the demand side of the market. Inequalities and shortages are related. Inequality in housing is partly a consequence, partly a cause of housing shortages. It is a cause in the sense that a more equal use of the housing stock would reduce the physical problems of overcrowding and sharing and so reduce the extent of any shortage, and a consequence because a shortage inevitably means that some households will end up sharing or in poor accommodation. Reducing inequalities involves improving the physical conditions of those who are poorly housed, improving choice and ensuring a closer relationship between housing costs, quality and ability to pay. As well as additional building and improvement, changes in the existing system of subsidies and the existing allocation of houses are needed. Indeed expanding investment alone will not solve housing problems because there is no guarantee that extra output will go to those who are worse housed, especially if built in the private sector. Policies to encourage supply therefore need to be accompanied by policies aimed at producing a fairer use of existing stock and reducing variations in housing payments. This in turn requires changes in our haphazard system of housing subsidies. The problems associated with existing subsidies are discussed in Chapters 4 and 5 and some possible reforms outlined in Chapter 7. The remainder of this chapter considers the extent to which we continue to suffer from a shortage of houses, a subject over which there is considerable disagreement.

Dealing with Housing Shortages

Whether a housing shortage exists depends on how it is defined. One approach is to compare the number of desired separate households with the available number of existing dwellings of some minimum standard. This 'social' approach to defining housing need differs markedly from the economic concept of housing demand which represents that portion of housing need which is backed by willingness and ability to pay. In the pure economic sense, a housing shortage only exists when there are more persons able and willing to pay at the going price than there are houses available. Further, given a normal functioning free market, such a shortage would be a purely short or medium term phenomenon, the excess demand in the long run either being satisfied by an increase in supply or choked off by a further increase in price. Market equilibrium would be restored at the point where effective demand equals the available supply. Some households may remain homeless or sharing in such a situation because they have insufficient income to add to effective demand or because while they have sufficient income they do not wish to spend more on housing. A shortage exists in the social but not the economic sense.

Chapter 2 looked at the factors that determine economic or effective demand and the working of the housing market. The remainder of this chapter examines the extent of housing need in the social sense and how far it has been met.

Housing Standards

Housing need depends upon the number and size of households and the minimum acceptable standard and size of housing required by households of a given composition. As discussed in Chapter 1, it has long been accepted that public policy should aim at providing some minimum standard of housing to all households, independently of their ability to afford such housing. There is less agreement about what constitutes minimum standards, however. Housing need cannot be defined without ambiguity and subjective judgement and, in consequence, as Tony Crosland has observed,

> There is no unique and objective way of setting a total housing target. We can easily set a minimum figure which will meet our most pressing and urgent needs. But above that minimum the target will depend on a set of personal and social judgements.[33]

Not all households want separate accommodation, needs are heterogeneous and personal preferences differ. Standards will also vary over time. With rising living standards, housing expectations rise and minimum standards have to be revised in line with economic progress and social aspirations. It is increasingly being accepted that standards need to be extended beyond the structure and amenities of the house itself to considerations of privacy, space, density and the environment. Unfortunately some of these lessons have been learned too late. Too many of our modern estates, particularly tower blocks, yesterday's solution to the problems of shortages in our congested urban centres, have become socially repressive and detested by many of their occupants.

In general, minimum standards have been determined by a mixture of social convention and economic well-being, representing a balance between what is socially desirable and what is economically feasible. In practice, a number of statutory criteria have developed retarding such minima. These relate, in particular, to the fitness of the dwelling, its amenities and overcrowding.

Unfitness is defined in relation to housing conditions which put at risk the health of its occupants. Unfitness, as defined in the 1969 Housing Act, relates to the state of repair, stability, freedom from damp, internal arrangements, natural lighting, ventilation, water supply, drainage and sanitary convenience, facilities for preparation and cooking of food and for disposal of waste. While these largely public health criteria have not changed from 1957 and there is no obvious case for revising them, a broader definition of unfitness taking into account other factors such as an adverse environment which affects the well-being of inhabitants might be adopted.

Houses which are not 'unfit' can still be unsuitable for habitation if they lack widely accepted essential basic amenities. Discretionary grants were first introduced by the 1949 Housing Act and then made available as of right for standard amenities in the 1959 Act. Currently, householders are automatically entitled to an improvement grant under the 1974 Housing Act in the absence of a fixed bath or shower, inside WC, hot and cold water supply, wash basin and sink. Grants are also available at the discretion of the local authority for a variety of items such as drainage, dampness or lighting. In general this definition of amenities conforms with views of what is an acceptable minimum, but it does not provide a complete definition of what is an acceptable dwelling for a particular household. For example, a tower block flat may not be unfit or lacking in amenities, but may provide inadequate accommodation for a family with children.

Overcrowding or over-occupation has been defined officially in relation to the number of persons per room, with a figure of more than 1½ persons per room representing overcrowding, or the bedroom standard relating the number of bedrooms to the size and structure of the household.

The question of involuntary sharing is more difficult to assess and there is no national or statutory standard. A variety of forms of sharing exist, some voluntary, some involuntary. A useful distinction is between couples, with or without children, single-parent families and single adults living as part of another household. It is probably reasonable to assume that the great majority of sharing couples and single-parent families are involuntarily sharing. As regards single adults, most of these will be adult children still living at home or elderly persons living with their married children or other close relatives. Many of these will be doing so voluntarily but some will not. There remains a small proportion of single adults who do not wish to share but are forced to do so because of lack of income or difficulty in finding alternative accommodation.

Homelessness is an extreme form of housing need but is not a category of need separate from those discussed above. It arises for a number of reasons but most often because of personal reasons that people previously sharing no longer find it tolerable to do so, or because of eviction.

Why Housing Shortages Have Persisted

On a number of occasions over the last two decades housing experts and politicians have predicted the end of the housing shortage. In order to meet housing need in the sense of each household having a separate dwelling of minimum quality suited to its needs, it would be necessary for governments to have brought demand into line with need. It has long been accepted, though not universally, that governments should intervene to reduce housing shortages but, despite such intervention and the intentions of public policy, housing shortages have always persisted. Throughout this century, this has been the most pressing housing problem.

Why is it that such shortages have persisted? It was argued in Chapter 1 that, left to itself, the market would be unable to provide housing of some relatively determined minimum standard for all households. This is partly because of the conditions of housing supply which are highly dependent upon wider economic factors such as the availability and cost of credit, income levels and the general level of economic activity which means that the building industry, more so than many other industries, is characterised by considerable instability. In consequence the level of private building changes erratically over time depending in particular on movements in the economy. Another reason is the maldistribution of income and wealth which means that, given the cost of a dwelling of a minimum standard, private enterprise cannot meet the needs of a large proportion of the population. Government intervention is therefore needed to remove shortages but such intervention has not been successful in providing an adequate supply.

One reason for this is that there are significant regional and sub-regional differences in income inequality and hence the ability of private forces to meet housing need. In areas of below average incomes, shortages are more likely to persist and the need for direct supply by government is greater. The resource costs of meeting housing need in areas where there is a high demand for public housing is therefore higher than in areas where incomes are greater and meeting such need therefore takes much longer.[34] Another reason why government intervention has been slow in reducing shortages is that there are conflicts in housing policy. One conflict arises, for example, between the provision of property rights through legislation concerned with security, housing costs and minimum standards and the level of private supply. Controls of various kinds imposed on the relationship between landlord and tenant have undoubtedly been a factor reducing the supply of privately rented accommodation. Again, as was seen earlier, the adoption of relatively high standards such as the low-density houses built to Parker Morris space and heating requirements has inevitably meant fewer houses actually built. Further, resources devoted to housing are inevitably in competition with other government expenditure. There is also a view that housing construction and capital spending on housing in general have suffered disproportionately in times of economic restraint and that governments have used housing as an instrument of economic policy with resources being spent on housing when the economy is healthy and restricted when it is not.

> Housing policy has always been considered as expendable, a suitable case for Treasury treatment as soon as the economy gets into difficulty . . . Housing programmes have many times been axed as part of the regulation of the economy, though in fact housing makes a very bad regulator.[35]

Outstanding Housing Need

How near are we to eliminating housing shortages? Table 3.1 showed an excess of households over dwellings up to 1971 but a small surplus of dwellings in 1971 and 1976. In 1951 there were about 800,000 more households than dwellings in England and Wales but by 1976 a surplus of dwellings of about 500,000. These figures show the 'crude' deficit or surplus of dwellings over households and a casual glance can easily give the impression that the physical housing problem has been largely solved and, in consequence, that the level of new investment in housing can be scaled down. Certainly this is a view that has recently been voiced in some quarters. The Nationwide Building Society, for example, drawing attention to the 1976 balance, suggested that 'the main future need will be to provide for the net increase in new households and for the renewal of the existing stock'.[36] Commenting on a set of cuts in public spending on housing imposed in early 1976, a *Guardian* editorial in July 1976 posing the question, 'Are we building more houses than we need?', replied that, 'the aggregate answer is probably, yes'.[37]

The crude figures, however, do not mean that we no longer suffer from a shortage of homes. There are a number of ways in which Table 3.1 overstates the surplus in 1976 and understates the deficit in earlier years. In the first place, some proportion of the housing stock at any one time should be vacant to allow for adequate mobility and improvement. Also, some houses will be empty because they are used as second homes. Indeed, in 1971, the Census found 676,000 vacant dwellings, giving a net deficit of 430,000 households over occupied buildings.[38]

Various estimates have been made of the vacancy rate required to allow the housing market to operate. In making an estimate of housing needs to 1980, Needleman in 1961 used a 4 per cent margin of vacancies for household movement, for the ownership of second homes and for excess houses in rapidly declining areas.[39] More recently a working party on London's housing needs suggested a figure of 4 to 5 per cent for London[40] and others have suggested 5 per cent for mobility and an additional 1 per cent for second homes.[41] The figure of 5 per cent now seems to have become widely accepted, if not official. In a recent speech, for example, Peter Shore, as Secretary of State for the Environment, spoke of '5 per cent plus an allowance for second homes'.[42]

Another important factor is that much of the existing housing stock remains unfit or lacking in basic amenities. Table 3.3 showed that in 1976 approximately 1.65 million households (9.4 per cent of all households) lived in unfit or substandard dwellings. In addition, some 1.1 million dwellings were in serious disrepair, though there is some overlap here with unfit dwellings. Finally, these figures also exclude the large number of dwellings on local authority estates which, though structurally sound and containing basic amenities, have severe environmental disadvantages. As well as the physical quality of accommodation, Table 3.3 showed an estimated 150,000 overcrowded households, 650,000 sharing and 360,000 concealed, though some of those sharing will be doing so voluntarily. In total, there were therefore approximately 2.7 million households living in unfit or overcrowded conditions or sharing in 1976, and these figures still exclude families living in housing of a good standard but ill suited to their needs.

Finally, these national figures conceal very wide regional and area variations. Housing remains imperfectly distributed relative to jobs, and some regions still have 'crude' shortages. The 1971 Census showed a 'crude' shortage in three major conurbations of 96,000 in Greater London, 3,234 in the West Midlands and 1,930 in Merseyside,[43] though these will be smaller now. There are also more localised shortages. While Lancashire, for example, had an overall surplus, six of the seventeen former county boroughs had crude deficits. Even in Kent, five local authorities showed an overall deficit. Measures of outstanding housing need must therefore include the sum of these localised deficits.

On the basis of these figures, it is possible to build an *approximate* global estimate of the extent of unmet housing need in England and Wales and the scale of housing provision required to tackle the most pressing housing needs. This can be done by comparing the size and physical adequacy of the existing stock with the number and sizes of households to be accommodated. A number of such estimates have been made in the past by estimating the addition to the housing stock needed to make good present shortages, allowing for the extent of unfit and substandard dwellings, overcrowding and involuntary sharing and purely regional and local housing shortages; for future needs arising through new household formation and replacement and for a margin of vacant dwellings adequate for mobility.[44] Table 3.9 gives an estimate of the extent of housing need as at 1976 and the scale of programme needed to meet such needs over the next decade, based on the most recent figures available. It must be emphasised that such estimates are very approximate and are subject to wide margins of error. A comparison of past forecasts of housing need with actual outcomes indicates the degree of error that can be involved. Housing need is wide and heterogeneous, estimates of the rate of obsolescence and household formation are inevitably uncertain, some of the information on which forecasts need to be based is imperfect and incomplete, and estimates are sensitive to underlying assumptions. Housing prophecy in the past has had a very poor track record. Nevertheless, such exercises are useful for indicating the broad scale of future investment needed to meet basic needs.

In 1976 there were an estimated 18.1 million dwellings and 17.6 million households in England and Wales, an apparent surplus of 500,000 dwellings. To obtain the number of desired separate households we need to add to this figure the number of concealed households, estimated at 360,000 (Table 3.3), giving 17.96 million households needing separate accommodation.[45] Allowing a vacancy reserve of say 5 per cent for mobility and second homes gives a total requirement of

18,860,000 separate dwellings. Given an existing stock of 18,100,000 this gives an additional requirement of 760,000 dwellings. In addition, there are 1,870,000 unfit or substandard dwellings in need of replacement or improvement.[46] Further, there are 150,000 overcrowded households, but this does not necessarily give rise to a requirement for additional building since, if these dwellings are vacated, they will become available for use by smaller households. This figure is therefore ignored. Finally, a figure for purely regional or local shortages needs to be added, say 100,000. This gives an estimate of the current shortage of approximately 2,730,000 dwellings.[47]

Of course, increasing the sound housing stock by 2,730,000 dwellings by a mixture of new building and improvement will not of its own deal with the problems of overcrowding and sharing and occupation of substandard accommodation. The new dwellings need to be of the right type and size and in the right areas and above all not be too expensive for households to buy or rent. The nature of the housing market is such that a surplus of houses can exist alongside homelessness and the occupation of inadequate housing.

In addition to meeting outstanding *current* requirements, a housing programme spanning, say, the next ten years would also have to meet *future* needs arising from further losses of homes through redevelopment and growing obsolescence and additions to need through new household formation. Annual losses to the housing stock through slum clearance, redevelopment and open space and road building can be assumed to continue at the current level of around 75,000 per annum.[48] As for obsolescence, the Department of the Environment's study group on social ownership has estimated the annual rate of houses becoming unfit but not cleared to be around 30,000.[49] In addition, an estimated 100,000 houses per annum are likely to fall into major disrepair.[50] The rate of household formation depends on rises in income, changes in demographic patterns, housing availability and the scale of the future housing programme and is particularly difficult to predict, especially in view of the likely growth of single-person households and the fact that household formation is partly dependent on the availability and cost of housing. Future household formation has been estimated at 149,000 per annum.[51] This gives a total of 3,540,000 units over the next decade to meet new requirements.

Table 3.9 therefore shows that a housing programme to meet current and future needs within ten years would require an average of 627,000 new or improved dwellings a year. The programme would require a mix of improvement and new building, though the ideal mix is a matter of

Table 3.9: An Estimate of Housing Needs, England and Wales, 1976 to 1986

	Extra Units Required	
(i) To Meet the Current Shortage		
Concealed households	360,000	
Vacancy surplus	400,000	
Replacement or improvement of unfit, substandard dwellings[a]	1,870,000	
Crude regional deficit	100,000	
Total programme to meet current requirements		2,730,000
(ii) To Meet Future Needs		
Losses through redevelopment, obsolescence	750,000	
Uncleared unfit housing	300,000	
Houses falling into disrepair	1,000,000	
Household formation	1,490,000	
Total to meet future requirements		3,540,000
Total current and future programme		6,270,000

Note: [a]890,000 unfit and 980,000 fit but lacking one or more basic amenities.
Source: See text and Table 3.3

dispute. Of the 890,000 currently unfit dwellings, many will need replacing. Of the 980,000 substandard dwellings, some will need replacing, some require extensive and others only relative minor improvement. To meet the regional deficit and vacancy reserve, new building is required.

As to the feasibility of such a programme, a comparison with the actual rate of building and improvement achieved in recent years indicates that it would require a substantial expansion over current and recent performance. Over the period 1972 to 1976 the number of units completed, new building and improvement combined in both public and private sectors, averaged 503,000 and the total had fallen below the average in 1975 and 1976.[52] On the basis of recent performance, therefore, the actual programme over the next decade is likely to fall well short of the target indicated in Table 3.9. If remaining areas of pressing need are to be largely removed, there therefore needs to be an expansion in the level of housing investment.

It is very difficult to predict the actual scale of housing investment over the next decade. This is determined by a great variety of factors, and will depend in particular on general economic circumstances, the rate of inflation, the willingness and ability of the government to increase public spending on housing investment and the state of the building and construction industry.

What is of interest is the extent to which the meeting of the target will depend upon increases in public spending on housing. Assuming that the private sector can contribute at the most 225,000 to 275,000 dwellings a year, say 135,000 to 160,000 new buildings and 90,000 to 115,000 improved, and the figure for improvement is particularly optimistic given the recent slump in the take-up of improvement grants, the remainder, some 350,000 to 400,000 units, need to come from the public sector. Over the last five years, public sector house completions have averaged only 117,000 units and improvements around 80,000 units, a combined total of the order of 200,000 units. Recent public expenditure White Papers, together with official Department of the Environment announcements and the new controls on public sector building, suggest that, on current plans, public sector new building is unlikely to exceed 100,000 a year in the next few years. If we assume an average of 100,000 a year for the next decade, this leaves 250,000 to 300,000 to be met by rehabilitation and improvement. This represents a four or five fold increase over the rate of rehabilitation achieved in 1975 and 1976 and would require a substantial increase in public expenditure on housing investment.

Whether we can meet remaining housing needs within some reasonable time span, would seem to depend crucially on the level of public investment that can be sustained and hence upon wider economic factors and the level of priority that governments feel should be afforded to housing. Certainly, our current level of housing investment is low by international standards. In 1975 we spent a lower share of gross domestic product on capital formation in housing than almost any other country in Western Europe: 4.4 per cent compared with, for example, 6.7 per cent in Italy, 5.3 per cent in the Netherlands and 7.2 per cent in France.[53] In addition, some contribution might be made by a more effective use of the existing stock. As argued in Chapter 5, the scope for this is widespread but heavily constrained by a variety of social, economic and political constraints. The changes in policy required would be unlikely to make a significant impact for a long time, though it is a possibility that would be facilitated by an expansion in the size of the housing stock.

Nevertheless, given the scale of programme required in relation to recent achievements and the considerable expansion in public sector activity that would seem to be required, it must be concluded that not only have we not yet solved the problem of the persistent housing shortage, but that we are unlikely to do so within the next decade. On the basis of the existing level of investment in housing, serious physical housing problems are likely to remain well beyond the mid-1980s with some, though a decreasing number of households continuing to live in unfit, substandard or overcrowded homes, share unwillingly or face serious restrictions on their mobility.

Moreover, the prospect of significant unmet housing needs remaining in 1986 is one predicted by the recent Green Paper on housing. In the Technical Volume, it is predicted that some 720,000 households are likely to remain unsatisfactorily housed in 1986 — living in unfit or substandard accommodation, overcrowded or sharing. Further, this total does not include households living in 'houses that are in poor repair, suffer from damp and the like, but are not unfit and have the basic amenities', or in houses with basic amenities 'of an antiquated and unreliable kind'.[54]

Housing as a Series of Local Problems

The previous section demonstrated that, contrary to the views of those who argue that there is now a housing surplus in Britain, serious shortages in fact remain and may well persist throughout the 1980s. Nevertheless, despite the continuing existence of a national shortage, there is now a widely held view that housing problems are essentially local in nature. We have already seen that there remain even crude local shortages, areas where there is an excess of households over dwellings. In addition, the other physical problems of unfitness, overcrowding and sharing are very unequally distributed between regions and districts. The housing Green Paper, for example, argued that we should no longer think

> only in terms of national totals. This may have made sense when there was an overwhelming absolute shortage of housing everywhere. It makes sense no longer. On the contrary, a national approach can draw attention and resources away from the areas with the most pressing needs.[55]

It is therefore increasingly accepted that we now have less of a single national problem than a series of regional and local ones and that, too often in the past, targets have been set on a purely national basis without consideration of whether resources should be concentrated in particular areas. Housing policy in the 1950s and 1960s was characterised by the 'numbers game' in which ambitious national targets were fixed — ranging from the Tory 1951 cry of '300,000 houses' to the

Crossman White Paper of 1965 which described the immediate target of 500,000 homes a year by 1970 as 'modest in the light of housing needs' — but rarely met. Emphasis has now shifted from crude quantitative targets at the national level to general guidelines regarding regional and local policy. At a speech in Birmingham in September 1976, Peter Shore, Secretary of State for the Environment, spoke of the need to

> cease to regard housing as a single national problem susceptible to national targets and national solutions, and instead to regard it as a series of interlinked and interacting local problems, with the amount of public financial support sensitively tuned to the housing needs of each area.[56]

This new policy direction has been accompanied by a number of moves designed to concentrate resources within areas where needs are apparently the greatest. This principle was already well established in improvement policy, General Improvement Areas being introduced in the 1969 Housing Act and Housing Action Areas in the 1974 Housing Act, both designed to concentrate assistance, with the aid of higher grants and a range of additional special powers, in small areas with particularly poor housing conditions. More recently, the level of local authority improvement has been controlled under section 105 of the 1974 Housing Act and the level of municipalisation constrained by various criteria through a variety of government circulars, though these controls were designed to influence the overall level of spending rather than the area allocation of funds. In August 1976, following a short freeze on all public housebuilding imposed by the Chancellor of the Exchequer in July 1976, a new form of control was introduced designed to concentrate building in 61 designated stress areas which were allowed to restart their programmes. In consequence, many authorities were effectively prevented from further building.

More recently, a new system of capital spending allocation has been introduced, Housing Investment Programmes, designed to improve the geographical distribution of resources for capital spending. Local authorities now have to draw up comprehensive local housing strategies, covering all housing provision within their boundaries, and these are now used as a basis for allocating loan sanction between authorities. In this way, local assessment is used as the basis for deploying resources, in principle, an improvement on previous methods, though the system has been criticised in various ways.[57]

Whatever the case for setting priorities for the allocation of resources, such policy gives rise to the problem of setting criteria for the determination of priorities. Drawing up a coherent and locally sensitive programme requires a systematic assessment of the scale depth of housing need by region and local area, but deciding what is a stress area and what is not may ultimately be a matter of judgement. In 1976, the list of stress authorities was drawn up on the basis of data about overcrowding and basic amenities from the 1971 census, and on information from regional offices, though the government made it clear that they would consider representations from other councils not included in the original list. The criteria used could be criticised on the grounds that the 1971 census information was out of date, that lack of amenities is primarily a case for rehabilation rather than new building, and that some districts were excluded despite evidence of overcrowding, substandard housing and a large waiting list.

In general, this new emphasis on the concentration of resources for housing investment in areas and on problems of greatest need is desirable. It can hardly be denied that some areas have more severe problems than others and that the intensity of housing need varies between areas. In this sense, national housing problems do consist of a series of local problems, but this should not hide the fact that such problems are not restricted to just a minority of areas, as is now often maintained. Evidence from housing analysts and pressure groups suggests that housing need remains more widespread than the government is prepared to admit. The analysis of the previous section suggests that on the basis of the assumptions employed and without changes in current policy, significant outstanding housing need will remain for many years. Moreover, in addition to the more traditional forms of housing stress of overcrowding, unfitness and lack of amenities, new problems are emerging, such as the rising level of disrepair especially in the private rented stock, and the extensive environmental and structural problems on many of our older and some new local authority housing estates. These needs will not be met without additional public investment.

Summary and Conclusions

There is now a large and growing body of opinion which argues that housing need in Britain is now largely residual in nature, confined to specific problems in a diminishing number of areas, and that the level of investment in housing, especially public investment, can in consequence be scaled down. In this chapter, it has been argued that this is far from being the case. Physical problems remain widespread with a significant proportion of the population continuing to live in houses which are unfit, lacking in basic amenities, in serious disrepair, overcrowded or situated in environmentally oppressive surroundings. Moreover, current housing problems are not restricted to these physical deficiencies. Housing is characterised by widespread inequalities which are reflected in variations in housing standards, in housing costs for equivalent accommodation, in housing access, and in the allocation of subsidies. Housing policy needs to aim not only at remaining physical problems, but also at reducing these inequalities. These require the maintenance of a high level of public investment in new building and improvement, changes in the management and administration of the existing stock and, above all, major changes in our current system of housing finance.

Notes

1. Central Statistical Office, *Social Trends, No. 6* (London, HMSO, 1975), table 9.6.
2. A.A. Nevitt, *Fair Deal for Householders*, Fabian Research Series 297 (Fabian Society, 1971).
3. Jane Morton, 'Europe. So Just How Does Britain Compare?', *Roof* (Shelter, May 1976).
4. A.A. Nevitt, 'Issues in Housing', in R. Davies and P. Hall, *Issues in Urban Society* (London, Penguin, 1978), p. 210.
5. D.V. Donnison, *The Government of Housing* (London, Penguin, 1967), p. 43.
6. Department of the Environment, *Housing Policy – A Consultative Document* (HMSO, Cmnd 6851, July 1977), para. 2. 04.
7. Ibid., para. 2.16.
8. C. Crouch and M. Wolf, 'Inequality in Housing', in P. Townsend and N. Bosanquet (eds.), *Labour and Inequality* (London, The Fabian Society, 1972), p. 31.
9. Concealed households are families headed by a married couple or lone parent living within another household, and not identified as a separate census defined household in its own right.
10. Overcrowding is defined as density of occupation greater than 1.5 persons per room. This includes fewer households than would be counted as overcrowded by use of the 'bedroom standard'.
11. J. Greve, *London's Homeless* (London, Bell, 1964).
12. Central Statistical Office, *Social Trends*, no. 8 (London, HMSO, 1977), table 9.11, p. 155.
13. Department of the Environment, *Poverty and Multiple Deprivation: Report by the Consultants* (1975) and Department of the Environment, *Second Report on Multiple Deprivation* (1977).
14. L. Syson and M. Young, 'Poverty in Bethnal Green', in M. Young (ed.), *Poverty Report 1974* (London, Temple Smith, 1974).
15. L. Syson and M. Young, 'The Camden Survey', in M. Young (ed.), *Poverty Report 1975* (London, Temple Smith, 1975).

16. Department of the Environment, *Birmingham Inner Area Study: A Social Survey* (1975).

17. Department of the Environment, *Lambeth Inner Area Study: People, Housing and District* (1974). See also, *Housing in Multi-Racial Areas* (Community Relations Commission, July 1976).

18. S.S. Duncan, 'The Housing Question and the Structure of the Housing Market', *Journal of Social Policy*, vol. 6, part 4 (1977), pp. 385-412.

19. J.B. Cullingworth (ed.), *Problems of an Urban Society*, vol. 2: *The Social Content of Planning* (London, Allen and Unwin, 1972), p. 102 and Duncan, 'The Housing Question and the Structure of the Housing Market', p. 391.

20. Office of Population Censuses and Surveys, *The General Household Survey, 1976* (London, HMSO, 1978), table 2.28, p. 41.

21. See, for example, Cullingworth, *Problems of an Urban Society*, vol. 2, p. 51.

22. Central Housing Advisory Committee, *Council Housing: Purposes, Procedures and Priorities* (HMSO, 1969), para. 96.

23. Cullingworth, *Problems of an Urban Society, Volume 2*, pp. 102-7.

24. Office of Population Censuses and Surveys, *The General Household Survey, 1976*, table 2.28, p. 41.

25. *Report of the Committee on the Rent Acts* (The Francis Report), (HMSO, Cmnd 4609, 1971).

26. C. Holmes, *Better Than No Place* (Shelter, 1971), table 20.

27. J. Edwards and D. Simpson, *A Study in Access: A Survey of Access to Housing in Liverpool* (Shelter Neighbourhood Action Report, report no. 6, Shelter, 1972).

28. S. Weir, 'Landlords Exploit Rent Act Loopholes', *Roof* (Shelter, October 1975), p. 11.

29. National Consumer Council, *Means Tested Benefits, A Discussion Paper* (London, 1976), p. 28.

30. See Table 4.7, Ch. 4.

31. National Consumer Council, *Means Tested Benefits, A Discussion Paper*, p. 28.

32. Department of Employment, *Family Expenditure Survey Report for 1976* (London, HMSO, 1977), table 33. It should be noted, however, that the Family Expenditure Survey may underrate the income elasticity of demand for housing.

33. A. Crosland, *Towards a Labour Housing Policy*, Fabian Tract 410 (Fabian Society, 1971).

34. Nevitt, 'Issues in Housing', p. 198.

35. F. Berry, *Housing: The Great British Failure* (London, Charles Knight, 1974), p. 223.

36. Nationwide Building Society, *Occasional Bulletins*, 134 (April 1976).

37. *Guardian* (15 July 1976).

38. Department of the Environment, *Housing Policy Technical Volume I*, table 1.5, p. 15.

39. L. Needleman, 'A Long term view of housing', *National Institute Economic Review*, no. 18 (November 1961).

40. Ministry of Housing and Local Government, *London's Housing Needs up to 1974* (Standing Working Party on London Housing, report no. 3, 1970).

41. H.W. Richardson and J. Vipond, 'Housing in the 1970s', *Lloyds Bank Review* (April 1970).

42. Department of the Environment, *Press Notice* (10 September 1970).

43. *Census 1971 England and Wales, Housing Statistics* (London, HMSO, 1974).

44. See, for example, Needleman, 'A Long Term View of Housing'; Richardson and Vipond, 'Housing in the 1970s', and D. Hoodless, 'What Size of Housing

Programme do we Need?', *Roof* (Shelter, March 1976).

45. If we assume that some separate households would prefer to share and not move into separate accommodation even if it were available, the extent of need would fall.

46. Department of the Environment, *Housing Policy Technical Volume I*, Table B.1, p. 159.

47. Ideally, such estimates should be made for each region separately, and national requirements obtained by summing net deficits across each region. To the extent that there are some regions where there is a surplus of 'good' dwellings over households (including concealed), the global requirement for replacement of unfit dwellings may be less than that shown in Table 3.9. Against this, the figure of 2,730,000 dwellings takes no account of dwellings which while not in poor condition, may nevertheless be environmentally unsuitable.

48. Department of the Environment, *Housing and Construction Statistics*, no. 13 (HMSO, 1st quarter, 1975). There may be some duplication here with the figure for unfit and substandard houses under 'current requirements'.

49. *Report of the Study Group on Social Ownership* (unpublished) quoted in Hoodless, 'What Size of Housing Programme Do We Need?', p. 45.

50. Hoodless, 'What Size of Housing Programme Do We Need?', p. 45.

51. Ibid., p. 45.

52. Table 1.1, Ch. 1.

53. Department of the Environment, *Housing Policy: A Consultative Document*, appendix 3, table 1(b).

54. Department of the Environment, *Housing Policy Technical Volume I*, ch. 3, para. 116, and table III.38.

55. Department of the Environment, *Housing Policy: A Consultative Document*, para. 2.16.

56. Department of the Environment *Press Notice* (10 September 1976).

57. See Ch. 7.

4 GOVERNMENT INTERVENTION IN PRACTICE – THE CURRENT SYSTEM OF FINANCE

The financial arrangements affecting housing in Britain are extremely complex. The existing system of housing finance consists of a great variety of aids and concessions, differing within and between tenures, and which have developed historically in a largely piecemeal manner. In general, these aids are distributed in irrational and indiscriminate ways with little regard to any principles of need or capacity to pay, efficiency or equity. Described by the late Tony Crosland as a 'dog's breakfast', it is not surprising that he saw housing policy aimed at dealing with remaining problems as needing 'above all, a reform of housing finance'.[1]

Such was the state of the financial arrangements underpinning housing policy that Tony Crosland eventually set up, in mid-1975, what was intended to be a fundamental review of housing finance to be undertaken by the Department of the Environment in conjunction with other Departments. In Chapter 7, we consider in some detail the results of that review, *Housing Policy, A Consultative Document*, published in July 1977 as a Green Paper.[2] This chapter first examines in some detail the financial arrangements affecting housing in each of the main sectors, and then looks at public expenditure accounting arrangements and trends in the components of housing expenditure.

The Present System of Housing Finance

Owner-Occupiers

Owner-occupiers receive help in a great variety of ways, though there is disagreement as to what constitutes their actual subsidy. The main form of financial assistance provided to householders with a mortgage is tax relief received on mortgage interest payments together with option mortgage subsidy. The option mortgage scheme operates by providing mortgagors the option of an ordinary mortgage with tax relief on the interest paid, or a mortgage at a lower, subsidised rate of interest which involves repayments equivalent to the net payments, after tax relief, paid by a standard rate taxpayer. There is no dispute that the net outgoings of home owners with a mortgage are reduced by the amount of tax relief claimed on mortgage interest payments. Moreover, mortgage interest has represented the only form of interest allowable against tax since the budget of March 1974, thus making this form of assistance unique to the purchase of a house.

Another form of help special to home owners is the absence of tax on the imputed income from house ownership and others have argued that it is this exemption rather than tax relief which represents the subsidy. Imputed income refers to the notional income received by home owners in the form of housing services whose 'imputed' value is equivalent to the market rent that would otherwise have to be paid for them. Until 1963, house owners had to pay tax on the value of their imputed rental income from ownership (under 'Schedule A') as part of a general system of taxing both actual and imputed income from real property. To the extent that owners pay tax on their imputed income in this way, mortgage interest incurred in obtaining that income represents a justifiable allowance against this tax, such that it is only one or the other which represents the subsidy and not both.

Nevertheless, up to 1963, owner-occupiers were considerably under-taxed on this basis because the imputed rent element was calculated on the basis of 1936-7 rating valuations which increasingly understated current market value rents. While Schedule A taxation was abolished in 1963, mortgage interest payments remained as an allowable expense against income tax.

The abolition of Schedule A taxation for owner-occupiers has meant that while house ownership provides considerable income in kind, it is not taxed.[3] The argument for taxing the imputed income from ownership is that taxes should be levied on the capacity to pay tax and that home ownership, which removes the need to pay rent, provides income in kind and so raises the taxable capacity of the owner, provided the costs necessarily incurred in obtaining the asset which yields imputed income is deducted in assessing tax. Owner-occupiers with real income from their home have a higher standard of living and a greater capacity to pay tax than non-owner occupiers with identical money incomes, yet in the absence of Schedule A taxation, they are treated identically for income tax purposes. This confers a considerable financial advantage on the home owner as is clear from, for example, a comparison with tenants, or landlords who have to pay tax on rent income, or with investors in shares who pay tax on dividends. The extent of this tax saving can be gauged from a comparison of two standard rate taxpayers with identical incomes, one buying and one renting his home. Suppose A has a gross income of £6,000 p.a. and rents a house for £1,000 p.a.

If the rate of income tax is 30 per cent and personal allowances amount to £1,000, A pays income tax of £1,500. If instead, A buys the house for say £10,000 and obtains a 100 per cent mortgage at a 10 per cent rate of interest, he pays mortgage interest of £1,000 p.a. which he can deduct to obtain taxable income and so pays only £1,200 in tax (30 per cent of £4,000), or £300 less than if he remains a tenant. While the mortgagor will have to pay some additional sum in capital repayments, this essentially represents a form of saving which yields a capital asset. The favourable tax position of an owner-occupier would also be made apparent with a similar comparison with a landlord.

Whether mortgage tax relief or the absence of tax on imputed income represents the actual subsidy to home owners depends on whether houses are regarded as an investment good which represents a form of saving and produces a stream of taxable income, or a consumption good like other consumer durables which are not taxed. If the purchase of a house is regarded as a form of saving, then it is the absence of Schedule A taxation which represents the subsidy, and tax relief if housing is considered an ordinary consumption good. This is a difficult issue to be dogmatic about.

Owner-occupiers also enjoy special financial benefits in other ways. First, they, in general, borrow money at below market rates of interest, largely at the expense of building society depositors. Secondly, owners are exempt from capital gains tax if the house is a sole or main residence. If house prices rise at a faster rate than all prices, such gains can be substantial. It is often contended that house purchasers do not benefit from any appreciation in the value of their house since moving from one house to another does not allow any realisation of these gains. However, this ignores the fact that rising house prices increase the costs of those buying in a later period and enable those who bought earlier to move to a more expensive house, without increasing the share of their income spent on housing. House price appreciation leads to a redistribution of income from new buyers to existing owners, from those buying for the first time later in life, towards those of the same generation who bought at an earlier date, and from tenants as a whole to owners as a whole.

Further, capital gains can be directly realised when house owners move to smaller houses or cheaper regions, or do not devote the entire gain to a subsequent purchase. A survey of house sales by the Department of the Environment in 1973 showed that the majority of owners do 'take some of the profits' on changing house:

Some of the most interesting results came from an analysis of the financial consequences of moves by owner-occupiers from one home to another. After paying off their previous mortgages and receiving their new mortgage advances, the majority realised more from the sale of their old house than they put towards the purchase of their present one. While some of this surplus would be absorbed by moving expenses and fees, the balance would be invested or spent. This means that, on the whole, funds were flowing from long term lenders into current expenditure as a by-product of the finance of housing through long-term loans from building societies and other sources, rather than in the reverse direction. Most families moving to more expensive homes were financing the difference in price by borrowing money, and in well over half the cases, they were borrowing more money than was needed purely for the difference in price.[4]

Even if the gain is not realised by householders themselves, it will be by their heirs. Moreover, the opportunity for taking out an annuity providing a guaranteed income on retirement on the value of the house is widening all the time, and tenants are unlikely to find a form of savings that offers such capital gains, or at least avoids a capital loss.

Owner-occupiers therefore receive financial assistance in various ways. They borrow money at below market rates of interest. They enjoy income tax relief on mortgage interest payments (with no question of undergoing a separate means test as does a tenant for a rebate or allowance), a regressive form of aid which benefits those with the largest mortgages and highest incomes most, while being exempt from tax on both the imputed rental income and capital gains that arise from personal ownership.

Further, these benefits are greatly enhanced by inflation. Apart from the benefit of being able to borrow at rates of interest that are often negative in real terms,[5] the share of income which the owner-occupier devotes to housing costs declines over the life of a mortgage. Mortgage repayments are normally fixed in money terms over the period of the loan, and only rise (fall) with increases (reductions) in interest rates, so that while initial repayments can be relatively high, they fall in real terms if prices rise and in relation to income as incomes rise, and cease when the mortgage is repaid and the house is owned outright. After a period of inflation, therefore, established owners can face relatively low outgoings, often lower than the rent paid by tenants. Further, owners acquire a capital asset, the value of which depends on the relative rates of increase of house prices and general inflation.

Tax relief is also a regressive form of subsidy. While tax relief on mortgages of £25,000 and above and for second homes was ended by the Labour Government in March 1974, tax relief is the higher, the higher the borrower's income and the larger his mortgage. The effect of tax relief is to lower the rate of interest actually paid on the loan. Thus the basic rate taxpayer pays a net interest rate of 7.15 per cent (with an 11 per cent nominal interest rate and a 35 per cent basic rate of income tax), while a mortgagor paying tax at the higher marginal rate of 80 per cent has his mortgage rate reduced to an effective 2.2 per cent by tax relief. This figure is further reduced to 0.22 per cent for someone on the highest marginal rate of taxation (98 per cent) for unearned income.

In 1975/6, mortgage tax relief plus option mortgage subsidy amounted to £957m or £174 p.a. per household with a mortgage.[6] The amount of assistance received by an individual household may vary widely from this average figure, and for a particular household, changes over time. The size of mortgage for a new buyer is determined by the current market price of the house when purchased. In the early stages of a mortgage, interest repayments and hence tax relief are high, but as the mortgage is gradually paid off, both the interest charges and the associated tax relief fall in money terms and more rapidly in real terms when prices are rising. An increase in the mortgage interest rate may increase interest charges temporarily, but the trend is still downwards. When existing houses are bought and sold, the house price received and paid will be the current market price. The actual size of mortgage and hence mortgage repayments to an individual household at a given point in time therefore vary widely according to when the house was bought, its price, the size of initial loan required and the mortgage interest rate. In turn, the amount of tax relief received depends on the size of initial loan and the amount of loan outstanding, the mortgage interest rate, and the mortgagor's marginal tax rate.

Local Authority Tenants

Local authority tenants pay rents that, on average, are lower than either historic costs or market levels. The full historic cost to the local authority of the provision of council housing consists of maintenance and administration, and the payment of interest on past loans obtained to finance building. The difference between this historic cost and the income from rents has been met by direct central government subsidies under a variety of Housing Acts and by local rates.

Table 4.1 shows the combined Housing Revenue Account of all local authorities in England and Wales for the three years 1967/8, 1973/4, and and 1975/6. This is a statutory account which local housing authorities have been required to keep by law since 1935. All costs incurred in the provision of local authority housing under successive Housing Acts must be debited to the account, and all rent and other income including Exchequer subsidies credited to it. The account must be balanced annually by reduction of any working balance and/or contribution from the general rate fund sufficient to meet any shortfall. Loans for new buildings are amortised over 60 years, the assumed life of dwellings. Authorities operate a 'loans fund' through which they borrow money for all capital expenditure at various rates of interest and for various periods, and then advance money from the loans fund to the various service accounts.

Table 4.1: Combined Housing Revenue Account of Local Authorities, England and Wales (£ million at outturn prices)

	1967/8		1973/4		1975/6	
	£	%	£	%	£	%
Expenditure:						
Supervision, management	45	8.4	126	10.4	253	12.8
Repairs, maintenance	87	16.2	203	16.8	340	17.2
Debt interest	389	72.6	827	68.5	1317	66.6
Other	15	2.8	51	4.2	66	3.3
TOTAL	536	100.0	1207	100.0	1977	100.0
Income:						
Rents	399	73.6	850	70.5	1115	56.1
Exchequer subsidy	96	17.7	237	19.7	633	31.9
Rate fund contribution	39	7.2	65	5.4	175	8.8
Other	8	1.5	53	4.4	64	3.2
TOTAL	542	100.0	1205	100.0	1987	100.0
Subsidies:						
Exchequer[a]	96	71.1	237	51.9	633	61.4
Rate fund contribution[a]	39	28.9	65	14.2	175	17.0
Rebates	—	—	155	33.9	233	21.6
TOTAL	135	100.0	457	100.0	1031	100.0

Note: [a]Excluding rent rebate.
Source: Department of the Environment, *Housing Policy, Technical Volume I*, table IV.9, p. 179.

Since the Houisng Rents and Subsidies Act of 1975 which repealed the 1972 Housing Finance Act, local authorities are obliged by law to charge 'reasonable' rents subject to their not being allowed to budget for a surplus on the housing revenue account. 'Reasonable' relates to the balance between the interests of tenants as a group and ratepayers as a group, *and* between the interests of one tenant and another. After allowing for government subsidies, each local authority balances its housing revenue account annually by means of rental income and rate fund contributions, the share of each lying within the discretion of the authority. While local authorities have freedom in principle to determine rent levels and what contribution should be made from the rates, this decision can and has been influenced by central government, by, for example, the imposition of a rent freeze by Statute, as in 1974, or the imposition of minimum or maximum rent increases by exhortation or threat of penalties by for example the tying of certain subsidies to a prescribed rent increase.

Tenants as a group pay that part of historically incurred costs not met by Exchequer subsidy or rate fund contributions. But because of rent pooling individual tenants do not pay the historically incurred costs of the house they rent. If they did so, tenants of pre-war houses would pay very low rents and tenants of post-war houses much higher rents. Under rent pooling, the rents of individual properties are not related to the historic cost of the property, but all costs are pooled and the rent requirement, after subsidy and any rate-fund contribution, spread over all properties. In this way, the rents charged for individual properties can be related to factors such as age, size, condition and location, rather than their historic cost.

The actual subsidies that a local authority receives depends upon a variety of factors, especially the time when they built up their housing stock and the then prevailing cost of building, interest rates and levels of central government subsidy, and vary widely between authorities. Prior to 1967, subsidies consisted of fixed annual payments for each completed house over a given number of years, irrespective of the cost of the house. The numerous acts passed simply altered the amount payable, though the 1961 Housing Subsidies Act did attempt to relate the subsidy more closely to local resources by varying the flat rate subsidy according to the state of the housing revenue account and introducing a supplementary subsidy in the case of especially high costs.

The 1967 Housing Subsidies Act represented the most clear departure from previous policies. The aim of the act was to encourage local authorities to provide housing to Parker Morris standards, and the subsidy introduced was for the first time directly related to the capital cost of providing such housing. The subsidy was prevented from being open-ended by the simultaneous introduction of the cost yardstick system designed to limit the capital cost of housing. Subsidies were also related to the interest rate payable, and were designed to change automatically with changes in interest rates.

The 1972 Housing Finance Act changed the system of subsidies in a number of radical ways. The power to fix rents was removed from local authorities and rents were to be set at 'fair' rent levels; where fair rents were greater than actual rents, they were to be raised in a series of stages. A new national statutory rent rebate scheme for public tenants and rent allowance scheme for private tenants was introduced, the former financed partly by the central Exchequer and partly by ratepayers, and the latter initially wholly by the Exchequer. With these changes, the subsidy system had to be recast and subsidies were related to the financial position of the housing revenue account, with local authorities having to make prescribed contributions from the general rate fund, another new departure.

The 1972 Act was repealed by the 1975 Housing Rents and Subsidies Act, though this was intended to be an interim measure. The act abolished 'fair rents' and restored to local authorities their earlier freedom to set 'reasonable' rents and make rate fund contributions at their own discretion. A new basic capital cost subsidy was introduced paid at the rate of 66 per cent of reckonable loan charges, together with a special 'high cost' element for authorities with very high costs.

A number of points arise from Table 4.1. On the expenditure side, debt charges represent the bulk of the cost of housing provision – 67 per cent in 1975/6. The remaining costs are supervision and management, and repairs and maintenance. The share of each has not changed significantly in the last decade. On the income side, gross rents accounted for about 56 per cent of income in 1975/6, Exchequer subsidies for 32 per cent and the rate fund contribution for 8.8 per cent. Over the last decade, the share of income provided by rents has fallen from 74 per cent in 1967/8 and that provided by Exchequer subsidy risen from 18 per cent.

The main explanation for these changes are to be found in the steady increase in the real costs falling on the housing revenue account. Costs have risen at a faster pace than inflation in general since the early 1970s. Between 1971/2 and 1974/5, the real cost per average local authority dwelling rose 30 per cent, but then remained constant at this new higher level between 1974/5 and 1976/7.[7] There were three main reasons for this jump in costs. First, house-building costs and land prices rose more rapidly than average prices, pushing up the capital cost of building. Secondly, the costs of management and maintenance rose, partly because of rising labour costs and the volume of work, but also

because of the expansion in 'support' services such as the administration
of the new rent rebate and allowance schemes, the expansion of housing
advice centres and social ownership programmes and the growing proportion of homes for the elderly and disabled requiring resident
wardens and other services. These have all required additional staffing,
and it is questionable whether the costs of these services should fall on
the housing revenue account at all, since these are not exclusively of
benefit to council tenants. The most important factor, however, was
the rising cost of loan charges after 1973 arising from the jump in
interest rates especially in 1973 and 1974 which increased the cost of
financing new debt at market rates of interest and the re-financing of
maturing older debt.

How have these rising costs been met? Local authority unrebated
rents rose by approximately 113 per cent between 1970 and 1976
while the index of retail prices rose by 114 per cent and average manual
earnings (before tax) by 139 per cent.[8] Changes in rent levels have
therefore kept pace with general increases in retail prices and have
almost kept pace with gross earnings over this period. Net earnings over
the period rose more slowly than gross earnings. During the 1960s rents
on average rose at a faster pace than earnings and prices.

The difference was therefore met by a steady increase in
Exchequer subsidy, whose share of costs rose from 18 per cent in
1967/8 to 32 per cent in 1975/6. The increase in subsidies to local
authority housing revenue accounts over this period gave rise to some
criticism — particularly in the press — that council housing is too
expensive and taxpayers pay too much.[9] But the above analysis puts
this view into perspective. Tenants' contributions have kept pace with
inflation, and the need for additional subsidy arose mainly as a result of
the interaction between inflation and changes in interest rates on the
costs of financing local authority debt.

One of the main reasons for the increase in subsidy over the period
1973 to 1976 was the impact of the increasing rate of inflation and the
accompanying increases in interest rates on loan charges. This induces
a phenomenon known as 'front loading' or 'bunching' of loan charges,
which means in essence that a rapid rise in the rate of inflation and
hence, interest rates, leads to loan charges rising at a faster rate than
inflation for a time. If the rate of inflation then stabilises or falls, loan
charges will rise at a slower rate than inflation and hence fall in real
terms. Provided rents are maintained in real terms, the real subsidy
required will subsequently fall. This is because a rising rate of inflation
and interest rate leads to a more rapid rate of repayment of loans.

Initially this pushes up debt charges but this is eventually offset by increasing incomes and the falling real value of loans. The time pattern of repayments in real terms is altered with more being repaid earlier and less later.[10] The reason why loan charges rose particularly steeply in the early 1970s was that there was a unique combination of a rising capital programme in real terms, a rise in costs relative to the general price level and a steep rise in interest rates.[11]

What constitutes the subsidy to local authority tenants? The subsidy can be seen as the difference between the actual and historic cost rent; as the difference between the actual rent and the rent obtainable on the open market, which may be above or below the historic cost of an individual dwelling depending on when the dwelling was built and pre-vailing local market conditions; or as the difference between actual rent and long run marginal cost, expressed on a current annual equivalent basis.

The total Exchequer subsidy and rate fund contribution to housing revenue accounts in the UK combined amounted to £1,066 in 1975/6 or an average subsidy per tenant (exclusive of rent rebate) of £173 a year.[12] This compares with the figure for tax relief plus option mort-gage subsidy of £970 or £174 per mortgagor. Local authority tenants also receive assistance in the form of rent rebates. The cost of rent rebates in 1975/6 was £256 p.a. which represented an average rebate per tenant of £41 p.a., though only approximately 20 per cent of tenants were in receipt of rebates. It is arguable whether rebates should be treated as a direct form of housing subsidy or part of the wider system of income support, an issue which is discussed further in Chapter 5.

As with the case of owner-occupiers, the actual rents paid and subsidy received by tenants vary widely and have not been systemat-ically related to individual need, income and quality of accommodation. One factor causing differences in rents is variations in the average cost of housing provision between boroughs and regions. These costs may vary either because of differences in the size of building and rehabilita-tion programmes or because of differences in the cost of building. Authorities with a large new or recent building or improvement programme in relation to their stock of dwellings will have higher average costs per dwelling than those with smaller investment pro-grammes. There are also very wide regional and area variations in construction and improvement costs. When authorities in high cost areas, such as London, also have relatively large new building schemes, their dwelling costs can be very high. Table 4.2 shows how

Table 4.2: Variations in Costs and General Subsidies by Type of Local
Authority, England 1974/5 (£ per dwelling)

	Average Costs	Average Exchequer Subsidy[a]	Average Rate Fund Contribution
Greater London Council	648	246	80
Inner London Boroughs	711	318	118
Outer London Boroughs	495	178	47
Metropolitan Districts	300	82	22
Non-Metropolitan Districts	289	71	17
Total, England	347	104	29

Note: [a]Excluding rent rebates.
Source: Department of the Environment, *Housing Policy Technical Volume II*,
p. 6.

wide the differences are between regions, and the extent to which
central government and rate fund contributions fail to even out
these differences sufficiently to generate similar rent levels between
areas.

Another reason for wide variations in rent levels is that rents have
generally been set at the discretion of local authorities (with the exception of the period of operation of the Housing Finance Act from 1972
to 1974) at levels that are 'reasonable' between tenants and ratepayers.
Moreover, the total subsidy available to an individual authority is only
partially related to its current housing needs, and not at all to the
incomes and circumstances of its tenants. Rather, subsidies are related
to the time when authorities built up their housing stock and the then
prevailing costs of building, interest rates and legislation regarding the
level of central government subsidy. Differences in rents also stem from
variations in the criteria used to determine rents, and differing policies
on rent rebates, rent pooling and rate contributions adopted by auth-
orites.

In consequence, rent levels vary widely. At April 1976, the average
weekly unrebated rent of a post-1964, three-bedroomed house was as
high as £10.80 in the London Borough of Hammersmith, £9.60 in
Wokingham and £8.40 in Brighton, and as low as £3.70 in Chorley
(Lancashire), £3.97 in South Derbyshire, and £4.10 in Carlisle, compared with an average in England and Wales of £5.74.[13] In 1975, it has
been shown that 9 per cent of rebated rents of local authority tenants
were under £80. p.a., 17 per cent were between £80 and £159 p.a., 47
per cent were between £160 and £239 p.a., and 27 per cent were more
than £240,[14] though these variations do not allow for size and quality

differences.

There are a number of important differences in the way housing is financed in the public rented and owner-occupied sector. First, while house buyers generally take out loans for a period of between 20 and 30 years, local authorities finance the construction of new council dwellings with loans from the consolidated loan fund which are repaid over 60 years, irrespective of the periods for which the authority itself may have borrowed from the capital market. In consequence, the public sector's outstanding debt on a particular dwelling would fall more slowly than a house purchaser's debt if he did not move over the course of the loan.

Secondly, all public sector housing debt is related to the 'historic' cost of construction. In contrast to owner-occupation where every time a house changes hands a new mortgage is based on the new current market price such that debt increases, when public tenancies change hands, the dwelling and the debt on it are not revalued to current market prices. The debt on a particular local authority house remains fixed in money terms, and so declines with inflation, and council house outstanding debts only rise when new houses are built. Mortgage debt, however, increases on houses changing hands, irrespective of whether additional houses are added to the owner-occupied stock. Indeed, while the outstanding debt on local authority housing revenue accounts rose by 59 per cent between 1970 and 1975, the outstanding mortgage debt of all owner-occupiers rose by 105 per cent over the same period. In 1975, the outstanding debt on mortgages and local authority housing stood, respectively, at £23,930 million and £11,459 million.[15]

Finally, in the public sector, the costs of housing provision within a local authority are pooled across all dwellings and tenants. The great advantage of this is that the benefit of lower historic costs on earlier houses can be used to even out the higher costs of current building. The loan costs of older housing are now minimal in relation to total loan charges. On the other hand, housing built more recently has very high loan charges, but by pooling, local authorities are able to spread most of this cost over their tenants. The effect is that older tenants are paying rents that are much higher than the historic cost of building their house in order to keep the rents of newer tenants below that which would be needed to pay the current cost of providing their house, after deducting Exchequer subsidy and rate fund contributions. In this way, all tenants are able to pay reasonable rents which reflect the pooled historic costs of housing to the local authority. This is in sharp contrast to the new owner-occupier who pays the current market price of accommodation and not the historic cost. While a mortgage also remains fixed in money terms, the savings accrue to the individual mortgagor, and when the house is sold, any capital gain is achieved at the expense of the next purchaser, and indirectly, the community, which is forced, by way of mortgage tax relief, to repeatedly and expensively subsidise a succession of occupiers of one private house. One of the great historical benefits of council housing is that the benefit of capital gains on houses built in the past are spread over all tenants. They do not accrue to an individual tenant but are socialised to the benefit of tenants as a group.

Private Tenants

There are a variety of categories of private tenant, none of which receive direct government assistance towards their rent, except in the form of rent allowances. Most tenants, however, have and still do benefit to a greater or lesser degree from rent control in some form, but rent control involves a subsidy from the landlord rather that the state as in the case of tax relief and general subsidy. There have been a variety of forms of rent control which have affected different types of tenant in different ways.

Rent control over privately rented houses was first introduced as a temporary measure during the First World War and, though more expensive houses were gradually freed, low rated property remained controlled throughout the inter-war period. At the outbreak of the Second World War there were some 4 million houses that had been controlled since the First World War. The Rent and Mortgage Interest Restrictions Act of 1939 froze rents at the pre-war level for all but about 100,000 privately rented houses with high rateable values. Rent control remained in force until the 1957 Rent Act, although the Housing Repairs and Rent Act of 1954 allowed landlords to increase rents if they could show that they had spent money on repairs. The 1957 Act abolished control automatically on dwellings with a rateable value of more than £40 in greater London and more than £30 elsewhere in England and Wales and permitted increases in the rents of houses remaining under control according to their gross values and state of repair. It also removed control from all houses let to new tenants.

Until the 1957 Rent Act, therefore, most tenants of unfurnished private dwellings were protected by rent controls which prevented properties from being let at more than the pre-war rent. While the 1957 Act led to a considerable relaxation of these controls, controlled dwellings were not completely phased out when the 1965 Rent Act introduced the 'fair rent' system. The 1965 Act restored protection over most privately rented, unfurnished properties, introducing the 'regulated tenancy'. The act provided for tenants and landlords of formerly decontrolled tenancies to apply for a regulated 'fair rent' to be determined on the basis of the 'age, character, locality and state of repair of the dwelling' while disregarding the value due to any local shortage of similar accommodation. Fair rents were intended to be fair to tenants and landlords, providing the latter with a reasonable return on capital equal to the market rent in long run equilibrium with any short run scarcity element excluded, and sufficient to encourage the landlord to continue to rent. In general, it has been estimated that registered fair rents have been about 20 per cent below market levels.[16] While a large number of properties have had regulated rents imposed, many have remained unregulated either because they have a gross rateable value too high to be covered by the act, or because their tenants have not taken advantage of their right of regulation. Furnished tenants remained unaffected by the act.

In 1972, the Housing Finance Act introduced procedures to speed up the conversion of those remaining controlled tenancies into rent regulation to be carried out in a series of stages. All existing controlled dwellings were to be gradually decontrolled until rents reached 'fair' levels. Furnished properties had never been subject to rent control or regulation except for the limited security of tenure provided under the Rent Tribunal procedure established by the Landlord and Tenant (Rent Control) Act, 1949. In 1974 Labour's Rent Act granted protection against arbitrary eviction to the furnished tenants of absentee landlords, thereby, in effect, providing for furnished tenants the same rights of security and regulation as enacted in the 1965 Act for unfurnished property. In the event, a number of loopholes have developed as a result of various exceptions permitted in the 1974 Act which have effectively precluded many tenants from protection.[17]

The impact of rent control is shown in theory in Figure 4.1. If the demand and supply for rented accommodation is given by the curves denoted D and S, the equilibrium market rent would be r_e and N_e the number of rented dwellings provided. Suppose r_e was considered too high a rent for tenants to pay and legislation set a maximum rent of r^*. Then each tenant receives a subsidy of $(r_e - r^*)$ from his landlord. The initial effect of rent control is to redistribute income from landlords to tenants. Further, lower rents will expand the demand for rental accommodation from ON_e to ON_b. This will cause an initial excess demand of $N_e N_b$ since the short run supply curve can be assumed to be

Figure 4.1: The Impact of Rent Control

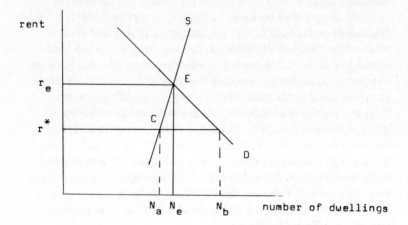

fixed at N_eE. The excess demand will mean that some rationing device other than price will be needed to allocate the available supply of dwellings. An entry price in the form of 'key money' may develop, or overcrowding may increase.

In the longer run, the reduction in rents, while helping low income tenants, will discourage the supply of homes for renting. Supply will eventually fall to N_a, either by rented houses being sold, or by houses falling into disrepair. The new short term supply curve will have shifted to the left at N_aC. The extent of the fall in supply will depend on the elasticity of supply. Since this is rather low, at least in the short run — a result mainly of the unfavourable tax treatment of landlords — the fall in supply may not be very great. Conversely, the effect of decontrol would not be to stimulate a very large increase in supply. To the extent that the elasticity of supply is greater in the long than the short run, however, decontrol would have a greater impact in the long run.

In general, therefore, the main impact of rent control has been to reduce the cost of housing to existing tenants, to redistribute income from landlords to tenants, to discourage new building of property to rent and to promote the deterioration in the quality of the existing rented stock, and its transfer into owner-occupation. But the precise extent of each of these effects is far from easy to establish, and is the subject of controversy. As a way of protecting tenants from the rents that would have emerged in a free market when rented accommodation is in short supply, rent control has been subject to a number of criticisms. First, because of the capricious nature of its distributional effects. Tenants are subsidised by their landlords, irrespective of their comparative incomes. By subsidising only one part of the rented market, rent controls also redistribute income away from landlords of controlled property to landlords of uncontrolled property and to existing owner-occupiers to whom unsatisfied demand is shifted. A fairer way of protecting tenants would have been by aid financed by taxation levied on the whole community. Secondly, because of its impact on the supply of accommodation to rent. There is little doubt that rent control has been one of the factors causing the decline in the availability of privately rented accommodation. But this is not the only factor and the decline was in fact under way before rent control was introduced.[18]

There are both demand and supply factors that account for the permanent decline of privately rented property. On the demand side, rising real incomes and changing economic and social patterns will have led to a switch in preference to owner-occupation. This preference for other forms of tenure has been reinforced by the greater financial benefits offered by owner-occupation and public renting, a consequence, in part, of our subsidy system. On the supply side rent control has reduced the rate of return on investment in housing, and legislation aimed at tenant security will have acted as a disincentive to landlords. Nevertheless, even in the absence of rent control, private landlords have been at a permanent tax disadvantage in relation to owner-occupiers, and alternative forms of investment have offered higher returns. Indeed it has often been the case that in order to give a private landlord a market return on the value of his house, rents would have to have been set that were higher than the cost to the tenant of buying the property at vacant possession value himself. The landlord would expect more from a tenant than the pre-tax interest (currently about 7½ per cent) which he would get if he sold the house and invested the proceeds in a building society. A tenant would therefore have to pay at least this and expect regular increases, while if he bought the property and qualified for tax relief he would have to pay only about 5½ per cent plus some capital repayment. Even with 'fair rents', landlords have in general been better off by selling properties, provided they can obtain vacant possession and so realise the 'scarcity element' on property ownership. Another important factor has been the impact of slum clearance policies which has affected this sector particularly heavily.[19] Since the Second World War, there has, indeed, been very little new building for private letting, and then predominantly at the luxury end of the market. But even without rent control, we would have experienced a decline in the importance of private letting.

A final disadvantage of rent control has been its impact on the maintenance of rented accommodation. A relatively high proportion of privately rented dwellings have been shown to be unfit, substandard or in serious disrepair and an important factor has been the low rents received for such property.

The private rented sector currently remains extremely heterogeneous in character. Table 4.3 shows approximately 2.8 million privately rented, housing association and tied dwellings in England and Wales in

Table 4.3: Sub-divisions of Privately Rented and Other Tenures, England and Wales 1966 to 1976 (thousand dwellings)

	1966 (April)	1971 (April)	1976 (End-Year)
Housing associations	130	180	250
Rented with job[a]	800	810	700
Rented unfurnished from a private landlord:			
controlled	1700	1200	375
regulated	1070	840	1115
Rented furnished (excluding 'tied' accommodation)	250	330	350
Total	3950	3360	2790

Note: [a]Including nearly 100,000 armed forces married quarters.
Source: Department of the Environment, *Housing Policy Technical Volume III*, table 1X.1, p. 62.

1976. There remain three main categories of private tenant; the few remaining controlled tenants paying something like the historic value at the time of letting, since decontrol only occurs with the death or moving of the sitting tenants, or when the tenancy moves into regulation when all the basic amenities have been installed; the regulated tenant, who pays a 'fair rent' which lies somewhere between the historic cost and current market value which is mainly set by the vacant possession value of sale to owner-occupation; finally, furnished tenants who often continue to pay high rents at current market value.

Table 4.4 shows the variations in rent paid by unfurnished and furnished private tenants and local authority tenants. Private rents vary to a much greater extent than local authority rents. The variations in

Table 4.4: Rents[a] of Private and Local Authority Dwellings, 1973 (£ a year)

	Lowest decile	Median	Highest decile
Private rented unfurnished	24	76	265
Private rented furnished	95	253	over 400
Local authority rented	69	168	260

Note: [a]Rent net of rebate or allowance.
Source: Department of the Environment, *Housing Policy Technical Volume III*, table 1X.3, p. 71.

rents in the unfurnished sector reflect the fact that this category contains controlled lettings which gives the low rents at the lower tail of the distribution; but it also stems from the tendency for rents to be raised (sometimes through registering a rent for the first time) when a new tenant comes. In most instances in recent years when a rent is first registered there is an increase compared with the rent previously charged. The unfurnished sector provides relatively cheap accommodation, though it is often of a very poor quality. Furnished accommodation was, in general, by far the most expensive.

Public Expenditure on Housing

The share of all public expenditure devoted to housing and the other main areas of social policy is shown in Table 4.5 for the years 1972/3 to 1978/8, together with the projected levels for 1978/9 and 1979/80. While housing ranks below education, health and personal social services and social security in importance, £4475 million was spent on housing in 1977/8, 8.2 per cent of all public spending. Housing's share of spending has also increased from 6.1 per cent in 1972/3.

The Main Components of Expenditure

Expenditure on the various components of the housing programme are shown in Table 4.6 for the period 1972/3 to 1977/8 together with their projected levels for 1978/9 and 1979/80, as set out in the 1978 Public Expenditure White Paper.[20] These annual White Papers show past levels and plans for public expenditure and its components. Table 4.7 shows the percentage composition of expenditure on housing. The most important items of spending are subsidies and local authority invest-

Table 4.5: Housing's Share of Public Expenditure, Great Britain, 1972/3 – 1979/80 (proportion of all spending %)

	1972/3	1973/4	1974/5	1975/6	1976/7	1977/8	1978/9	1979/80
Housing	6.1	7.7	9.7	8.4	8.7	8.2	8.1	8.2
Education	14.9	15.1	14.1	14.3	14.8	14.7	13.9	13.8
Health and personal social services	12.6	12.8	12.1	12.4	13.0	13.6	13.0	13.0
Social security	20.7	20.0	19.7	21.1	22.6	24.3	24.2	24.1
All other expenditure	45.7	44.4	44.4	43.8	41.2	39.2	40.8	40.9
TOTAL[a]	100	100	100	100	100	100	100	100

Note: [a] All programmes excluding debt interest, and the contingency reserve for 1978/9 and 1979/80.

Source: *The Government's Expenditure Plans, 1978/9 to 1981/2 Volume II* (HMSO, Cmnd. 7049 – II), Table 5.1, p. 134.

ment, though their relative shares have changed significantly over the period shown. Subsidies for local authority housing are defined to include central government and rate fund contributions to local authorities to meet the difference between rental income and the cost of local authority housing, and subsidies to meet the cost of the rent rebate and allowance schemes for council, housing association and private tenants. Most of the cost of these income-related subsidies is met by central government. Of these separate items, Exchequer subsidies are by far the most important. While subsidies accounted for 27 per cent of all spending in 1972/3, their share rose sharply to 42.5 per cent in 1977/8. In real terms, subsidies more than doubled in value over this six-year period. The explanation for this substantial rise in subsidy has been discussed in earlier sections of this chapter.

The White Paper also includes as subsidy, the option mortgage subsidy paid to owner-occupiers who choose an option mortgage rather than a conventional mortgage eligible for tax relief on mortgage interest payments. A major anomaly in the White Paper has been that while option mortgage subsidy has been included as subsidy, mortgage tax relief has not. This is because such relief is not paid directly to mortgagors but is potential tax not collected by the Inland Revenue. This anomaly has been partly corrected in the 1978 White Paper which includes mortgage tax relief on public expenditure though it still does not appear in the main table.[21] Table 4.6 incorporates tax relief for comparative purposes, but it is not included in the totals.

Turning to investment, Table 4.7 shows that local authority net investment in land acquisition and new building accounted for 39.2 per cent of all spending in 1972/3 but had fallen to 31.5 per cent in 1977/8. Within this total, the building of new dwellings is the most important. While the volume of new building rose noticeably in 1975/6 and 1976/7 it has fallen back in 1977/8. Until July 1976 when the government imposed new controls on new building in designated non-stress areas, spending on new building by local authorities was, at least in principle, unrestricted and central government had imposed no fixed ceilings. Nevertheless, governments have relied on a variety of indirect controls over local authority building such as the cost yardstick which imposes financial limits on the cost of each dwelling, and the power of the Secretary of State for the Environment to reject Compulsory Purchase Orders and veto building plans. Part of the reason for the fall in the volume of new building in 1977/8 over 1976/7 lies in these new controls which have curtailed building in non-stress areas, and part in the shortfall of actual investment over that planned in the

Table 4.6: Public Expenditure on Housing, Great Britain (£ million at 1977 survey prices)

	1972/3	1973/4	1974/5	1975/6	1976/7	1977/8	1978/9	1979/80
CURRENT EXPENDITURE								
Subsidies:								
general	673	824	1277	1353	1464	1440	1465	1463
rebates, allowances	173	396	404	384	444	467	481	499
Total subsidies	846	1220	1681	1737	1908	1907	1946	1962
Option mortgage subsidy	57	94	118	139	158	154	154	129
Mortgage tax relief	745	950	1095	1100	1175	1055	n.e.	n.e.
Total current expenditure[a]	930	1377[b]	1850	1918	2113	2109	2147	2139
CAPITAL EXPENDITURE								
Local authority investment:								
Land, new dwellings, other	1434	1431	1655	1893	1813	1496	1539)	
Acquisitions	60	92	308	195	104	56	92)	2233
Improvements	505	684	585	492	449	432	521)	
Total gross local authority investment	1999	2207	2548	2580	2366	1934	2153	2233

Sales (land & dwellings)	– 205	– 110	– 55	– 69	– 63	– 86	– 154	– 160
Improvement grants from local authorities:	214	285	217	89	80	91	155	157
Local authority lending for house purchase: gross	284	475	786	443	210	157	143	143
Repayments	– 269	– 282	– 184	– 260	– 257	– 251	– 220	– 199
Net lending	15	193	602	183	– 47	– 94	– 77	– 56
Loans & grants to housing associations	178	180	256	375	424	475	481	503
Total capital spending (net)	2195	2750	3751[c]	2996[d]	2757	2366	2555	2675
TOTAL[a]	3125	4127	5601	4914	4870	4475	4702	4814

Notes: [a] Excluding mortgage tax relief, but including administration.
[b] This total includes £29m temporary grants to building societies.
[c] Including £70m for acquisition of new dwellings from the private sector, £188m government lending to building societies, and £183 other (net) lending.
[d] Including £ –162m other (net) lending.
n.e.: not estimated

Source: *The Government's Expenditure Plans, 1978/9 to 1981/2, Volume II*, table 2.7.

Table 4.7: Composition of Public Expenditure on Housing (percentage)

	1972/3	1974/5	1975/6	1976/7	1977/8	1979/80
Subsidies for local authority housing	27.0	30.3	34.2	39.2	42.5	40.8
Option mortgage subsidy	1.8	2.2	2.7	3.2	3.4	2.7
Administration	0.9	1.0	0.9	1.0	1.1	1.0
Total current spending	29.7	33.5	37.8	43.4	47.0	44.5
Local authority investment on land, new dwellings (less sales)[a]	39.2	29.6	35.9	35.9	31.5	
Local authority acquisitions	1.9	5.8	3.8	2.2	1.3	43.0
Local authority improvement	16.2	10.9	9.7	9.2	9.7	
Improvement grants	6.8	4.1	1.8	1.6	2.0	3.3
Local authority net lending for house purchase	0.5	11.3	3.6	-1.0	-2.1	-1.2
Housing associations	5.7	4.8	7.4	8.7	10.6	10.4
Total capital spending	70.3	66.5	62.2	56.6	53.0	55.5
Total	100	100	100	100	100	100

Note: [a]Including 'other investment', mainly slum clearance.
Source: Table 4.6.

previous year's White Paper. Indeed many local authorities underspent their housing capital allocations in 1977/8. For example, Reg Freeson, the Minister for Housing announced in October 1977 that while the government had budgeted for about 90,000 council house tenders in England in 1977, the actual figures would only be about 75,000.[22] The explanation for the shortfall is not entirely clear. One view is that it was the result of the widespread switch in political control from Labour to Conservative in the local elections of May 1977. Another is that it is the 'Government's bureaucratic controls, notably the housing cost yardstick and the housing investment programmes'.[23] There is evidence that there will also be a substantial shortfall in actual over allocated capital spending in 1978/9.

Net investment figures are derived by deducting income obtained from the sale of council houses to tenants. In past White Papers, the sale of council houses has been assumed to bring income to local authorities equal to the price at which houses have been sold. But in terms of public spending, because most sales are financed by council mortgages, the receipt from sales is offset by such lending. In the latest

White Paper[24] this 'associated lending' is included as an offset and has the effect of reducing the recorded benefit in earlier years quite substantially.

Another item of local authority investment is the acquisition of existing dwellings. This accounted for only 1.3 per cent of all spending on housing in 1977/8 after falling from its peak of 5.8 per cent in 1974/5, a year when the newly returned Labour Government gave considerable emphasis to municipalisation. Since 1974/5, the purchase of existing dwellings from private owners has been restricted in a variety of ways. Local authorities require loan sanction to proceed with acquisition and under various Department of Environment *Circulars*, general approval has only been given for certain categories of property including those left empty for more than six months and houses in Housing Action Areas.

A further form of local authority investment is improvement of older housing, both the rehabilitation of houses bought from private owners and the modernisation of older council owned estates. This accounted for 9.7 per cent of all housing expenditure compared with 16.2 per cent in 1972/3. Under section 105 of the 1974 Housing Act, spending on local authority improvement has been controlled since mid-1975.

The other major investment item is loans and grants to housing associations. Spending in support of housing associations has increased from 5.7 per cent of the total in 1972/3 to 10.6 per cent in 1977/8. Nearly all of the increase has taken the form of new capital grants introduced in the 1974 Housing Act aimed at stimulating housing association activity. Grants to housing associations take a very different form from local authority subsidies. The main element is the capital grant which meets in a single lump sum the difference between the total cost of building or rehabilitating a dwelling and the loan which could be met from a fair rent for the house *less* the cost of management and maintenance. The grant is designed to pay more or less the whole subsidy at the start of each scheme rather than spend it gradually over many years as in the local authority sector. In addition, there are loans borrowed from local authorities or the Housing Corporation to finance the debt remaining after the capital grant.

Final items of spending are improvement grants to private owners, and local authority lending to private individuals for house purchase. The figure for improvement grants shows only the government's contribution through the grant towards the cost of work and not the owner's own contribution. The proportion of total spending devoted to improvement grants has fallen steadily from the peak year of 1972/3 when it reached 6.8 per cent to 2.0 per cent in 1977/8. Local authority net lending for house purchase covers gross lending offset by repayments on loans. This form of spending became very important in 1974/5 when the government used this to try and make up some of the sharp fall in building society lending. In the years 1976/7 and 1977/8, repayments of home loans actually exceeded new mortgages, a situation that is apparently planned to continue until 1981/2. This item therefore has the net effect of reducing public borrowing.

Changes in Spending Over Time

Tables 4.5 and 4.6 show two main trends in housing expenditure over the period 1972/3 to 1977/8. The period 1972/3 to 1974/5 saw a substantial increase in the real value of the housing programme from £3125m in 1972/3 to £5601m in 1974/5, and a rise in housing's share of all spending from 6.1 per cent to 9.7 per cent. 1974/5 proved a peak year for housing. Since 1974/5 real expenditure on housing has fallen in each year to £4475m in 1977/8, and its share fallen to 8.2 per cent. These trends are the result of a number of factors.

In volume terms, housing expenditure jumped by 32 per cent in 1973/4 over 1972/3 and by 35 per cent in 1974/5 over 1973/4. Of the increase between 1972/3 and 1973/4, higher subsidies, especially on rebates and allowances, accounts for over a third. The remainder is made up of an increase in local authority lending for private purchase, a small increase in improvement grants and a fall in income from council house sales.

The increase between 1973/4 and 1974/5 is due, in the main, to a number of new measures taken by the new Labour Government of February 1974 designed to revive a deteriorating housing situation. The boost to the housing programme took the form of an impetus to local authority lending partly in order to offset the heavy fall in building society lending, a new encouragement to municipalisation by local authorities, and a new emphasis on housing association activity. In consequence local authority lending rose substantially in 1974/5 over 1973/4, the value of acquisitions by local authorities rose from £92m to £308m and grants and loans to housing associations rose from £180m to £256m. Local authority investment in new dwellings also rose slightly as a result of the steady revival in local authority building, though this did not peak until 1975/6 and 1976/7, years of substantial increase over the previous three. The new government also introduced a rent freeze which combined with the continuing impact of inflation and rising interest rates, led to a 63 per cent increase in Exchequer subsidies over 1973/4.

Since 1974/5 there has been a steady fall in housing expenditure. This is partly a result of general cuts in public spending, but also a number of special factors. The cuts in the planned housing programme over this period imposed as part of the wider economic policy of cutting and restraining public spending was concentrated in certain spending areas. Table 4.6 shows a sharp fall, in particular, in the rate of acquisition, local authority improvement and above all, local authority mortgage lending. Together, these fell in value from £1,679m in 1974/5 to £645m in 1977/8. These were all the result of changes in government policy, and these items bore the brunt of cuts, together with new building to some extent in 1977/8. The burden of the cuts has therefore fallen heavily on investment.

There have also been other factors working to reduce expenditure on housing. There has been a steady fall, for example, in the take-up of improvement grants, partly as a result of deliberate government policy, introduced in the 1974 Housing Act of tightening the conditions on grants to counter the abuses prevalent in the boom of the early 1970s. Again, falls in interest rates since 1975 have led to some restraint in the growth of local authority subsidies, though they have still risen over the period. Finally, in both 1976/7 and 1977/8 there was a shortfall in actual over planned spending. A comparison with the 1977 White Paper given in the latest White Paper shows an overall shortfall of 5½ per cent in 1976/7 and 1977/8.[25] In 1976/7 this 5½ per cent was made up of a 2 per cent shortfall in gross investment by local authorities, a 10 per cent fall in publicly financed housing association investment, an 8 per cent fall in local authority mortgages and a 34 per cent shortfall in improvement grants.

As a net result of these factors, housing expenditure in 1977/8 was higher than in both 1972/3 and 1973/4 but lower than in the three years from 1974/5 to 1976/7. But whether housing has suffered more or less heavily than other programmes is not easy to determine, given these other factors. Table 4.6 shows that between 1972/3 and 1977/8 public expenditure on housing rose by 43 per cent while all public spending rose by only 5.3 per cent. Between 1974/5 and 1977/8, housing has fallen 20 per cent and all spending by 6 per cent, but 1974/5 was an especially good year for housing.

One noticeable feature of trends in expenditure that is apparent from Tables 4.6 and 4.7 is the steady fall in investment as a proportion of all expenditure on housing. After rising from a low of £2,177m in 1972/3 to a peak of £2,955m in 1974/5, gross public sector investment by local authorities, new towns and housing associations has slumped to only £2,459 in 1977/8. As a proportion of all expenditure, investment has fallen from 70 per cent in 1972/3 to 60 per cent in 1975/6 and to only 55 per cent in 1977/8. This compares with the share of subsidy of 30 per cent in 1972/3 and 42.5 per cent in 1977/8. If tax relief is included and rebates and allowances excluded from subsidy, general subsidies exceeded gross public sector investment in 1977/8 for the first time. As a ratio of subsidy defined in this way, gross public sector investment has fallen from 1.5 in 1972/3 to 0.9 in 1977/8.

A final consideration, and one that is particularly important in considering the economic consequences of public spending on housing, and indeed all services, is the need to distinguish those payments which represent transfer payments from those which represent a direct use of productive resources by the government. Transfer payments are payments for existing assets and simply lead to a transfer of income from one section of the community, via taxation and subsidies, to another, and the individuals who benefit remain free to spend the income in the way they choose. They therefore do not involve the direct use of resources of manpower, materials and land by the government. Transfer payments include subsidies to tenants and owner-occupiers, the purchase of land, the acquisition of dwellings, and loans to private individuals for house purchase. These amounted to £2,107m in 1977/8, 47 per cent of all spending. The purchase of goods and services directly, and so direct consumption of resources by public bodies, includes investment in new building and improvement by local authorities and housing associations, and improvement grants, which accounted for the remaining 53 per cent of spending. Any change in the share of all housing spending to GNP is therefore a poor guide to changes in the growth of the use of resources by housing because of the faster growth in the transfer payment element. Where the growth of housing spending, including transfers, does make an economic impact, however, is on the need for changes in general taxation to meet such growth. Housing expenditure is high in public expenditure terms, but less important in terms of its demand on real resources.

Notes

1. A. Crosland, *Guardian* (15 June 1971).
2. Department of the Environment, *Housing Policy, A Consultative Document* (HMSO, Cmnd 6851, 1977).
3. The favourable tax position of owner-occupation has been pointed out by a

number of writers, especially A.A. Nevitt, *Housing, Taxation and Subsidies* (London, Nelson, 1966); and also holds in the United States – H. Aaron, 'Income Taxes and Housing', *American Economic Review*, vol. 60, no. 5 (December 1970), pp. 789-806.

4. Department of the Environment, *Press Release: Chains of Sales in Private Housing* (9 September 1973).

5. J. Foster, 'Redistributive Effect of Inflation on Building Society Shares and Deposits: 1961-74', *Bulletin of Economic Research*, 28 (1976), has estimated that over the perid 1961 to 1974, the redistribution from lenders to building societies to borrowers was over £3 billion (in 1963 prices), with the gainers being younger and higher income groups and the losers elderly and low income groups.

6. See Table 5.3. Ch. 5.

7. M. Smith and E. Howes, 'Current Trends in Local Authority Housing Finance', *Centre for Environmental Studies Review*, no. 3 (May 1978).

8. See Table 2.6. Ch. 2.

9. See, for example, Christopher Booker and Bennie Gray in *The Observer* (11 May 1975); Jeremy Gates, 'Lost Millions – Now Council Tenants Must Share the Bill', *Daily Express* (13 June 1975); Joe Rennison, 'Council Rents We Cannot Afford', *Financial Times* (21 June 1975).

10. See D. Webster, 'Council House Costs – Why We Should All Calm Down', *Roof* (Shelter, October 1975).

11. Department of the Environment, *Housing Policy Technical Volume I* (HMSO, 1977), pp. 189-93.

12. Table 5.2, Ch. 5.

13. Chartered Institute of Public Finance and Accountancy, *Housing Statistics (England and Wales)*, part I.

14. National Economic Development Office, *Housing For All* (October 1977), table 3.3, p. 13.

15. Housing Centre Trust, *Guide to Housing* (1977), p. 210.

16. *Report of the Committee on the Rent Acts* (The Francis Committee) (HMSO, Cmnd 4609, 1971).

17. S. Weir, 'Landlords Exploit Rent Act Loophole', *Roof* (Shelter, October 1975).

18. See, for example, A. Murie, P. Niner and C. Watson, *Housing Policy and the Housing System* (London, Allen and Unwin, 1977). Ch. 6.

19. See Table 6.2, Ch. 6.

20. *The Government's Expenditure Plans, 1978/9 to 1981/2* (HMSO, Cmnd 7049, January 1978).

21. Ibid.

22. Department of the Environment, *Press Release 533* (12 October 1977).

23. 'Memorandum by Shelter', *Second Report from the Expenditure Committee* (House of Commons Paper 257, HMSO, 1978), appendix 13.

24. *The Government's Expenditure Plans, 1978/9 to 1981/2*.

25. Ibid., table 2.7.

5 THE IMPACT OF SUBSIDIES

Chapter 4 showed that housing is heavily subsidised and in a great variety of ways. It is often argued that the existing system of housing finance lies at the roots of many of our housing problems. Indeed, much of the evidence to the Department of the Environment's housing policy review was swift to point to the inequities and irrationalities of our financial support. What then has been the impact of the existing system of subsidies? In this chapter, consideration is given to the effect of housing subsidies as they have evolved, and the extent to which they have promoted – or hindered – the achievement of housing objectives. In general, our housing finance system has been criticised on the grounds of its inefficiency and inequity – its impact on the level and the distribution of housing provision. Each of these is therefore considered in turn.

How Efficient is the Current System of Housing Finance?

As discussed in Chapter 1, the efficiency argument for subsidies of some kind is that the level of investment would be inadequate without them. The equity argument relates to the distribution of resources and the inability of lower income groups to exert an effective demand for accommodation of some minimum quality. The aim of demand subsidies such as mortgage tax relief or the remission of Schedule A tax on owner-occupied properties is to increase demand. These in turn will increase supply or house prices, or these in some combination. Supply subsidies, such as Exchequer subsidies to local authority building (though these can also be seen as demand subsidies to the extent that they enable rents to be kept below the cost of provision), are aimed at stimulating supply directly.

But have the subsidies used been effective? There are a number of aspects of efficiency that are important in relation to housing including the impact of subsidies on the level and structure of housing investment, on the distribution of resources between housing and other activities, on house prices, and on the level of occupation. Each is considered in turn, and it will be seen that there are a number of ways in which existing aids and concessions have been inefficient in their impact.

Investment in Housing

There is little doubt that the level of investment in housing has been greater than it would have been in the absence of these financial aids. The population is therefore better housed, on average, than would otherwise have been the case. Investment in housing over the last 30 years has gone into owner-occupied and local authority housing and not into the privately rented sector. In the local authority sector, supply depends in particular upon the initiative of local authorities and the level of government financial support. The increase in the volume of local authority housing has been a direct result of government intervention and the redirection of resources through taxation, though its need has arisen partly as a result of the steady decline in the availability of privately rented accommodation. Without such redirection what would have happened is a matter for speculation, though it is unlikely that the resources guided into public sector dwellings would have been taken up by private renting or owner-occupation to the same extent.

The lack of investment in the privately rented sector, both in new housing and improvement and maintenance, has been due to a combination of factors such as rent control which has affected supply directly, and policies towards other sectors which have switched demand away from private renting. In the absence of direct public sector provision, and in other forms of intervention, it is most unlikely that private forces would have been able to sustain an adequate supply of accommodation to rent.

The expansion of owner-occupation has been partly a result of subsidies and partly other factors such as the general growth of incomes and the steady decline in the availability of privately rented accommodation. It has been contended that aid to owner-occupation is necessary to the maintenance of supply in this sector. The recent Green Paper on housing, for example, has stated that 'The Government consider that . . . continuance of mortgage tax relief and option mortgage subsidy is vital to the growth of home ownership', and that a cut in assistance would lead to a fall in investment.[1]

While some aid is necessary in order to assist certain categories of owner-occupier such as first time buyers, it is not the case that aid in its existing form and at its existing level is necessary either to maintain supply or encourage home ownership. In the last decade, increases in subsidies have not led to an increase in the rate of new building. Mortgage tax relief more than doubled between 1968 and 1974 (from £342 million to £777 million at constant prices), while the value of new housing produced annually fell by 14 per cent (from £1,696 million to £1,467 million).[2] Of course, the ratio of tax relief to new investment can vary for a number of reasons such as changes in interest rates and the number of mortgagors, which are independent of the relationship between subsidy and investment. The real cost of tax relief in recent years has risen largely because of real increases in house prices, higher mortgage rates and because of the increase in the velocity of transfers within the housing stock. A very large proportion of mortgage finance and so tax relief goes to finance the transfer of households moving from one house to another rather than purchases by first-time buyers. Unlike the public sector where outstanding debt grows only as a result of capital spending on new building or improvement, debt grows in the owner-occupied sector through changes in ownership. Currently only one in five new mortgages from building societies is used to finance the purchase of new houses. Increasing tax relief is thus being used to finance other consumption and the exchange process and there is little evidence of any direct benefit to new construction. The period since the early 1970s has therefore seen a steady growth in the ratio of subsidy (tax relief and option mortgage subsidy) to investment.

Partly as a result of this growth in the cost of housing subsidies, there has been a growing concern about the slice of the nation's resources that is being absorbed by housing finance. Between 1963 and 1973, the proportion of investment funds from all financial institutions (other than banks) absorbed by loans to house purchase increased from 25 per cent to 36 per cent, an increase of 33 per cent.[3] This has been the result of the increased volume of transfers among existing owners or existing houses changing hands, and being financed with bigger mortgages and at higher prices. In the last decade this shift of capital funds into housing has probably not restricted the availability of capital for industrial purposes because industrial investment has slackened while savings have increased. In the next decade, however, the Green Paper has estimated that the annual volume of gross funds needed to finance loans for house purchase will rise by 50 per cent from £6,000m in 1976 to £9,000m in 1986. It is doubtful whether such an increase could be sustained without serious consequences for investment elsewhere in the economy, particularly if the demand for industrial investment revives, yet the Green Paper suggests the need to tap new sources of funds in the City to channel more funds into the finance of owner-occupation.[4]

A similar increase in subsidies has arisen in the public sector. Subsidies for local authority housing more than doubled between 1968 and 1974 (from £386m to £824m at constant prices) while the value of annual investment (new and improvement) fell by 13 per cent (from £2,029m to £1,756m).[5] The ratio of investment to subsidy has therefore declined in this sector as well. Nevertheless, the view that high subsidies are needed to sustain investment has more force in the public sector. As the Green Paper's Technical Volume has put it,

> The guiding principle throughout has been that Exchequer subsidy should meet enough of the outgoings not covered by rents to prevent undue discouragement of new building as a result of the size of the residual burden falling on the rates, or on other tenants through 'pooling'.[6]

In the period since the early 1970s it seems to have been the case that the rise in subsidy costs has led to a restraint in public sector investment because of the need to limit public spending on housing within an overall ceiling. But the main reason for this is not that local authorities have not tried to embark upon new building but that they have been discouraged by central government because of the additional subsidy it would have entailed. As we have already seen in Chapter 4, the extra subsidy in this period arose not because of low rents – which kept pace with inflation between 1970 and 1976 – but because of the effect of the forward bunching of interest charges through the escalation of inflation and interest rates, higher management and maintenance costs, and higher construction costs.

Subsidies and House Prices

Whatever the arguments about the need for some kind of subsidy to owner-occupiers, it is clear that existing levels of subsidy are not sustaining a high and buoyant level of investment. In addition, the form that financial assistance has taken for owner-occupation has led to higher house prices than would otherwise have prevailed. Subsidies to demand, as we have seen, increase supply and price in some combination. A special feature of housing is that demand subsidies have a relatively weak impact on supply, especially in the short run and even in the long run.

The demand for owner-occupation as opposed to other forms of tenure arises through a number of factors; a preference for home ownership, difficulties in obtaining housing in other sectors, but particularly the special financial benefits offered by owner-occupation including its relative tax advantages, the ability to borrow money at less than market rates of interest which make it an attractive investment, and perhaps in recent years, the increasing realisation that houses are a good hedge against inflation. Some of these financial benefits are the result of independent economic factors which may of their own lead to changes in house prices in relation to other prices, but others – including the benefit of tax relief – have arisen through direct government policy in housing.

While tax relief and the other financial benefits offered by owner-occupation have stimulated demand in this sector, supply from new construction and transfers from other sectors have not kept pace. Excess demand has occurred both in particular short periods and over the longer term. The rate of increase of house prices has therefore fluctuated. Over long periods, house prices have risen more quickly than inflation. Over the period 1958 to 1975, for example, the price of new houses rose by 411 per cent, while the index of retail prices rose by 180 per cent and average earnings by 351 per cent.[7] The average annual rate of increase in the retail price index was 6.2 per cent between 1958 and 1975 compared with 10 per cent for house prices and 9.1 per cent for earnings. Some of this relative increase in house prices is due to an increase in the quality of houses because of such items as central heating, double glazing, improved plumbing and electrical systems, but it is difficult to make a precise estimate of the increase in quality.[8] But another important factor has been the high demand for owner-occupied housing, a demand stimulated by government subsidies.

It can be argued, therefore, that the favourable financial treatment of owner-occupation, in stimulating the demand for houses to buy has maintained a higher rate of building than otherwise, but has also increased prices. Some of the benefit of tax relief has therefore shifted, through higher house prices, from buyers to existing owners, builders and landowners. Moreover, most of the gain has gone to land-owners and existing home owners rather than builders, and to that extent rising prices have had less of an impact on building, and maybe even a positively harmful effect. These long term incentives to demand have therefore been partially self-defeating. Tenure choice and the proportion of households who can afford to buy have not been increased, but decreased as the demand for housing by the well off has been encouraged and inflation in house and land prices fuelled.

As a result of the growth of home ownership and the increase in house values in relation to other assets, the last 15 years have seen a massive shift in the makeup of personal wealth away from shares to dwellings. As the Royal Commission on the Distribution of Income and Wealth has shown, the proportion of personal wealth held in dwellings and land has doubled from 27 per cent in 1960 to 47 per cent in 1974 while the proportion held in company securities has halved from 23 per cent to 11 per cent.[9] While this shift has been encouraged by the replacement of personal shareholders by institutional shareholding and the low profitability and confidence of industry, a major factor has been the ability of house purchasers to borrow at relatively low rates of interest combined with the tax advantages of home ownership which has made investment in housing relatively profitable.

Excessive subsidy to owner-occupation has also had other undesirable consequences for resource allocation. First, it has been one of the factors causing increasing public expenditure on housing, particularly since 1970, through its contribution towards inflation in house and land prices. Increases in house prices, particularly between 1970 and 1973, have increased acquisition costs to local authorities and housing associations and increased the cost of building (especially through increases in land prices) and improvement in the public sector. There has also been a substantial increase in the cost of tax relief to the Exchequer, which rose from £540m in 1969/70 to £1,095m in 1975/6 in constant prices (Table 5.3), though some of this increase is due to higher tax rates and higher mortgage rates as well as higher house prices.

Secondly, it has been one of the factors encouraging the decline in the stock of privately rented unfurnished accommodation. While the privately rented sector has been in long term decline for a variety of reasons, excessive subsidies to owner occupiers have encouraged this decline by reducing the demand to rent and making it more profitable for landlords to sell. It is also the case that this process of decline was given a powerful boost by the house price boom in the early 1970s, by increasing the gain to landlords from selling with vacant possession. Thirdly, it has tended to encourage a shift of resources into the more expensive end of the housing market.

Subsidies and Under-Occupation

A further important criticism of the form that subsidies have taken is that they have encouraged under-occupation and the waste of limited housing space. Table 5.1 shows that, using the bedroom standard as a measure of ideal size, 62 per cent of households in 1974 lived in accommodation above that standard, 23 per cent had 2 or more rooms above it and 6 per cent of households had accommodation below the

Table 5.1: Bedroom Standard[a] of Households, 1974 (percentages)

By Tenure	Bedrooms Below Standard		Bedrooms Equal to Standard	Bedrooms Above Standard		All
	2 or more	1		1	2 or more	
Owned outright	1	2	17	41	39	100
Owned with mortgage	—	3	26	46	24	100
Local authority tenants	1	7	45	36	12	100
Privately rented, unfurnished	1	6	35	39	19	100
Privately rented, furnished	1	19	62	14	4	100
ALL	1	5	32	39	23	100

Note: [a]Bedroom standard is 1 separate bedroom for each adult or married couple and for each pair of adolescents of same age and sex and pairs of children below 10 years irrespective of sex.
Source: Central Statistical Office, *General Household Survey*, 1974.

bedroom standard. The table shows that the incidence of under-occupation is most prevalent in the owner-occupied sector. The bulk of under-occupation is by one or two person households living in 3 bedroom houses.

The Green Paper's Technical Volume shows that 70 per cent of all small households living at low densities (one-person households with 5 rooms or more and two-person households with 6 rooms or more) were owner-occupiers, and that such households were one-fifth of all owner-occupiers, a higher proportion than in all other tenures. The majority of these households (70 per cent of the one-person households and 50 per cent of the two-person households) were of pensionable age.[10] In contrast, under-occupation is least prevalent in the public and privately rented furnished sector. Overcrowding, on the other hand, is especially common in the privately rented furnished sector.

This maldistribution of housing space is partly the result of existing subsidies. Under-occupation within the owner-occupied sector partly reflects a natural preference for greater space, but it also reflects existing financial arrangements. Tax relief, which benefits those with the largest mortgages and highest incomes the most, has been a permanent encouragement to under-occupation and over-consumption and hence building for under-occupation. Some of the increase in supply of owner-occupied housing in recent years will have gone towards improving housing provision for those who were already well housed rather than those who are poorly housed. Tax relief is an inducement to trade up especially in times of inflation when houses provide a good investment, and scarce building resources are therefore being used up without increasing the supply of housing directly to those in greatest need. The filtering process, whereby households moving to better property release housing to those of lower income, works only slowly and is likely to have only a marginal impact.

The relatively lower, but still significant under occupation in the privately rented unfurnished sector is mainly due to successive rent control which has discouraged mobility. There is a high concentration of elderly tenants in such accommodation. Under-occupation in the local authority sector is low in comparison with other sectors, largely because of the greater emphasis on matching households to houses. Nevertheless there is undoubtedly scope for improving transfer arrangements when households move through the life cycle, a situation that is sometimes discouraged by the lack of significant variation in rents between properties of different size, inefficient management, and the general lack of smaller units of accommodation.

To what extent would more efficient use of the existing stock contribute to the reduction in overcrowding? In the case of London, it has been shown that if the occupancy rate in the owner-occupied sector (0.55 according to the 1971 Census compared with 0.75 for local authority dwellings, 0.59 for privately rented unfurnished and 0.86 for privately rented furnished) were raised to the average for all tenures, it could accommodate 440,000 extra people, while if the occupancy rate in the furnished sector were lowered to the average, extra accommodation would have to be found for only 150,000 people.[11] Space standards could therefore be improved in principle, without new building, for those in relatively overcrowded conditions with only a marginal reduction in the space available to owner-occupiers.

There is undoubtedly scope for making better use of the housing stock, though there are a number of practical obstacles to any significant reduction in under-use. There is, for example, a significant mis-match between dwelling and household size, and in particular, a considerable shortage of smaller dwellings. Many households may be under occupying by preference; and others because they are deterred by the cost and inconvenience of moving. In the privately rented sector, landlords may prefer to leave part of a large house vacant, hoping to gain full vacant possession. Mobility both within and between sectors is very restricted. In the privately rented unfurnished sector, low rents often act as a disincentive to move as do the difficulties of finding alternative accommodation. Local authority tenants in general find it difficult to obtain transfers between authorities, and within their own authority, sometimes as a result of inefficiency in management, but also because of the shortage of accommodation, especially smaller units. Owner-occupiers, in general, lack the incentive to move down market. Such immobility as well as limiting the scope for a more effective use of the housing stock, is inhibiting to general economic efficiency. More efforts should be made to promote greater mobility by encouraging under occupiers to move, or let spare accommodation by taking lodgers or converting their premises into smaller, separate dwellings.

Summary

Overall, therefore, some forms of financial aid to housing have been inefficient; resources have been allocated in ways which have had undesirable and unintended consequences. Subsidies have led to an increase in total housing investment and a shift in its structure towards owner-occupation and local authority renting and away from private letting. They have encouraged the decline of the privately rented sector and a steady deterioration of the quality of privately rented accommodation. Some of the impact of owner-occupier tax concessions has been felt in higher house prices which has in turn increased public spending on housing. Further, by encouraging upward trading in the owner-occupied sector, existing aids have increased the level of under-occupation and led to a waste of space. Under occupation has also arisen in rented accommodation because of general immobility. Too many resources have been channelled directly or indirectly into improving the housing conditions of those already well housed, and enhancing the wealth of those already well endowed especially land-owners, developers and better off owner-occupiers.

Are Subsidies Fairly Distributed?

It has been argued above that housing subsidies have been inefficient in their impact, but it might be contended that some of these efficiency losses could be justified if the system had led to a favourable redistribution of income. So what have been the redistributional consequences of housing finance?

The distributional aspect of housing finance is very important, since one of the main aims of government intervention is to secure greater equality in the allocation of housing resources than would result in a free market situation, and ensure that whatever assistance is used to promote this aim provides equity of treatment between different householders. One statement of housing objectives, in the White Paper *Fair Deal for Housing*, for example, pointed to the need for 'a fairer choice between owning a home and renting one' and 'fairness between one citizen and another in giving and receiving help towards housing costs'.[12]

What is meant by equity? The question of equity is essentially separate from the question of redistribution. A subsidy is inequitable if it provides a different level of aid to two households that are in identical circumstances with respect to income, household size and housing situation. Equity is therefore concerned with ensuring fairness of treatment between households. Redistribution is concerned with providing a more equal distribution of housing resources.

There are a number of different ways of looking at equity or fairness. Equity can be seen in terms of the allocation of subsidies, i.e., that subsidies should be proportionately or progressively related to income, need, and housing services obtained. However, since this may not account for variations in housing costs or payments, equity may alternatively be seen in the extent to which subsidies ensure that housing costs are similar for households with similar accommodation, household size and income, or for households of given size and accommodation, costs are proportionately or progressively related to income. In this sense, subsidies may have to vary between similar households because costs vary. Again, equity might be seen in terms of the allocation of resources directly, i.e., that services should be distributed according to social need, independently of income, though this involves a value judgement about where to draw the line between what level of housing provision is necessary to provide for basic need and what is above this level.

It is difficult to go very far in discussions about fairness without meeting widespread misconceptions. The most popular view about housing finance — at least among non-council tenants — that council tenants are uniquely over subsidised, feather bedded and Jaguar owning, while owner-occupiers are self-sufficient and self-sacrificing, still seems to persist. The implication of this view that council tenants, as a group, get too good a deal is that their subsidies should be reduced in relation to other groups. This view has sometimes even received official backing. The main sources of inequity as set out in *Fair Deal for Housing*, for example, were seen by the then Conservative Government as the indiscriminate way in which Exchequer subsidies to the council sector were allocated between authorities and tenants, in which the burden of paying for the subsidies was distributed, and in the excessively high level of subsidy to this sector in total. While there was support for the view that subsidies were inequitable and anomalous and that reform was overdue in both sectors, the Housing Finance Act of 1972 which followed the White Paper aimed exclusively at reform in the local authority sector. The act was designed to raise public sector rents and reduce subsidies to this group while ignoring completely subsidies to owner-occupiers, and is a good illustration of the partial approach so often adopted in housing policy.

Whichever concept of equity is adopted, there is no doubt of the considerable lack of fairness in current financial arrangements. This is clear from a simple comparison between those households with high incomes paying very little for good quality housing and those facing heavy payments out of low incomes for poor housing. But just how widespread are such inequities? As the misconception about council tenants cited above demonstrates there is little agreement about where the most serious inequities lie and about what reforms are needed. This is partly a consequence of the inevitable value loaded nature of the issue, but also of the difficulties of establishing with precision the actual impact on equity and income distribution of present and past policies. Indeed the Technical Volume of the recent Green Paper has gone so far as to argue that 'there is no incontrovertible way of making the comparison between home owners and local authority tenants to show the extent of the advantage of one group over the other — or even to show which group does better'.[13] Despite this convenient agnosticism by the Department of the Environment, it will be argued here that we can identify the extent of inequality in housing finance sufficiently to be at least able to point in the direction in which we should be moving.

This is not to deny that there are conceptual and data problems associated with measuring the equity with which housing aid is distributed, and that results are sensitive to the assumptions and method adopted.

Tax Relief and Local Authority Subsidies — the 'Historic Cost' Approach

One widely used approach for comparing home buyers and local authority tenants is simply to compare the average level of tax relief per mortgagor with the average level of Exchequer subsidy and rate fund contribution per tenant. Tables 5.2 and 5.3 show the total and average levels of assistance, in current and constant prices, provided in this form between 1967/8 and 1976/7. Over the period subsidies measured in this

Table 5.2: Exchequer Subsidies and Rate Fund Contributions Received by Public Sector Tenants, UK, 1967/8 to 1975/6 (per annum)

| | Current Prices | | | | Constant (1976) Prices | | | |
| | Total | | Average per Dwelling | | Total | | Average per Dwelling | |
	Excluding Rent Rebates £m	Rent Rebates £m	Excluding Rent Rebates £m	Rent Rebates £m	Excluding Rent Rebates £m	Rent Rebates £m	Excluding Rent Rebates £m	Rent Rebates £m
1967/8	200		39		487		95	
1968/9	231		44		520		99	
1969/70	281		51		615		112	
1970/1	311		55		645		114	
1971/2	328		57		616		107	
1972/3	324	77	56	13	567	142	98	24
1973/4	432	176	73	29	698	291	118	48
1974/5	827	220	137	36	1128	312	187	51
1975/6	1066	256	173	40	1214	250	197	39

Source: Department of the Environment, *Housing Policy Technical Volume I*, table IV.4 and IV.8.

Table 5.3: Tax Relief and Option Mortgage Subsidy, UK, 1967/8 to 1976/7 (per annum)

	Current Prices		Constant (1976) Prices	
	Total £m	Average per Mortgagor £m	Total £m	Average per Mortgagor £m
1967/8	180	38	445	94
1968/9	200	41	470	97
1969/70	245	49	540	108
1970/1	300	58	620	119
1971/2	330	62	635	119
1972/3	395	73	710	131
1973/4	560	101	925	167
1974/5	770	136	1075	190
1975/6	970	174	1095	197
1976/7 (Estimates)	1240	214	1240	214

Source: Department of the Environment, *Housing Policy Technical Volume II*, table VI.26 and *Parliamentary Question*, 27 July 1976.

way increased substantially. Tax relief and option mortgage subsidy more than quadrupled at current prices, and rose by 146 per cent in real terms. Average tax relief increased 357 per cent at current prices and by 107 per cent in real terms. This substantial increase is explained by the steady increase in the mortgage interest rate over the period, from 8.5 per cent to 10.5 per cent, the increase in the basic rate of income tax and the fall in tax thresholds (especially in respect of higher rates of tax), and the increase in house prices. Similar rises occurred in subsidies to local authority tenants. Average subsidy (excluding rebates) rose 343 per cent in current prices and 107 per cent in constant prices over the same period. The main reasons for these increases were the increasing costs of new construction and increasing loan charges due to rising interest rates.

Comparisons for the same year show that in 1975/6 total Exchequer subsidies and rate fund contributions (excluding rent rebates) to local authority tenants amounted to £1,066m and a further £256m in the form of rebates. In comparison, tax relief and option mortgage subsidy amounted to £970m. The average subsidy per tenant amounted to £173 and rebates to £40, while the average mortgagor received £174 in the same year.

The main area of dispute in respect of this method of comparison is whether rent rebates should be counted as subsidies in the case of tenants. Many have argued that rent rebates should not be treated as subsidies since they are an essential part of our system of income maintenance, aimed at giving income support to low income families. The Fabian Society, for example, in its evidence to the housing policy review has maintained that 'It would be wrong to regard rent rebates and allowances as a housing subsidy when they are part of the complex tangle of welfare benefits which are intended to alleviate poverty.'[14] In contrast, the Building Societies Association, in their evidence to the review has contended that rebates should be counted as housing subsidies.[15] Another area of disagreement has arisen over the number of dwellings that should be used to estimate the average value of tax relief. In general, the number of dwellings used has been the number of mortgaged dwellings, the number on which relief is actually claimed, but the Buildings Societies Association have argued for the use of all owner-occupied dwellings or 75 per cent of them.[16] These issues are of less importance however than the question of the validity of the method itself for establishing the extent of equity between the two main housing sectors.

The Green Paper's Approach

Certainly this method of comparing the relative level of assistance provided to tenants is not the only one available. In its analysis of fairness, the Technical Volume of the Green Paper used five measures of comparative assistance between local authority tenants and home owners: the total assistance provided through subsidies or tax relief to each; the average assistance per household; the proportion of total costs met by assistance; the average net housing costs borne by households out of their own incomes after allowing for assistance; and the minimum rates of assistance provided. Table 5.4 summarises the results of each comparison in 1975/6.

Total assistance in each sector is approximately similar; the average assistance per household is similar if the average figure in the case of owner-occupiers is based on mortgagors actually in receipt of tax relief and not all owner-occupiers; as a proportion of outgoings, assistance is higher in the case of tenants; average net housing costs, after assistance, are higher for owner-occupiers; the potential minimum level of assistance provided is zero in each sector.

None of these measures however is a satisfactory indicator of fairness between local authority tenants and home owners. There are a number of weaknesses common to each. In the first place, they do not relate assistance to what is actually being consumed and so the benefits of living in each sector. The average quality of accommodation and services provided in each sector, the physical quality, size and amenities

Table 5.4: Comparative Assistance, Local Authority Tenants and
Owner-Occupiers 1975/6: The Green Paper Estimates

		Local Authority Tenants	Owner-Occupiers
Total assistance	£m	1066	957
Average assistance per household	£	173	174(96)[a]
Assistance — as proportion of outgoings	%	41	27
Average net housing costs	£	229[b]	263[c]
Potential minimum assistance provided	£	0	0

Notes: [a]The figure outside the brackets relates to owner-occupiers with a
mortgage and the figure in brackers to all owner-occupiers.
[b]Gross rent plus costs of upkeep not included in rent, but excluding rent
reba:es.
[c]Mortgage interest charges and expenditure on upkeep and insurance, but
excluding transaction costs and capital repayments.
Source: Department of the Environment, *Housing Policy Technical Volume II*,
ch. 5.

offered by accommodation, and the access, mobility, social status and
legal rights of households differ widely between each sector. In terms of
these characteristics, the benefits of owner-occupation are greater on
average as we shall see. Further these measures do not allow for
differences in average incomes, and tenants have considerably lower
incomes, on average. Thirdly, the owner-occupier enjoys the benefit of
ownership of a capital asset, such that a proportion of his outlay should
be considered a form of savings. The only measure to make allowance
for this is the fourth which deducts transaction costs which can be
regarded as part of the expense of acquiring a marketable asset, and
capital repayments which can be regarded as payment for the progressive acquisition of an asset.

Fourthly they treat subsidies and costs in a purely static way and do
not allow for variations in payments and assistance over time. They also
conceal very wide variations within these averages, both between and
within tenures, and between different parts of the country. Further, on
the cost side, one reason why the proportionate contribution towards
costs is higher in the case of publicly rented housing is that the average
cost of public sector dwellings are higher than owner-occupied
dwellings. This is partly because there is considerably more building for
public renting at high density in inner urban areas where costs are high
because of land shortages, high density building and slum clearance. In

the inner London boroughs, for example, where average costs per local authority dwelling are twice the national average, there are roughly two local authority tenants to every home owner. Costs are also higher in the public rented sector because local authorities incur extra costs in providing for special needs including 'sheltered' accommodation for the elderly and specially designed accommodation for the disabled.

Finally, these approaches are based on actual costs, or assistance actually received. The problem with this is that the financing and charging methods operating in the two tenures are so different that such a simple comparison fails to measure the effective relative degree of assistance. Local authorities apply charging principles related to historic construction costs, while owners' payments are related to the purchase price of the house which is greater than historic cost paid by the first occupier. A more appropriate comparison would require taking a position where both could be treated on an equivalent basis.

The 'Market Value' Method

An alternative approach to overcome this last point is to estimate subsidies in each sector as the difference between what is actually paid and what would be paid in the absence of financial aid from governments. This 'market value' approach requires estimating the value of payments in a free market situation. Subsidies in the public sector are taken as the difference between the market rent that would be paid in the absence of government intervention and the actual rent paid. The appropriate subsidy in the case of owner-occupiers is then the lack of tax on the imputed rental income from ownership together with the absence of tax on accrued capital gains. In this way both tenants and owners are placed on an equivalent basis for comparison.[17]

One attempt by Odling-Smee to measure the total level of subsidies in each housing sector, including the privately rented sector, estimated the total subsidy to housing to be over £5,000m in 1973, though the author emphasised throughout how tentative the estimates inevitably were.[18] Table 5.5 shows these estimates of the average subsidy in each sector. The subsidy to tenants is derived from estimates of market rents based on estimates of house prices which are freely determined by supply and demand.[19] On this basis, the average subsidy to tenants of local authority and private controlled dwellings was estimated to be about the same at £260 to £280 p.a. in 1973; to tenants of uncontrolled, private unfurnished dwellings substantially less at £170 p.a. while tenants of private furnished dwellings received no subsidy on average. The source of subsidy to the average local authority tenant is

Table 5.5: Estimated Average Housing Subsidies per Sector, Market Value Method, and Average Income 1973

	Subsidy	Income[a]
Local authority tenants	260 – 280	2021
Tenants of privately rented controlled dwellings	260 – 280	)
Tenants of uncontrolled privately unfurnished dwellings	170	) 1701)
Tenants of furnished dwellings	0	1812
Owner-occupiers	280	2432

Note: [a]Median gross income per household, *Family Expenditure Survey,* 1973, table 1.
Source: J.C. Odling-Smee, 'The Impact of the Fiscal System on Different Tenure Sectors', in *Housing Finance* (Institute of Fiscal Studies publication, no. 12, September 1975).

about 10 per cent as a direct cash payment in the form of a rent rebate, about 20 per cent from direct central government in subsidies, and the remainder (about 70 per cent) a subsidy given by the local authority itself, financed partly out of rates, but mainly out of the accrued capital gains on its housing stock. All of this subsidy comes from public authorities and hence from general taxation.

Private tenants of unfurnished dwellings received subsidies from public authorities through direct cash payments in the form of rent allowances (about 5 per cent of the total subsidy on average for controlled tenancies and 10 per cent for uncontrolled tenancies) and partly through its loss of tax revenue because landlords pay income tax on the basis of actual rents rather than the higher market rents (about 30 per cent of the total subsidy for each type of tenancy). They also receive subsidy from landlords (about 65 per cent of total subsidy on average for controlled tenancies and 60 per cent for uncontrolled tenancies) who receive lower rents than in the absence of rent control. The owner-occupier is subsidised by the government by being relieved of income tax on net market rent and accrued capital gains tax. These two elements were estimated to be worth £280 p.a. in 1973, of which income tax relief accounted for about 40 per cent and capital gains tax relief for about 60 per cent.

These estimates suggest that owner-occupiers, local authority tenants and tenants of private, controlled tenancies receive subsidies of a similar order of magnitude on average; tenants of private, unfurnished, uncontrolled tenancies receive a smaller subsidy, and tenants of furnished dwellings receive none. Odling-Smee points out, however, that this understates the relative financial advantage of being an owner-occupier rather than a tenant because it does not allow for the accrued real capital gains from owner-occupation arising because house prices tend to rise in real terms. This, however, is not necessarily a consequence of government intervention in housing markets.

While this method provides a more consistent approach to comparing fairness in the allocation of subsidies, it suffers from the practical disadvantage that the results are highly sensitive to the underlying assumptions used to estimate market rents. In particular, hypothetical market rents were estimated on the basis of prevailing house prices in the owner-occupied sector on the grounds that these are broadly market determined, but these might be very different in the absence of government assistance. If such assistance were removed, demand and supply would change throughout the housing market in all tenures, and actual market rents might settle at very different levels from the hypothetical ones estimated from current house prices. Because the long run supply of housing is unlikely to be perfectly price elastic, house prices would be lower in the absence of tax relief and other tax concessions, while if market rents were charged for rental accommodation, the demand for home ownership would be affected. Moreover, this approach still fails to reflect differences in the quality of service provided in each sector, differences in relative incomes, variations over time and variations around these averages.

In relation to services provided, Chapter 6 shows that in terms of quality of accommodation, as measured by unfitness, amenities and overcrowding, owners enjoy a higher standard than local authority tenants, while private tenants are housed in the poorest accommodation, on average. In terms of other services including security and mobility, owner-occupiers get the best deal and private tenants the worst. In relation to income levels, Table 5.5 shows that private tenants are poorer than public tenants and owner-occupiers better off than public tenants, on average. In aggregate terms *between* sectors, therefore, the system of current subsidies is regressive, owner-occupiers receiving the highest subsidy as well as having the highest incomes. Private unfurnished tenants, in contrast, have lower incomes than local authority tenants, on average, but receive less in subsidy. We have already seen in Chapter 3 that rented accommodation houses a disproportionate number of poor households.[20]

In conclusion of this static comparison of the average level of subsidy *between* tenures, while owner-occupiers have the highest incomes and enjoy greater mobility and a better quality of accommodation than local authority tenants, they receive a similar level of subsidy. Private tenants, in contrast, have lower incomes still, generally live in poorer and more overcrowded accommodation, lack security yet receive the lowest subsidy on average. Among private tenants, furnished tenants are particularly poorly treated. The system of finance is therefore broadly regressive between tenures, owner-occupiers receiving more help in relation to their income and accommodation services enjoyed than local authority or private tenants.

Subsidies and Incomes Within Tenures

In determining who benefits from our system of housing finance, it is also important to consider variations in subsidy and household payments *within* tenures. As regards housing costs in the local authority sector, households may be paying very different rents for basically similar accommodation, not only between different areas, but sometimes within. Rents vary because the costs of housing prvision vary between authorities, because the level of Exchequer subsidy also varies, and because of differences in local policy on rate contributions, rent pooling and rent rebates. Subsidies vary because these are related mainly to the time when the authority built up its housing stock and the then prevailing costs of building, interest rates and level of central government subsidy rather than to local needs. Subsidies are not distributed in such a way that rents are systematically related to income.

Further, rents in the private sector vary widely, and to a greater extent than local authority rents.[21] Again there are wide differences in the level of mortgage outgoings and tax relief between households buying their houses. This is mainly because mortgage repayments are related to the price of a house when bought, and the initial size of loan. They are normally fixed in money terms over the period of the loan, and while initial repayments can be high they diminish in real terms if prices rise and as a proportion of income if money incomes rise, and cease when the mortgage is repaid and the house is owned outright. Correspondingly, the level of tax relief falls in money terms as the interest component of repayment falls, and in real terms with inflation. Recent purchasers will therefore receive most tax relief, those with older mortgages less, and those who have paid off their mortgages, none. In market value terms, the incidence of subsidy will be more systematically related to the capital value of the house.

How then are subsidies distributed within tenures in relation to the incomes of households? One attempt to measure the incidence of subsidies on an historic cost basis is given in the Green Paper's Tech-

nical Volume for the year 1974/5. The total housing subsidy to be
allocated, for England and Wales, is £1,476m made up of £650m in tax
relief on mortgage interest, £68m in option mortgage subsidy, £518m
in Exchequer subsidies to local authority and new town housing
revenue accounts, £133m in rate fund contributions to housing
revenue accounts and £107m in rent rebates. Table 5.6 shows the
distribution of these subsidies by ranges of income of head of household and wife in the case of owner-occupiers with a mortgage and local
authority tenants.

Table 5.6: Distribution of Subsidies by Income Range, 1974/5,
England and Wales

Income of head of household and wife	Owner-Occupiers Average Tax Relief and Option Mortgage Subsidy		Average General Subsidy	Local Authority Tenants		
				Average Rebate[a]	Average Total Subsidy	
		Proportion of Average Income[b]				Proportion of Average Income[b]
£	£	%	£	£	£	%
Under 1000	59	n.e	120	46	166	n.e.
1000-1499	73	5.8	132	48	180	14.4
1500-1999	91	5.2	152	28	180	10.3
2000-2499	104	4.6	137	7	144	6.4
2500-2999	101	3.7	147	—	147	5.3
3000-3499	129	4.0	154	—	154	4.7
3500-3999	129	3.4	148	—	148	3.9
4000-4999	148	3.3	164	—	164	3.6
5000-5999	179	3.3	) 154	—	) 154	n.e.
6000+	369	n.e.	)		)	
ALL	141	—	139	23	162	—

Notes: [a]Averaged over all tenant households in the range, not just over the
number of households receiving rebates.
[b]Taking average income in each income cell as the mid-point of the range.
n.e. — not estimated.
Source: Department of the Environment, *Housing Policy Technical Volume I*,
tables IV. 34 and IV. 35.

This shows that the average level of mortgage tax relief (and option
mortgage subsidy) rises fairly steeply with income from £59 per annum
when the head of houehold's income is under £1,000, to £369 per
annum in the case of incomes of over £6,000. If relief were restricted
to the basic rate of income tax, average tax relief in the highest
income range would be £275, still more than lower income groups.

Nevertheless, tax relief rises less than proportionately with income and so falls over the income range as a percentage of income.[22] In contrast, subsidies to local authority and new town tenants, before rent rebates, rise only slightly with income. Subsidies, including rebates, fall slightly in absolute terms as income rises, and fall sharply as a proportion of income.[23]

These figures, while subject to margins of error due to the methodology employed to derive them, suggest that while poorer owner-occupiers receive considerably less subsidy in absolute terms than richer owners, poorer tenants receive only slightly less subsidy than those better off, before rebates, and slightly more, after rebates. While the average subsidy is similar in the two sectors, if the progressivity of housing subsidies is measured in conventional, proportional terms, subsidies to local authority tenants are much more progressively distributed than those to owner-occupiers.

It is important to note that this result is at variance with the conclusions of the government's official analysis of the redistributional impact of government activity, the annual studies by the Central Statistical Office published in *Economic Trends* which aim to show the impact of public spending and taxation on the distribution of income.[24] The studies set out to allocate the money spent and received by government to different households, categorised by size and income. In allocating housing subsidies, the studies have included only Exchequer and rate fund contributions to housing revenue accounts and rent rebates, and have always ignored subsidies to owner-occupiers, a position for which they have long been criticised.[25] By leaving out tax relief in this way, quite apart from the method used, the studies have always been able to conclude that housing subsidies are progressive, a situation shown to be considerably less than the truth by the housing Green Paper.

That the subsidy to local authority tenants is progressively distributed is confirmed by a recent study which attempted to measure its distribution by income group on the basis of the market value approach. In this case, subsidy is measured as the difference between the open market and the actual rent charged. Using data for 1968, this study showed that the estimated subsidy as a proportion of income fell from 30 per cent in the case of households with income less than £500 p.a. to 4.3 per cent in the case of households with income greater than £3,000 p.a.[26]

Variations over Time

A final qualification to these estimates of the equity of housing finance is that they present only a static view. They relate purely to the situation in a single year, yet subsidies and housing costs for all households change quite significantly over time. These single year comparisons, therefore, cannot show relative levels of assistance over longer periods of time.

The time profiles of housing costs and assistance provided towards these costs vary significantly between tenants and owner-occupiers. In terms of housing costs, in the early years, the repayment of a mortgage combined with the relatively minor costs of insurance and maintenance involve the house purchaser in higher annual outgoings than the payment of rent by tenants. However, these outlays diminish in real terms over time as prices rise, and as a proportion of income, if incomes rise, and eventually become insignificant when the mortgage is fully repaid. In contrast, renting involves lower annual payments at first, but rents tend to rise in line with inflation and eventually become greater than the purchaser's costs, usually before purchase is complete. When the mortgage has been fully repaid, the buyer's housing costs are insignificant, he owns a capital asset, but tenants continue to pay rent.

In dynamic terms, the choice between buying and renting can therefore be seen as a choice between the foregoing of present consumption in favour of higher consumption later in life for the purchaser, and higher consumption now with relatively lower consumption later for the tenant. The trade-off is unlikely to be one for one, however, for the financial savings later from buying may in total outweigh the initial losses.

One way of estimating relative costs is to calculate the discounted value of lifetime housing payments in the case of the tenant and the owner-occupier, after allowing for the effect of the acquisition of a capital asset in the case of the owner-occupier. Of course, such estimates would not indicate the extent to which differences in relative costs are the direct result of differences in subsidies between the sectors, and to what extent they are due to wider factors including the rise in house prices in relation to other prices, changes in interest rates and general rises in prices and incomes. They could also not be used on their own to argue that one group is better off than another in terms of subsidy, but they would be useful for illustrating the relative costs of house purchase and renting over time in terms of housing payments.

In practice, estimates of these discounted costs depend on a great number of factors, including the life expectancy of the householder, changes in interest rates and rates of inflation in house prices, rents, maintenance costs and all prices, all of which are very difficult to predict. The calculations will also be sensitive to the choice of discount rate used to discount the value of costs accruing in the future. These costs will also be affected by changes in government policy which affect subsidies, tax relief, tax levels, and of the decisions of individual households about movements between dwellings. Leaving aside households who switch tenures, an important factor is also the frequency of movement by owner-occupiers.

One attempt at this approach compared the discounted value of relative housing payments between the tenures over time, basing the comparison on two householders respectively buying and renting a similar house in 1964. The relative costs of buying and renting were estimated for three separate periods, 1964 to 1970, 1964 to 1973 and 1964 to 1988, the final year of mortgage repayments. Up to 1973 actual rates of inflation in rents, house prices and general prices were used; after 1973, comparisons were based on three different assumptions about the future rate of inflation. Using a real discount rate of 3 per cent, it was found that, deducting the net value of the house to the owner at each stage from his accumulated payments, purchasing on a mortgage gave better value than renting in each of the three sub periods examined.[27] There is therefore good reason to believe that while the house purchaser faces higher initial outgoings than a local authority tenant for similar accommodation, an inter-temporal comparison would show that the accumulated costs of owner-occupation are less than renting if the value of the asset acquired is included in the calculation.

Summary

In summary, determining the extent to which housing subsidies are equitably distributed is made difficult by a number of conceptual and empirical problems and the sheer complexity of housing finance. Nevertheless, certain features are clear. The main conclusion that can be drawn is that subsidies are distributed in haphazard, unsystematic and indiscriminate ways. Some elements are progressive, some regressive. Overall, housing finance is regressive in impact. Owner-occupiers are noticeably better off than local authority tenants on average, yet receive at least a similar level of subsidy. Private tenants have lower incomes still, contain some of the poorest households and are less adequately housed yet receive unambiguously the least assistance. Within tenures, tax relief is worth more in absolute terms to those with the highest incomes, though it may fall slightly as a proportion as income rises. Subsidies to local authority tenants are more progressively distributed. Rent rebates are progressive, being absolutely and proportionately of greater help to lower income tenants, but they suffer from the major problem of low take-up. Subsidies as a whole are distributed quite indiscriminately and are not related in any systematic way to income, need or the quality and services of accommodation provided. The assertion of the Green Paper that 'much of the debate on "equity" in housing is sterile: it is an attempt to compare chalk and cheese. . . . There are fundamental differences between the two tenures which must defeat any attempt to draw up an incontrovertible "balance sheet"'[28] is unfounded and seems to be simply a convenient way of evading the need for major reforms, reforms which may be politically embarrassing.

Notes

1. Department of the Environment, *Housing Policy – A Consultative Document* (HMSO, Cmnd 6851, 1977), para. 5.30, p. 37 and para. 2. 14, p. 6.

2. Fabian Society, *Evidence to the Department of the Environment's Review of Housing Finance* (March 1976), p. 10.

3. National Economic Development Office, *Finance for Investment* (May 1975), ch. 6.

4. Department of the Environment, *Housing Policy Technical Volume II* (HMSO, 1977), table VII, 19 and para. VII. 61.

5. B. Kilroy, 'Subsidies: Value for Money', *Roof* (Shelter, March 1976), p. 38.

6. Department of the Environment, *Housing Policy Technical Volume I*, ch. 1, para. 22.

7. Building Societies Association, *Facts and Figures*, no. 3 (July 1975), table A.

8. C. Whitehead, *The UK Housing Market* (Saxon House, 1974), has quoted the Department of the Environment as saying that the quality of the housing stock has been increasing at 4 per cent per annum, although other estimates are less than half this amount.

9. Royal Commission on the Distribution of Income and Wealth, *Report No. 4* (HMSO, Cmnd 6626, October 1976).

10. Department of the Environment, *Housing Policy Technical Volume I*, table II.16 and II.17, pp. 68, 69.

11. D. Webster 'House Prices and Allocation: The Case for Action on the Demand Side of the Market', *Housing Review* (January-February, 1975).

12. *Fair Deal For Housing* (HMSO, Cmnd 4728, 1971), para. 5, p. 1.

13. Department of the Environment, *Housing Policy Technical Volume II*, ch. 5, para. 75, p. 18.

14. The Fabian Society, *Evidence to the Review of Housing Finance*.

15. The Building Societies Association, *Evidence to the Review of Housing Finance* (March 1976).

16. Ibid., annex 2.

17. See, for example, C. Whitehead, 'Neutrality Between Tenures: A Critique of the Housing Policy Review Comparison', *The Centre for Environmental Studies Review*, no. 2 (Centre for Environmental Studies, December 1977).

18. J.C. Odling-Smee, 'The Impact of the Fiscal System on Different Tenure Sectors' in *Housing Finance* (Institute of Fiscal Studies Publication, no. 12, 1975).

19. The hypothetical market rent in 1973 was estimated on the basis of assumptions of an 11 per cent interest rate, an average 8 per cent annual increase in house prices and an average life of the existing housing stock of 50 years and an annual yield of 4 per cent.

20. Table 3.7, Ch. 3.

21. Table 4.4, Ch. 4.

22. Though, because of problems of incomplete data on which these estimates are based, the figures in Table 5.6 probably overstate average tax relief in the lower income ranges and understate it at the top end; see, for example C. Boyd 'A Fair Share?' *Roof* (Shelter, September 1977).

23. There are conceptual problems associated with the allocation of subsidies between tenants, quite apart from empirical difficulties. Conceptually, the subsidy to an individual tenant could be taken as the difference between the historically incurred cost of the dwelling and the actual rent, but this would mean that tenants of older property are not subsidised at all because the rent they pay is greater than the historic cost. In general, some averaging procedure of costs and subsidies over tenants is therefore employed. See Department of the Environment, *Housing Policy Technical Volume I*, ch. IV, para. 90 for the procedure adopted.

24. See, for example, 'Effects of Taxes and Benefits on Household Income 1975', *Economic Trends*, no. 278 (December 1976).

25. See, for example, A.L. Webb and J.E.B. Sieve, *Income Distribution and the Welfare State* (Occasional Papers in Social Administration, no. 41, London, G. Bell and Son, 1971).

26. L. Rosenthal, 'The Regional and Income Distribution of the Council House Subsidy in the UK', *The Manchester School*, vol. XLV, no. 2 (June 1977).

27. S. Lansley and G. Fiegehen, *One Nation? Housing and Conservative Policy*, Fabian Tract 432 (Fabian Society, September 1974).

28. Department of the Environment, *Housing Policy — A Consultative Document*, para. 6. 41, p. 49.

6 HOUSING TENURE – CURRENT ISSUES AND TRENDS

The nature of our tenure system and its future development has become an increasingly important aspect of housing policy. This is partly because of the increasing attention given to the question of equity in housing and the relative costs and advantages offered by different sectors, partly because of the problems posed by the decline in the private rented sector, and partly because of concern about future trends and in particular the role to be played by the publicly rented sector. A major area of debate in recent years has been the extent to which a genuinely fair choice exists between tenures, and whether owners and tenants receive equal help from the state in relation to their needs and ability to pay. The question of relative financial support was examined in Chapter 5, where it was concluded that aid is not distributed equitably between tenures. There is little doubt that one of the main sources of inequality in housing lies in our system of tenure. Each sector differs widely in the physical quality of accommodation provided, in the legal, social and financial benefits they offer and in the way in which dwellings are allocated, yet for a large section of the population, no choice exists between them.

This chapter reviews briefly the development of our present tenure structure, examines a number of characteristics of each tenure and considers a number of contemporary questions about the future role of existing and alternative forms of tenure.

The Existing Tenure Pattern

How It Has Changed

The housing market in Britain is divided into three major sectors, owner-occupation, private renting and local authority renting. Table 6.1 shows trends in the tenure structure of the housing stock since 1914. The current most widespread forms of tenure are local authority renting and owner-occupation. Both have become increasingly important since 1914 almost entirely at the expense of the privately rented sector whose dominant pre-First World War position has been gradually eroded.

Table 6.1: The Distribution of the Housing Stock by Tenure, 1914 to 1975, England and Wales (percentages)

		1914	1938	1960	1971	1975
Owner-occupied	%	10	32.5	43.8	52.6	55
Local authority rented and new towns	%	–	9.6	24.7	28.7	28.9
Privately rented and miscellaneous	%	90	57.9	31.5	19.3	16.1
All		100	100	100	100	100
Total stock, millions		7.9	11.4	14.6	17.1	18.0

Source: Department of the Environment, *Housing Policy Technical Volume I*, table 1.23, p. 38.

The components of these changes in the housing stock by tenure are given in Table 6.2. This shows that the growth of owner-occupation is explained by both new building, which accounted for some 64 per cent of the increase in the number of owner-occupied dwellings between

Table 6.2: Components of Change of Housing Stock by Tenure, 1914 to 1975, England and Wales (millions)

	Owner-Occupied	Local Authorities and New Towns	Private Landlords and Miscellaneous	Total
1914-1960				
New building	+ 3.1	+ 3.4	+ 1.0	+ 7.5
Purchases (+) or sales (–)	+ 2.6	+ 0.2[b]	– 2.8	0
Demolitions and changes of use[c]	– 0.1	neg.	– 0.7	– 0.8
Net	+ 5.6	+ 3.6	– 2.5	+ 6.7
1960-1975				
New building[a]	+ 2.6	+ 1.6	+ 0.3	+ 4.5
Purchases (+) or sales (–)	+ 1.1	+ 0.1	– 1.2	0
Demolitions and changes of use	– 0.2	– 0.1[d]	– 0.8	– 1.1
Net	+ 3.5	+ 1.6	– 1.7	+ 3.4

Notes: Neg. — negligible.
[a]Includes conversions.
[b]Mainly requisitioned during the Second World War and subsequently purchased.
[c]Includes 0.2 million destroyed by air raids.
[d]Mainly 'pre-fabs'.
Source: Department of the Environment, *Housing Policy Technical Volume I*, table I. 24. p. 39.

1914 and 1975, and by transfers from other sectors, which accounted for the remainder. The main explanation for the growth of local authority housing has been new building. In contrast, in the privately rented sector, the period 1914 to 1975 saw new building of 1.3m, mostly pre-1938, but a loss of 4.0m through sales to other sectors and a loss of 1.5m through demolition and change of use.

This shift in the tenure structure of the housing stock has been influenced by the nature of government policy and its interaction with market forces together with rising real incomes over the period. The rising importance of owner-occupation is due to a steady expansion in demand for houses to buy resulting from rising real incomes, the special financial advantages offered by buying relative to renting, and general difficulties of access to other sectors. The increase in the size of the local authority sector is due to a variety of subsidies to supply combined with a continuing high demand for local authority homes to rent. The steady loss of privately rented accommodation is due to a mixture of supply and demand factors. Supply has been discouraged by rent control, the disadvantageous tax position of the private landlord, alternative and more profitable forms of investment, the transactions costs associated with private renting, and also slum clearance and redevelopment programmes which have affected private letting particularly heavily. On the demand side, rising real incomes and changing economic and social patterns have switched natural preferences away from renting, while the greater financial and other benefits of owner-occupation and public renting due to the nature of the subsidy system have depressed demand. Rent control is often claimed to be the most important factor, but 'demand' factors and demolition polices are also significant. Even without rent control, owner-occupation would have expanded at the expense of private renting.

Differences in Housing Conditions by Tenure

There are major differences in the type, size and standard of accommodation between tenures. In 1971, for example, the General Household Survey showed that about 28 per cent of owner-occupied dwellings were detached houses compared with 1.1 per cent of local authority and new town dwellings, and 6 per cent of privately rented unfurnished. In contrast, only 2 per cent of owner-occupied dwellings were purpose built flats compared with 23 per cent of local authority dwellings and 14.6 per cent of dwellings rented unfurnished and 7 per cent furnished from private landlords. Owner-occupied dwellings are predominantly detached and semi-detached houses, while local authority dwellings are mainly semi-detached and terraced houses and purpose built flats, and privately rented unfurnished dwellings largely terraced houses, and furnished, mainly non-purpose built single rooms and small flats. There are also wide differences in the size of accommodation. The great proportion of large houses are owner-occupied. The most common type of dwelling in the public rented sector is the three-bedroomed semi-detached or terraced house, though the proportion of purpose-built flats is higher than in the other sectors. Privately rented accommodation is the most heterogeneous.[1]

Most important is the variation in the physical standard, condition and density of dwellings in each sector. Table 6.3 shows the extent of

Table 6.3: Unfitness and Lack of Amenities by Tenure, England and Wales, 1976 (thousands, percentages in brackets)

	Owner-occupied	Rented from Local Authority	Other Tenures[a]	Vacant	All Tenures
Unfit dwellings	310(3)	49(1)	384(16)	151(30)	894(5)
No fixed bath in bathroom	302(3)	47(1)	526(17)	126(25)	901(5)
No inside WC	407(4)	161(3)	471(19)	129(26)	1638(9)
Lacking one or more basic amenities	547(5)	280(6)	640(26) 7	166(33)	1633(9)
All dwellings	10125(100)	5067(100)	2444(100)	497(100)	18133(100)

Note: [a]Mainly privately rented, but includes accommodation rented with job or business, and miscellaneous tenures.
Source: Department of the Environment, *Housing Policy Technical Volume I*, table II.4, p. 56.

unfitness and lack of basic amenities by tenure. Poor housing is heavily concentrated in the privately rented sector. 16 per cent of privately rented accommodation was unfit in 1976 compared with only 3 per cent of owner-occupied and 1 per cent of local authority rented dwellings. Privately rented dwellings accounted for 39 per cent of all dwellings lacking one or more basic amenities but only 13 per cent of all dwellings. Further in 1976, 50 per cent of owner-occupied dwellings had full central heating compared with 29 per cent of local authority and 16 per cent of privately rented dwellings.

A similar picture emerges from a comparison of levels of occupation. Overcrowding is concentrated in rented accommodation. It has been shown that 70 per cent of owner-occupiers with a mortgage and 80 per cent of outright owners have enough space to allow them one or more spare bedrooms, compared with 48 per cent of local authority tenants, 58 per cent of private unfurnished and 18 per cent of furnished tenants.[2] The 1971 Census showed that in England and Wales, 8.1 per cent of households renting privately furnished accommodation were living at densities of more than 1½ persons per room compared with 1.4 per cent of households renting privately unfurnished accommodation, 1.8 per cent of local authority tenants, and 0.5 per cent of owner-occupiers. Both in terms of the bedroom standard and density levels, shortage of space is most common among tenants of privately furnished dwellings and least common among owner-occupiers.[3] As Table 5.1 indicates, low densities of occupation are most prevalent in the owner-occupied sector and least common in households renting from local authorities and private furnished accommodation.

Variations in Income and Socio-Economic Group by Tenure

Another important feature of our tenure system relates to the distribution of households by income level between different sectors. Table 6.4 shows household income at the 10th, 50th and 90th percentiles within each of the five main tenures.[4] This shows that the median household income of households buying their own houses is 59 per cent higher than local authority tenants, 109 per cent and 54 per cent more than private unfurnished and furnished tenants, respectively, and 37 per cent higher than outright owners. Mortgagors are considerably better off than households in each of the other sectors. Among the remaining groups, outright owners have the highest incomes, on average, while local authority and privately rented furnished tenants are better off than unfurnished tenants. As regards the dispersion of income within each sector, mortgagors have incomes that are relatively narrowly dispersed. Above the median, local authority tenants, furnished tenants and outright owners are less dispersed by income than private unfurnished tenants. The local authority sector contains a smaller proportion of households with higher incomes than each of the other sectors with the exception of those renting unfurnished.

It is useful to compare changes in these relative incomes over time. Table 6.5 shows the ratio of the income of local authority tenants, private unfurnished tenants and outright owners to the income of households with a mortgage at the 10th, 50th and 90th percentiles for 1953/4, 1963 and 1975. In general, the incomes of households buying their own homes with a mortgage have grown at a faster pace than those of households in the other sectors. In consequence, the ratio of the

Table 6.4: Household Income and Tenure, 1975

percentile	Local Authority Rented	Other rented Unfurnished	Rented Furnished £ per week	Owned with Mortgage	Owned Outright
10	17.70	14.50	19.70	52.80	19.50
50	57.00	43.30	58.60	90.40	66.20
90	113.60	108.80	119.00	154.00	133.70
			percentage of median %		
10	31.1	33.4	33.6	58.4	29.5
50	100	100	100	100	100
90	199.3	251.3	202.9	170.3	202.0

Source: Estimated by linear interpolation from Department of Employment, *Family Expenditure Survey Report,* 1975, table 1.

Table 6.5: Incomes of Households in Different Tenures as a Percentage of the Income of Purchasing Households, 1953/4, 1963, 1975 (percentages)

	10th percentile			median			90th percentile		
	1954/4	1963	1975	1953/4	1963	1975	1953/4	1963	1975
Local authority rented	71.6	47.1	33.5	83.3	77.2	63.1	86.6	73.3	73.7
Other rented unfurnished	42.8	35.5	27.5	73.0	68.0	47.9	83.3	70.3	70.6
Owned with mortgage	100	100	100	100	100	100	100	100	100
Owned outright	44.1	43.7	36.9	81.2	71.1	73.2	104.3	89.6	86.8

Source: Department of Employment, *Family Expenditure Survey Reports:* estimated by linear interpolation.

median income of council tenants to purchasers has fallen from 0.83 in 1953/4 to 0.63 in 1975; of other unfurnished tenants from 0.73 in 1953/4 to 0.48 in 1975;and that of outright owners from 0.81 in 1953/4 to 0.73 in 1975. The faster increase in the incomes of mortgagors as a group has reflected the general tendency for better off local authority and private tenants to move into owner-occupation and poorer private tenants to move into the local authority sector. An important reason for this pattern has been the steady rise in the proportion of local authority tenant households with economically inactive heads, from 25 per cent in 1968 to 35 per cent in 1975. This is a result of both the increase in the proportion of retired households and of women with dependent children on supplementary benefit in this sector.

The effect of these trends has been a steadily increasing segregation of households by income between the two major sectors. While there is some overlap of incomes between households buying and renting their homes, this has become steadily smaller, as shown in Table 6.6. In 1953/4, for example, an estimated 32 per cent of households buying their own homes had incomes that were less than the median income of local authority tenants. By 1975, this proportion had fallen to 11 per cent. Again, in 1953/4, 21 per cent of households buying their home had incomes less than the median income of private unfurnished tenants, a proportion that had fallen to 5 per cent by 1975.

Table 6.6: Proportion of Purchasing Households with Household Income Less Than Particular Percentiles in the Rented Sector, 1953/4 to 1975 (percentages)

Percentiles	1953/4	1963	1975
		Local authority rented	
25	12	8	2
50	32	29	11
75	59	56	42
		Other rented unfurnished	
25	7	4	1
50	21	19	5
75	52	47	32

Source: Department of Employment, *Family Expenditure Survey Reports:* estimated by linear interpolation.

There is, moreover, every reason to believe that this trend will continue. Owner-occupation is increasingly only available to renting households with higher incomes. It has been estimated that in 1971, only 8.6 per cent of all public tenants and 12.8 per cent of private tenants were sufficiently young (less than 50) and had sufficient income to buy a median priced house.[5] The privately rented sector will continue its long term decline, and the most likely pattern of change is a continuing movement of poorer private tenants into the local authority sector and those with higher incomes in both rented sectors into owner-occupation. Again, it is only the better off local authority tenant who can afford to purchase.

As a result of these changes, the tenure composition of poor households has shifted over the period. Table 6.7 shows the tenure composition of the poorest 10 per cent of all households in 1953/4, 1963 and 1975. Expressing this as a ratio of the tenure composition of all house-

Table 6.7: Tenure Composition of the Poorest 10 per cent of
Households, 1953/4 to 1975

	1953/4		1963		1975	
	Poorest 10% %	Risk of poverty ratio	Poorest 10% %	Risk of poverty ratio	Poorest 10% %	Risk of poverty ratio
Local authority rented	13.3	0.7	28.1	1.0	44.7	1.4
Other rented unfurnished	55.5	1.3	38.9	1.5	22.8	2.1
Rented furnished	2.0	0.7	2.1	0.8	4.2	1.0
Rent free	4.2	1.3	5.8	1.5	3.9	1.4
Owned with mortgage	4.4	0.3	2.6	0.1	1.8	0.06
Owned outright	20.6	1.3	22.5	1.2	22.6	1.1
All	100.0	1.0	100.0	1.0	100.0	1.0

Source: Department of Employment, *Family Expenditure Survey Reports*,
estimated by linear interpolation.

holds in each year, also shown in Table 6.7, then provides an indication
of the relative risk of poverty by tenure in each year and over time.
Thus in 1975 while the local authority sector accounted for 31.8 per
cent of *all* households, it accommodated 44.7 per cent of *poor* households. The tenure composition of the poor has changed significantly
over the period. In 1953/4, 13 per cent of the poorest decile lived in
the local authority sector, and 56 per cent in other rented unfurnished
accommodation, proportions which had changed to 45 per cent and 23
per cent respectively by 1975. The relatively high proportion of the
poor living in dwellings owned outright reflects the high proportion of
retired households in this type of accommodation. The risk of poverty
has also changed. The risk of poverty among local authority tenants
doubled over the period, and among other rented unfurnished households increased markedly. In contrast, the risk of poverty among
owners with mortgages was not only well below average at the beginning
but fell steadily over the period.[6] Between 1967 and 1975 the proportion of all households receiving supplementary benefit living in the local
authority sector increased from 45 per cent to 57 per cent.[7] In terms of
socio-economic group, though council housing now represents 29 per
cent of the housing stock in England and Wales, the General Household
Survey shows that it housed 59 per cent of unskilled manual workers in
1975 and 46 per cent of semi-skilled, compared with figures of 52 per
cent and 42 per cent in 1971. In 1975, 80 per cent of households in
council accommodation were skilled, semi-skilled or unskilled manual
workers.

Future Tenure Patterns

An important aspect of housing policy is the question of the future mix and role of different tenures. Present trends are towards a situation where the great majority of households will live in owner-occupied or publicly rented dwellings. As privately rented accommodation continues to decline, these will become the two main choices for households. The implications and desirability of this situation is a matter of contention. Some would argue that attempts should be made to revive the privately rented sector, others that it should be encouraged to run down and its role adopted by the public rented sector or the expansion of alternative forms of tenure such as housing associations. Others argue that the public rented sector itself should be run down. We therefore consider, next, the respective roles of each of the three main sectors and alternative tenures and how they are likely to develop, together with some of the main areas of debate.

Owner-Occupation

Recent years have seen growing support for the view that owner-occupation should continue to expand, though there is disagreement about how quickly and to what extent, and about what supporting government measures are needed. Both major political parties are supporters of home ownership and are committed to its encouragement. In the past, however, it has been the Conservative Party which has been the most enthusiastic about the virtues of owning one's home, this being the major ideological basis of their housing policy, a reflection of their belief in the principle of a 'property owning democracy' and their opposition to central and local government intervention. The housing policy of successive Conservative governments has been marked by direct and indirect encouragement of home ownership. In their 1970 to 1974 administration, policy included the encouragement of council house sales by the giving of general consent to sell to sitting tenants at a discount of up to 20 per cent, requests to local authorities to release land for private housebuilding and recommendations that they should build for sale, and the passing of the Housing Finance Act which shifted the balance of financial advantage further in favour of purchase rather than renting. During the period there was a sharp increase in the proportion of new dwellings built for sale.[8] The Conservatives have always supported a substantial role for owner-occupation.

While the Labour Party has always supported home ownership, they have also argued the need for a large public sector in housing. Nevertheless, recent statements and policy initiatives by the Callaghan government

suggest that Labour may be moving towards greater preference for
home ownership. In a speech in 1976, Peter Shore, Secretary of State
for the Environment, claimed that 'owner-occupation not only makes
economic sense for the individual and the community, it also satisfies
deep rooted aspirations in our people', and spoke of present trends
taking us towards a figure of 70 per cent owner-occupation by the end
of the century.[9] This view was reinforced in the housing Green Paper
which declared that 'for most people, owning one's home is a basic and
natural desire, which for more and more people is becoming attain-
able'.[10] This is also an indication of the convergence in housing policy
that has emerged in recent years between the leadership of the two
main political parties, with both now being major supporters of home
ownership as in some sense the 'desirable' or 'natural' form of tenure.
The consequence of this emerging consensus is considered in this
chapter and Chapter 7.

Access to Owner-Occupation

The Green Paper gave a good deal of attention to the need for
extending owner-occupation and improving access to it. It emphasised
the importance of building societies adopting more socially responsible
policies by providing more low start mortgages, offering higher percentage mortgages, extending lending on older properties and encouraging
greater co-operation between building societies and local authorities.
These, the Green Paper, claims, would help into home ownership those
who might not otherwise have been able to buy, and help those who
might have bought but with great difficulty.[11] In addition, the Green
Paper proposed new forms of financial assistance for the first time
buyer, and in February 1978, the Home Purchase Assistance Bill was
introduced providing assistance to first time buyers who have been
saving to buy their own home. The bill provides for a cash bonus up to a
maximum of £110 and for a loan of up to £600 interest free for 5
years, to those who have saved for 2 years and have kept at least £300
in savings for 12 months before seeking a loan. The scheme is to come
into operation in 1980, and it is estimated that 40 per cent of all first
time buyers will benefit. The aim is to help into home ownership the
marginal buyer, and ease the burden in the early years of those who can
barely afford to buy. The Conservatives have for some time supported
considerably more generous policies including direct subsidies to
building societies to hold down the mortgage interest rate, and larger
contributions to first time buyers' deposits.

   This act can be criticised on a number of grounds. It does nothing for the potential first-time buyer who is unable to save. It will also be of little benefit to those who want to buy older properties in innner city areas. This is because building societies have long been reluctant to lend in certain areas, particularly inner cities, a policy which has become known as 'redlining'.[12] Studies have found that only 15 per cent of house buyers in inner Birmingham and 17 per cent in inner Walsall have managed to obtain a building society mortgage, compared with 75 per cent of first time buyers in England and Wales as a whole.[13] The scheme is designed to benefit relatively substantial savers who are able to get a building society mortgage, and the majority of home buyers in inner urban areas will not be in a position to benefit. Further, the cost of the proposal, estimated at around £100m in the first year of operation, is to be met from existing housing expenditure provision and so is introduced at the expense of other areas of spending. In addition, as we have argued in Chapter 1, subsidies of this kind do not necessarily improve the access of lower income groups. It is most unlikely that the scheme will do more than marginally increase the number of mortgages taken up in the 1980s.

The basic objective of extending the choice of home ownership should be supported, but it is most unlikely that these policies will make a significant difference to the chances of the low paid and those wanting to buy older houses. Building society lending policy has generally been inflexible and rigid, and has worked to the disadvantage of certain groups including black households, the low paid and those with fluctuating earnings. One survey has shown that while 73 per cent of white home-buyers' mortgages came from building societies, for example, the figure for West Indians was 51 per cent and for Asians, 43 per cent.[14] The General Household Survey shows that 80 per cent of professional households are owner-occupiers compared with only 20 per cent of unskilled manual workers. Building societies have also discriminated against certain types of property especially older property and conversions. Redlining has contributed towards the decline of some of our inner cities, aggravated urban decay and frustrated improvement policies. To provide greater choice, exhortation is not enough. Past attempts to persuade building societies to adopt different policies have proved ineffective, despite the ever present threat of greater control.

Local authority mortgages have been made available to assist purchasers who could not get conventional mortgages, but these have been drastically cut from the peak year of 1974/5 when £786m was loaned to over 100,000 borrowers, comprising 14 per cent of all mortgage advances. In 1977/8, only £157m was loaned, and this is projected to fall to £143m in 1978/9, helping only some 25,000 mortgagors.[15] To try and fill the gap created by these cuts in lending, the government negotiated a support lending scheme in 1976 whereby the building societies agreed to relax their normal lending criteria and make loans of £100m to buyers nominated by local authorities. In 1977 £157m was agreed under the scheme, but the evidence suggests that the scheme is not working as planned. Building societies have not eased their lending criteria — at least to any extent — to include applicants who would previously have obtained a local authority mortgage. A monitoring exercise of the scheme by the Department of the Environment in September 1977 has revealed that only about 70 per cent of the quota will have been spent, that only some 35 per cent of referrals by local authorities have resulted in offers, that building societies were reluctant to lend above 90 per cent and were still taking a conservative view of properties needing improvement and in poorer areas.[16]

In view of the weaknesses of existing policies of exhortation and new financial assistance to ease access to owner-occupation, various alternative proposals have been made. Some have argued for more direct control or nationalisation of building societies that are powerful financial institutions receiving substantial state patronage and support, for example in the form of preferential taxation, yet are not publicly accountable in any way. Another alternative is the expansion of local authority lending, by, for example, requiring building societies to provide local authorities with a significant proportion of their funds (up to 20 per cent) for lending to house buyers. This would be a particularly effective way of ensuring that loans are available to marginal and currently disadvantaged buyers, for older properties and at 100 per cent where necessary, and would relieve the building societies of any anxiety about the security of loans on older properties or to lower income households. The main barrier to such a scheme is that under the current rules of public expenditure, whether a local authority guarantees a mortgage or simply acts as an agent of the building society, local authority lending is counted as public expenditure whereas support lending is not.[17] This is a serious anomaly in accounting arrangements, and should be amended.

As well as the need for new directions in policy to extend access to home ownership, there is an important need for policies that provide greater equality of advantage between sectors. As we have seen, owner-occupation offers superior benefits, financial and social, and the provision of a fair and equal choice between tenures depends upon the evening out of these benefits. The recent Green Paper on housing, however, has rejected the case for the reform of existing financial arrangements and supports the *status quo* (see Chapter 7). It also rejects the view that the preference for home ownership derives particularly from the financial benefits of ownership and suggests that a more likely reason is the 'sense of greater personal independence that it brings'.[18] Indeed, critics of the Green Paper's approach have argued that it is biased towards home ownership, is lukewarm towards public sector housing and will reinforce the current trend towards the division of society by income and class between the two main sectors.[19] The Green Paper together with recent speeches by ministers suggests that the government is adopting a new emphasis in policy which stresses the importance of home ownership but which has failed to set out a coherent and positive role for the public sector.

This position must have implications for the future growth of home ownership. On present policies, and assuming that sales of council houses rise to 20,000 a year by the end of the 1970s, the Green Paper predicts a tenure mix by 1986 of 59 per cent owner-occupation, 33 per cent public sector and housing associations and 8 per cent privately rented.[20] But this does not take account of the effects of the Green Paper's proposals to make access to owner-occupation easier. The Building Societies Association, in their comments on the Green Paper, have argued that 'the Green Paper has seriously underestimated the demand for owner-occupation'.[21] The failure to deal with the relative inequities between each sector will maintain the preference for owner-occupation. Nevertheless the growth of home ownership will depend in the main on the supply of mortgage finance and houses. In Chapter 5 we saw that even on the basis of a simple projection of past and current trends, the annual volume of funds needed to finance loans for purchase would be 50 per cent higher in 1986 than in 1976. The growth in the stock of owner-occupied dwellings depends on the rate of new building and the transfer of homes from the rented sector. Since the transfer from private renting is likely to slow down with the decline of this sector, the future trend of owner-occupation will depend particularly on the number of council house sales.

One of the problems of existing trends, and trends that can only be accelerated by proposals in the Green Paper, is the tendency towards a polarisation of society by income and class between the two major sectors. As long as the choice between renting and buying is biased in favour of buying, and the actual access to owner-occupation is restricted, there will be a tendency for those who can make a choice to opt for house purchase. As the Green Paper has pointed out, one of the consequences of the continuing growth and wider access to home ownership could be gradually to narrow the social make-up of the public rented sector unless tenants can be offered more varied housing opportunities and a greater degree of personal independence and control over their home.[22]

The trend towards polarisation would be reinforced by the selling of council houses, by the continuing decline of the privately rented sector, and by a failure to tackle some of the problems of council housing.

The Local Authority Sector

Throughout this century, the provision of municipal rented housing on a large scale has been a central plank of government policy aimed at ensuring decent housing at a cost that households can afford, though Labour administrations at both central and local level have always given greater emphasis towards municipal housing. Council housing has always had its critics, but recent years have seen a growing opposition from a number of quarters. Critics have argued that tenants are over subsidised and cosetted members of society, that council housing costs the taxpayer too much, that estates are badly designed, poorly constructed and badly managed, and that home ownership is in any case a superior and preferred form of tenure and should be encouraged. The advocates of this view have variously argued for a reduction in subsidies, higher rents, a halt to new building, and the gradual reduction in the size of the public sector through council house sales on a large scale, thereby limiting the role of the local authorities to catering for the needs of the poor and disadvantaged.

The Sale of Council Houses

These policies have been supported by leading Conservative politicians who, in recent years, have called for the partial or complete disposal of the council stock and the rundown of the role of local authorities as providers and managers of housing for rent. Timothy Raison, opposition Environment spokesman in a speech in December 1975, for example, argued:

Council tenants should be given a legal right to buy the houses in which they live on generous terms. Possible methods of doing this would include discounts on market price based on the number of years that the family has lived in their home or a gradual build up of equity stake by transferring rent payments to mortgage payments.

Conservative held Councils are now adopting policies of sales at discount prices. Horace Cutler, while opposition leader, and now leader of the Greater London Council, promised 'the sale of the century' if the Conservatives won control of County Hall which they did in May 1977. This policy is in line with the Conservative Party's firm belief in the basic virtue of home ownership and the dislike of market intervention.

The housing policies of recent Conservative governments have been marked by direct or indirect encouragement of home ownership and the promotion of council house sales. Table 6.8 shows the boost to sales that took place during the 1970 to 1974 Conservative administration. This followed the general consent to local authorities, given in 1970, that houses may be sold at full market value, without restriction, or at as much as 20 per cent below that value on condition that the house is offered back to the Council if it is re-sold within five years of the original sale.[24] This pre-emption clause is designed to prevent the owner selling at a profit within the five year period. A further circular issued in 1973 enabled councils to increase the discount to 30 per cent, but only with Department of the Environment consent. The Labour Government of 1974 has done nothing to rescind this general consent, though its Department of the Environment Circular 70/74 did emphasise the remaining need for rented accommodation in some areas and that it would be generally wrong for local authorities to sell houses in such areas. The Green Paper on housing was only lukewarm in its opposition to sales in areas of stress.[25]

Table 6.8: Sales of Local Authority Dwellings

	Number[a]	As a percentage of the local authority Housing stock
1966	3776	0.1
1967	3042	0.1
1968	8302	0.2
1969	7342	0.2
1970	6135	0.1
1971	16393	0.4
1972	42867	1.0
1973	30588	0.7
1974	3327	0.1
1975	1990	0.04

Note: [a]Excluding sales by New Towns
Source: Department of the Environment, *Hansard,* 2 August 1976.

This policy of council house sales has not only received support from the Right. In December 1975, Frank Field, Director of the Child Poverty Action Group, in a pamphlet published by the Catholic Housing Aid Society and entitled *Do We Need Council Houses?*, saw selling council houses as a way of redistributing wealth and providing a direct attack on the cycle of poverty, and as a way of extending individual freedom by relieving tenants of what he described as the 'serfdom imposed upon them by their council tenancies . . . and the petty rules and restrictions imposed by bureaucracy'. And in addition to these views, there has been support, across party boundaries, for equity-sharing schemes and local authority building for sale, some of the arguments for and against which are similar to those for selling council houses.

These views have received stern opposition from those who support the need for a large and growing local authority rented sector. This alternative view holds that council housing has been of massive benefit, providing, in general, good quality accommodation for a significant portion of the population who would otherwise have been very poorly housed; and in so doing, has helped to break the association between poor housing and poverty; that council housing is not unduly expensive and wasteful of resources, and that allowing the local authority sector to be run down to a 'residual' role, providing merely a kind of safety net for disadvantaged groups would have serious social and economic repercussions. As one report has argued, 'Whatever shortcomings council housing may have in the particular conditions of today, its achievements must be regarded as among the successes of British social policy . . . It would be disastrous if the council house sector became a refuge for the poor.'[26]

The main arguments used by those in favour of council house sales on a major scale is that owner-occupation is a preferred form of tenure, that owner-occupation is cheaper for society, that sales would extend freedom, reduce 'serfdom' and redistribute wealth, and that such a policy would not seriously accentuate housing stress in areas of shortage. Each is now considered in turn.

The Preference for Owner-Occupation. Those who argue the virtues of home ownership point to its undoubted popularity, that owners are prepared to pay a higher proportion of their incomes to buy, and that it encourages independence. There is no doubt of a considerable unsatisfied demand to buy. The building societies have regularly produced survey results to show that home ownership is a preferred form of tenure. A survey carried out in 1975 by the British Market

Research Bureau for the Housing Strategy Committee of the National
Economic Development Office, for example, found that 96 per cent of
existing owner-occupiers had a preference for owner-occupation compared with 40 per cent of council tenants and 36 per cent of private
tenants. In contrast, 55 per cent of council tenants exhibited a preference for council renting. The survey also showed that 92 per cent of
owner-occupiers were 'very' or 'quite' satisfied with their housing while
74 per cent of council tenants felt this way.[27]

This is hardly a surprising result. The main reason why there is an
observed preference for owner-occupation as a tenure is that most of
the advantages, housing, social and financial, lie with home ownership, a
situation that is not a 'natural' one but one created and perpetuated by
successive government policy. The choice between owning and renting
is not and never has been an equal one. Given the ability to choose, and
this opportunity has been and remains very limited, it is not surprising
that households opt for owner-occupation.

According to the *Housing Consumer Survey*,[28] the major advantages
of owner-occupation were perceived as being the freedom to decorate
(mentioned by 22 per cent of all respondents); a saving or investment
(22 per cent); independence (20 per cent) and a feeling of security (14
per cent). The *Survey* indicated a wide awareness of the financial
benefits of home ownership. Over a lifetime, owner-occupation offers
a better financial deal than renting, especially in times of inflation.
Actual payments may well be less over time, and buyers end up with
an asset, while tenants pay rent indefinitely. There is no reason in
principle why tenants should not have greater freedom and independence, and many tenants already enjoy 'freedom to decorate'.
Certainly the extent to which council tenants are inhibited is almost
certainly exaggerated. Poor management, bureaucratic incompetence
and petty restriction do exist, but probably not on a widespread scale,
and these can be rectified by the extension of tenant participation,
greater self management and maintenance among tenants, and
improved transfer and allocation policies rather than the disposal of
the council stock.

Another important reason why preference lies with owner-
occupation is that, as we have seen, owner-occupation offers a wider
choice of dwelling and higher physical standard of accommodation.
Most owner-occupied dwellings are detached or semi-detached houses,
while over 50 per cent of local authority dwellings are flats or terraced
houses. Owner-occupation, in general, offers more spacious accommodation, often a better environment and a much higher chance of a

garden, though not necessarily better internal amenities. The preference for owner-occupation may therefore simply reflect a preference for houses over flats, or a house with a garden at a lower density rather than for a particular tenure.

The Financial Consequences. It is often claimed that owner-occupation costs the community less than public housing. As well as the question of whether there is an economic gain to society from the selling of council houses, there is the additional issue of whether it is cheaper for society to build new houses for sale rather than rent.

Recent years have seen considerable debate as to whether the cost to public funds of a new house built for sale is less or more than the cost of a house built for council renting. Discussion has typically centred on a comparison between the immediate cost to the Exchequer of tax relief on a new house sold which is considerably less than the subsidy cost in the first year of an equivalent house built to let at a reasonable rent. Thus a householder purchasing a £15,000 house with a 90 per cent mortgage and a 9 per cent interest rate would receive tax relief of approximately £420 p.a. if he were a standard rate taxpayer (currently 34 per cent). In contrast, the subsidy on the local authority dwelling would be much higher. Assuming a pooled rate of interest of say 11 per cent, debt repayments in the first year would be about £1,650, and assuming a rent of £520 p.a., the subsidy in the first year would be of the order of £1,200 (ignoring management and maintenance costs). One reason for this is that council housing is financed by borrowing at nearer the market interest rate, which is in excess of the interest rate paid by mortgagors. The tenant's contribution is low in the first year because he pays a reasonable rent.

Over time, these relative contributions will change significantly. Assuming that rents rise in line with inflation, and they have more than done so in the last two decades, and interest rates do not rise, the annual subsidy to the local authority dwelling will fall over time in real terms with inflation and as debt is paid off. In the case of the owner-occupied dwelling, the cost of tax relief will also fall in real terms with inflation, unless interest rates rise, until the house changes hands (on average, after seven years) and a new mortgage is taken out which requires additional tax relief. Over time, therefore, the relative cost of subsidy will depend on rates of increase in house prices, rents and prices in general, changes in interest rates, the discount used to arrive at present values, and the frequency of reselling, and it is extremely misleading to make first-year comparisons only. Table 6.9 gives one example, which for the rates

Table 6.9: Total Payments Made on a £14,000 House, over 60 Years, in Council Tenancy, Owner-Occupation and Equity Sharing (all figures in £ p.a. at year 1 prices)

	Council Tenant		Owner-Occupier		Equity Sharing	
			Tax	Net		Net
	Rent	Subsidy	Relief	Payment	Subsidy	Payment
1	350	1423	509	1154	966	752
2	350	1239	458	1048	848	699
3	350	1079	412	961	746	656
4	350	921	371	878	646	614
5	350	791	333	805	562	577
7	350	563	266	671	415	511
10	350	304	189	516	247	433
15	350	22	333	803	178	577
25	350	−233	333	803	50	577
35	350	−315	333	803	9	577
60	350	−349	189	516	−80	433
Total over 60 years	21000	−4329	19716	47670	12023	34335

Note: A rate of interest of 11 per cent and a rate of inflation of 10 per cent are assumed. Owner-occupiers and equity sharers change dwellings every 10 years, and the dwelling price increases at the annual rate of inflation. The Council is assumed to repay its loan by equal annual instalments. Management and maintenance costs are not included, and no discounting has been done.
Source: London Boroughs Association, *Evidence to the Review of Housing Finance* (1976), table 15.

of inflation and other assumptions chosen, shows that over a 60 year period, the cumulative subsidy is much higher in the case of owner-occupation. With other assumptions, a different picture might emerge.[29] A particular weakness of the comparison given in Table 6.9, for example, is that no discount rate has been used to convert future subsidies into present values, and discounting would have the effect of reducing the relative subsidy in the case of owner-occupation. Whether one form of tenure is cheaper than another in terms of public subsidy is therefore not a question that it is possible to be dogmatic about. Moreover there are many other issues involved in deciding whether greater emphasis should be given to building for sale or rent, including the ability of households to purchase rather than rent, and the relative social consequences.

As a result of these changes over time, and the cross subsidising of new houses by existing dwellings in the public sector through rent pooling, the average level of subsidy in 1975/6 was £173 p.a. per council tenant and £174 p.a. per mortgagor.[30] No such mechanism exists for evening out payments between recent and earlier house buyers. In terms of outstanding debt, the average outstanding debt on a council house was under £2,000 in 1975 while the average building society mortgage outstanding was £4,260. This is because the debt on a local authority dwelling is fixed in money terms, and so falls with inflation, while rents keep pace with inflation. While a mortgage is also fixed in money terms, every time a dwelling changes hands, the mortgage is increased to the new inflated house price, such that mortgage debts per house tend to rise with inflation, whether or not any additional houses are added to the stock. Council house outstanding debts only rise when new houses are built, and if no more local authority dwellings were built, debt would eventually disappear.

What about the sale of existing council houses? When sold, the initial cost of tax relief may be greater than the Exchequer subsidy given, especially in the case of earlier built houses. Further, selling involves a perpetual subsidy liability that the Exchequer did not have before since the house will require additional tax relief each time it changes hands.

In addition to the Exchequer cost, there is the gain or loss to the local authority and this depends on whether the mortgage is provided privately or by the local authority. If the mortgage is obtained from a building society, the gain or loss can be seen by a comparison of the net capital sum received after repayment of the outstanding debt, and the annual cost of maintenance with the ongoing annual loss of revenue from rents, and subsidy. Because most tenants buy their homes with a local authority mortgage,[31] the gain or loss can alternatively be seen as the difference between the annual mortgage repayments received and the costs of maintenance and management with the rent and subsidy foregone. In general such comparisons would show a gain to the local authority in the first year because repayments and management and maintenance costs will usually be greater than the income lost in rents and subsidy. Over time, however, these annual comparisons would eventually show a loss with inflation as rents rise above mortgage repayments. Sales therefore become less financially attractive to the Council the longer it looks ahead. One attempt to measure the net effect of these flows over time has suggested that, on the basis of the assumptions used, and these are inevitably tentative, sales involve a net loss for local authorities.[32] The public expenditure consequences are therefore very complex. The initial gain to the local authority in the first few years may be offset by the extra cost to the Exchequer especially if the house is fairly old, and by future losses of rent income.

There is also the question of the financial consequences of sales on a large scale. The possible consequences for other investment of a substantial increase in mortgage lending have already been considered in Chapter 5. Further, there is no possibility of building societies funding more than a small proportion of council house sales. As Crofton has shown, to fund the sale of all council dwellings in the UK, even with large discounts, would yield a mortgage requirement that is greater than building society total assets. Even selling a quarter of the stock over ten years would mean that finance for new mortgages would be entirely taken up in purchase of existing owner-occupied or council house dwellings, thus putting an almost complete stop to new private building. If council house purchasers were to move as often as other mortgagors, at least every eight years, the mobility rate among the 25 per cent of houses sold would be 200,000 a year (one-eighth of one-quarter of 6.5 million) which alone would use more than the annual increase in the number of building society mortgages.[33]

Finally, a major financial benefit of a large public sector — that the benefit of lower historic costs on earlier built dwellings can be used to even out the higher costs of council building by rent pooling — would be lost by the disposal of the stock on any scale. It is in this way that the capital gains that accrue when building costs and house prices rise can be shared throughout the local community of council tenants. In the owner-occupied sector, in contrast, house price inflation benefits existing owners at the expense of new buyers. In addition, the advantage that subsidies go to finance new building, and not transfers as is the case in the owner-occupied sector, would be lost. Disposal even partially, of our council stock would involve trading in the strengths of our existing system of housing finance for two of its major weaknesses.

The Redistribution of Wealth. An argument that has been used in favour of sales especially on a massive scale, is that it would lead to a redistribution of wealth towards those who have least wealth. The extent of any wealth redistribution depends on the prices at which houses are sold, which are sold and who buys them. The local authority sector contains a disproportionate number of retired and low income households most of whom would not be in a position to buy, even if houses were sold at large discounts. Moreover, many of the higher income households are in fact larger households containing more than two adults and two earners.

The available evidence on sales also shows that it is the better and more desirable properties that are sold. In Birmingham between 1966 and 1971, of the 10,000 council properties sold, with the exception of one block of four flats, tenants bought only houses, and 98 per cent had their own gardens. Most of those sold were also in certain preferred areas.[34]

This policy therefore represents an extension of choice and wealth for the minority of higher income tenants living in better quality accommodation. It would leave local authorities increasingly catering for lower income families with a generally poorer quality stock of dwellings, and would accentuate not relieve problems of management and maintenance. A more socially divisive policy could hardly be conceived. A policy of sales offers no prospect of redistribution to poorer tenants or to those in less desirable property, and no such prospect for tenants of private landlords or tied accommodation. Moreover there is some evidence that poorer tenants tend to live in the worst accommodation, such that the process of redistribution itself would be inequitable. Far from changing inequalities in a fundamental way, either a partial sales policy or a more radical overall disposal would maintain existing inequalities within the council sector, and given that the average rateable value of local authority housing is somewhat less than that of mortgaged dwellings, with existing owner-occupiers too. The objective of reducing wealth inequalities is more effectively achieved by wider policies of redistribution.

Serfdom. Another argument used for sales is that there is widespread discontent among council tenants. It is claimed that tenants have a strong desire for independence and are inhibited by lack of mobility and the petty restrictions imposed by local authorities, which reduce them to the status of serfdom.[35]   It cannot be denied that there are problems associated with lack of mobility and poor management, but these may be exaggerated, and some discontent may be a reflection of the type of accommodation offered rather than management. The *Housing Consumer Survey*, as we have seen, showed that 74 per cent of council tenants were 'very' or 'quite' satisfied with their housing and 17 per cent were 'rather' or 'very' dissatisfied.[36]

The main reasons for dissatisfaction were poor facilities and dislike of the neighbourhood. On the basis of evidence of housing preferences and aspirations, it can be argued that local authorities have been too limited in the range of accommodation they have built, and have built too many flats, too many high rise blocks, too many large estates and too many dwellings without gardens. One reason for this is that the type of building allowed has been dictated by central government controls including the cost yardstick that have limited local flexibility. Another reason is that local authorities have always faced a trade off between the number of dwellings built and hence the number of people housed, and the quality and density of building. It may be that with the benefit of hindsight we have swayed too far in the direction of maximising housing gain, at the expense of environmental quality in particular.

Local authority accommodation perhaps too often consists of a flat in a high density estate with little open space. But it is the case that most council housing especially outside London is low rise and of satisfactory design and that most tenants live in happy settled communities without social problems. As Table 6.3 shows, a very low proportion of council dwellings are unfit or substandard. Space standards are lower in relation to owner-occupation, but this reflects the better use of stock achieved rather than overcrowding.

It is easy to point, as the media generally does, to the problems of high density estates which lack amenities and are environmentally oppressive. Problem estates are generally associated with the built form and design of the estate and the local situation with respect to environment, employment, shopping and transportation. Other factors that may cause problems include the level of child density; the quality of building which may be below average because it was built when subsidies were low, and the yardstick was particularly restrictive; and the fact that some estates have almost entirely housed families from slum clearance areas. In the future the creation of difficult estates can be avoided by a greater emphasis on small estates, on low rise, low density and higher quality building, with adequate local community and play facilities, and on more careful allocation policies. However often such situations receive widespread publicity, they are the exception and not the rule, and they must be distinguished from the wider problem of dissatisfaction among tenants.

Apart from these problems that are associated with the environment and structure of the accommodation offered, the main issues are mobility, tenant status and rights, and allocations policies. The mobility of council tenants is often limited, and can be improved by a more effective use of the existing stock, more efficient management especially more effective transfer policies, and the building of more dwellings in areas of shortage. Recent restrictions on new building and improvement will inhibit mobility as do sales of council dwellings.

As regards tenant status and rights, the problems created by bureaucratic restrictions can be easily exaggerated. Many so-called restrictions
are designed to improve peace and privacy and maintain the environment, by, for example, restrictions on external decorations and the
parking of lorries, and owner-occupiers with leases face similar restrictions. Recently, many authorities have been introducing new and less
rigid and paternalistic tenancy agreements. There are now growing
demands, by, for example, the National Consumer Council and the
Department of the Environment Housing Services Advisory Group, for
a national Tenants' Charter with liberal conditions of tenancy which
would include greater flexibility over repairs and decorations, the
receipt of compensation when leaving for major repairs carried out, and
the stressing of the landlord's duties and tenants' rights as well as
tenants' obligations. In addition, there are demands for the opening up
of all waiting and transfer lists, the abolition of residential qualifications, and the introduction of security of tenure. Many of these
proposals have been included as recommendations in the housing Green
Paper.[37]

Where problems of management do exist, they can be effectively
dealt with in most cases by the extension of greater involvement and
freedom through tenant participation in management, and the promotion of co-operative management. Selling council houses is a drastic
solution, and not necessarily effective. Such changes are already taking
place in many areas, and should be encouraged.

The Effect on Housing Stress. Finally, what impact would the selling of
council houses have in dealing with the problems of homelessness, overcrowding and poor quality housing in areas of housing stress and
continuing shortages? It is in these areas that the pressing need is for
more houses to rent. Selling council houses would limit the scope and
flexibility of local authorities for dealing with, however imperfectly,
these housing problems with which they are best equipped to cope, and
limit, not extend, the chances of decent housing for those families who
are the most poorly housed.

This is because sales reduce the number of houses which become
available to those on local authority waiting and transfer lists. The loss
of capacity depends upon the rate at which vacancies occur, but
currently the wholesale disposal of the council stock would involve a
permanent loss of about 150,000 re-lets a year arising from moves, since
the national vacancy rate has been about 4 per cent on average. Further,
sales reduce the range of housing available, since only the most desirable

properties are sold.

Summary. The selling of council houses cannot therefore be justified on economic or social grounds. Even in the short run, sales will not be strikingly beneficial to local authorities if they are financed by local authority lending, while to the Exchequer, the additional tax relief required will often be greater than the subsidy saved. In the long run, the balance may go either way. Only better off and younger tenants would be able to afford to buy, and only the better properties would be sold, thereby restricting the range of local authority accommodation and the social mix of tenants. By reducing the number of re-lets, the chance of improved housing for those on waiting and transfer lists who cannot afford to buy would be reduced.

Equity-Sharing Schemes

In the last few years, interest has developed in a form of tenure known as equity-sharing, an intermediate hybrid tenure whereby an occupier can half buy and half rent his home. Such schemes have the backing of the Labour Government in its Green Paper and the Conservative opposition, and are now being adopted by a number of local authorities. The idea was pioneered by Birmingham City Council who have offered 'half-and-half' mortgage schemes on newly built houses whereby occupiers acquire a long lease for half the freehold value of the house (with a local authority mortgage) and pay half the rent they would otherwise have paid as a tenant. Under the Birmingham scheme, occupiers are responsible for repairs and maintenance and are largely free from standard tenancy conditions. At any future date, purchasers can acquire the remaining half share. A number of local authorities have since introduced such schemes and the Housing Corporation are also sponsoring forms of housing association equity-sharing.

Equity sharing is not really an alternative form of tenure in the way that housing associations or co-operatives are, but rather a way of providing a stepping stone to full owner-occupation. Occupiers under such schemes can either buy the rented portion of their house or use the capital gain on selling to move to a 'full' house. To the individual, such schemes provide an opportunity to begin purchase but at the cost of higher housing outgoings. In general, the initial payments, part mortgage and part rent, are about double the rent that would otherwise be paid,[38] though, over time, mortgage repayments would fall in relation to the rent.

To the local authority, there is an initial financial gain, especially if the tenant gets a mortgage from a building society, because the rate fund contribution towards the cost of a newly built house is halved and the authority does not have to bear the cost of management and maintenance. Whether the authority continues to benefit depends on whether the occupier remains in the scheme. If the occupier buys the 'rented half' or behaves like the average mortgagor and moves after about seven years, the gain is ended because the authority loses the surpluses it would have obtained through increases in rents. Moreover, the central government would also find that initial savings in subsidy might be offset by higher tax relief payments in later years, depending on the rate of movement. Table 6.9 shows that over a 60 year life, given current tax-relief arrangements and movement every ten years, the undiscounted total public subsidy under an equity-sharing scheme could be greater than under a normal council tenancy.

The advantage of equity sharing on new houses is that marginal buyers are assisted into home ownership and that there are savings in public funds in the early years of such schemes. Over time, however, these savings could be converted into losses. Moreover, if the house is bought outright and sold, it goes into the ordinary housing market at a price out of the reach of the income group for whom it was originally designed. Further, the arguments against council house sales also apply to turning over existing council stock to equity sharing.

Local Authority Housing in the Future

A particularly disturbing trend and one that would be accentuated by sales on any scale is towards the concentration of low income groups in the council sector. Table 6.7 shows that the council sector housed 45 per cent of the poorest decile of households in 1975 compared with 31 per cent of all households, and that the risk of poverty among council tenants has been rising steeply in the last 25 years. This is a trend that has been caused by the tendency of low income private tenants to become council tenants as the privately rented sector has declined, while better off tenants from both sectors have moved into home ownership. This trend is likely to continue, especially with the continuing decline of the privately rented sector and would mean that society would become steadily segregated by income into the two major sectors. This is a serious prospect that would frustrate wider objectives of social equality, especially in the context of existing sectoral inequalities.

Such a trend would mean that local authorities would increasingly cater for the poor and the disadvantaged — one parent families, the elderly and handicapped, thereby reducing local authority housing to a largely welfare role. This trend would have serious repercussions. Local authority housing would increasingly become a residual sector which would further reduce its status, heighten divisions in society, widen stigma and encourage social and economic isolation. It would restrict the ability of local authorities to devolve management and other functions to tenants, and so inhibit the extension of independence and control to tenants. It would also limit the rent paying capacity of tenants and increase the proportion receiving rebates and supplementary benefit rent additions. To quote Aneurin Bevan who first rejected the view that councils should build only for lower income groups,

> As a result, you have colonies of low income people living in houses provided by local authorities, and you have the high income groups living in their own colonies. This segregation of the different income groups is a wholly evil thing from a civilised point of view . . . It is a monstrous infliction upon the essential psychological and biological oneness of the community.[39]

There are a number of steps that can be taken in an attempt to reverse such a trend, and ensure a greater social mix on council estates. But most important of all is the need to create a fairer and more equal choice between the main sectors by eliminating the various legal, social and financial inequities that exist. Equality of treatment and benefit is a prerequisite for preventing council housing descending slowly into a residual welfare housing sector. It is possible to deal with the relatively inferior legal and social position of tenants, and steps are being taken to improve the rights and status and mobility of public tenants, and extend freedom and independence. More will also need to be done to improve the environmental and internal amenities offered by some council accommodation. Regrettably, however, the recent Green Paper on housing has rejected the opportunity of taking action to reduce the excess financial benefits of owner-occupation, and this will remain a serious obstacle to creating fairness.

The trend towards welfare housing is also one that will inevitably be reinforced by the traditional policy of allocating council housing on a strict basis of need. This poses an important dilemma for housing policy. Encouraging and maintaining a wider social mix on council estates requires allowing access to groups other than those most in need, a clear break with traditional allocations policy. Making public sector housing available to a more diverse section of the population is essential if the council sector is to remain a major housing sector, and may be justified on longer term grounds even though such a broadening of the housing responsibilities of local authorities might initially prove to be at the expense of those most in need.

The Privately Rented Sector

The Current Role of Private Renting

The current and future role of the privately rented sector is a very important policy issue, and one which has important implications for the publicly rented sector. The current role of the privately rented sector is a diverse one, and it houses a great variety of household types. There are now some 1.85 million conventional private tenancies — of which about 1.5 million are let unfurnished, and 350,000 are let furnished — and a further 700,000 tied lettings, including a substantial number of lettings by public bodies such as the armed forces.[40] The legal relationship between landlord and tenant now largely depends on whether the landlord is resident or non-resident. Full Rent Act protection, at least in principle, is enjoyed by tenants of non-resident landlords, the majority of whom (about 1.4 million) are regulated tenants liable to pay 'fair rents' and who enjoy full security, and the remainder (about 400,000) controlled tenants whose rents are fixed in relation to 1956 gross rateable values and a proportion of some of the costs of subsequent repairs and improvements. Tenants of resident landlords, about 200,000, have the limited protection under the Rent Acts of being able to apply to the Rent Tribunal for suspension of a notice to quit and the fixing of a reasonable rent.

Most private tenants fall into one of three categories. First, elderly and middle aged single people and childless couples who are long standing private tenants and who cannot afford home ownership. Many of these occupy older housing under controlled or regulated tenancies, which is in poor repair and/or lacking amenities, and exhibit little mobility. Secondly, newly married couples or young single people setting up home for the first time, and many of whom will be private tenants for only a short time before becoming home-owners or council tenants. Thirdly, those who are highly mobile because of their job or studies. Most tenants in the second two categories are in furnished and multi-occupied flats, or lettings of resident landlords, and are very mobile. In view of the greater advantages offered by owner-occupation and council renting, it is not surprising that the tenants of private landlords have become increasingly the young and mobile, the elderly and immobile, those who cannot become local authority tenants or home-owners and those who do not want to. Many of these groups will continue to require rented accommodation, being too old, too im-mobile or too poor to be able to become home-owners.

Problems in the private rental sector concern both its size and quality. The sector has been in steady decline over a long period of time since before the First World War and now accounts for about 14 per cent of the housing stock. The combination of factors which account for this decline have already been discussed. In addition, as Table 6.3 shows, it contains a high proportion of property in a poor state of repair and lacking amenities. The low level of maintenance and im-provement is due to a number of factors. First, the lack of financial incentive. The rate of return on expenditure on improvement and repair is low. Fair rents are designed to provide sufficient income for repairs, and problems are less serious in the case of conversion from controlled to fair rents, but there is evidence of only small rent increases as a result of improvement. Moreover, there is no provision for depreci-ation allowances on improvement, and improvement grants only cover a proportion of the cost of improvement. Private landlords have proved to be very insensitive to the use of such grants except in the case of vacant possession. Secondly, the excess demand for rented accommoda-tion, especially in inner cities, has meant that landlords are in a seller's market and therefore under no economic pressure to improve their property. Finally, the evidence on landlords suggests that many are small scale, old and female and that they have acquired their property by inheritance, and may neither have the resources, expertise or interest to undertake major repair work.

Currently, the privately rented sector performs important housing functions, housing many groups who require rented accommodation and providing flexible arrangements for newly formed and mobile households, who are often not eligible under existing policies for public sector housing. Its contraction has caused problems for some of these groups, and any further decline, without a corresponding improvement in access to alternative forms of accommodation, will accentuate housing stress for those dependent on it.

The Revival of Private Renting

Like all housing issues, the question of the future role of the privately rented sector is a highly contentious one. Views vary between those who argue that attempts should and can be made to maintain and even expand the volume of private renting, and those who say that its decline should be encouraged by an extensive programme of municipalisation. There is also the further question of how much needed improvements and repairs can best be achieved.

Those who wish to revive the private rented sector have argued for changes in current legal and financial arrangements that would provide new incentives to existing landlords to continue to rent, and to potential, especially resident, landlords to enter the market. Proposals for revitalisation have included the reduction or even elimination of both Rent Act protection and rent regulation. One commentator, for example, as a start towards complete decontrol, has argued for the indexation of fair rents to an appropriate price index with more regular adjustment than the current every three years; the replacement of current security of tenure with fixed term leases of about three years, and the introduction of direct subsidies to tenants (or landlords) from central government at least comparable to the effective subsidies enjoyed by local authority tenants and owner-occupiers.[41] Such subsidies could take the form of tax relief on rents in the case of tenants and the removal of the present relative tax disadvantage of landlords by withdrawing at least part of the requirement to pay tax under Schedule D on rental income, and to pay capital gains tax. Alternatively, financial benefits could be made more equal by removing some of the tax and financial advantages of other forms of tenure.

Others have argued for new forms of 'landlordism' such as 'sale and lease-back' or 'part-equity' schemes. Sale and lease-back schemes would involve the purchase of the freehold by local authorities and the giving of letting rights to landlords; the landlord would have a capital sum and a rental income while the local authority would have control of the property and a ground rent income. Part equity schemes would involve local authorities in selling an equity share in one of its properties to a private landlord who guaranteed to rehabilitate it and provide a new letting.[42]

It is far from clear to what extent existing and potential landlords would respond to such initiatives. Landlords vary from those owning many properties to small landlords — charities, small companies and individuals — renting one or two houses on a relatively permanent basis, to owners who let on a temporary basis. We have little detailed information about landlords, but that which is available from the General Household Survey suggests that over 50 per cent of tenants, especially in the furnished sector, rent from an individual landlord rather than a corporate body. The response of different landlords would inevitably different.

Some evidence about the response to imposition and removal of protection can be inferred from the 1957 and 1974 Rent Acts. Those who favour the removal or relaxation of protection have often blamed the 1974 Rent Act for 'drying up' the supply of furnished accommodation. It is, however, unlikely that the act gave more than a slight impetus to the long term trend of decline. There were signs of an immediate withdrawal of lettings when the act was first passed, and since then there has been a drop in advertised lettings especially in London, though one important reason for this will have been the additional security provided under the act to furnished tenants of absentee landlords. By extending security the act has reduced the frequency with which furnished dwellings change hands. Some fall in lettings may also have been caused by the misunderstandings, fostered by highly misleading Press reports, surrounding the act, which in fact extended the rights of resident landlords and made it easier to gain possession from unsatisfactory tenants. Indeed, the figures for the annual loss of privately rented dwellings were in fact most rapid following the removal of protection in the 1957 Rent Act, the act designed specifically to revive the supply of privately rented accommodation. The loss of privately rented dwellings rose from 180,000 p.a. between 1951 to 1956 to 200,000 p.a. from 1956 to 1960, and is now running at about 100,000 p.a. The reason lies partly in the easier obtaining of vacant possession under the provisions of the 1957 Act. Further relaxation of protection might simply hasten the rate of decline by increasing insecurity, harassment and evictions.

The impact on tenants might also be serious. Given the high proportion of low income and elderly tenants living in privately rented accommodation and the low take up of rent allowances, there is little scope for significant increases in rents without causing widespread hardship, more overcrowding and homelessness. Any stimulus to new investment by increasing the rate of return on letting could therefore only be achieved by substantial public subsidies the suitability of which are highly questionable. Indeed, it has been argued that 'The only way by which housing provided by private landlords could be prevented from disappearing almost completely would be to allow landlords a degree of freedom to exploit their tenants that nobody with any social conscience could tolerate.'[43] One must therefore be sceptical about the feasibility of restoring a significant role to the privately rented sector, quite independently of its desirability.

Municipalisation

An alternative approach to the problems of the private rented sector is
the acquisition of such dwellings by local authorities. One argument for
municipalisation is simply that new incentives such as those cited above
would be unlikely to halt, let alone reverse, the loss of privately rented
accommodation, except in marginal cases, and it is important to
preserve such accommodation for renting. Other arguments are more
fundamental. Some have a basic opposition to the principle of private
renting on the grounds that the interests of landlords and tenants are
irreconcilable. As the Fabian Society has put it, 'The relationship
between the private landlord, interested in a house as an investment
producing income or capital gain, and the tenant who looks to the
house as his home, is one which has always contained the ingredients of
conflict.'[44] Successive legislation has been needed in order to reduce the
consequence of such conflict by regulating the power of landlords and by
the granting of rights to tenants, but such regulation has never proved
fully effective. Despite the provisions of the various Rent Acts, families
are still harassed and evicted to suit the financial convenience of landlords and a high proportion of privately rented property is in poor
repair. Examples of the evils of the privately rented sector are numerous
and were particularly well documented in the Milner Holland Report
on housing in Greater London in 1963.[45] Nevertheless there is also
evidence that exploitation tends to go hand in hand with scarcity and
that where there is no scarcity, 'relations between landlords and tenants
are surprisingly good.'[46]

The basic case for social ownership is that it would end the basis for
conflict and so end such abuses. Other arguments in favour of absorbing
such property into the publicly rented sector are that this is the most
effective way of rationalising rents and improving the take up of rent
allowances, that it would enable allocation of housing by need, that it
would ensure more effective control of overcrowding, that it would
provide greater security, and would enable the maintenance and
improvement of property to higher standards.[47]

While the case for municipalisation is a powerful one, this policy is
not without its limitations. In the first place, it would be a very long
time before such accommodation could be absorbed especially in those
areas such as parts of inner London where private renting is the pre-
dominant form of tenure and the problems of housing access are most
serious. We have seen that the current and projected rate of acquisition
is very slow and has fallen sharply from the peak of 1974/5.[48] To step
this rate up would be very costly in terms of public expenditure, both

in terms of initial purchase and future repair and improvement, though there are ways in which the burden of the cost of acquisition could be reduced by, for example, the use of some form of non-negotiable bond, financed largely by rent income from the property.

Secondly, the speed with which municipalisation can take place is constrained by the ability of local authorities to cope with the additional management required in terms of allocation, improvement and repair. Municipalisation on a major scale would also require local authorities to improve residential mobility, and to widen their areas of responsibility to young childless couples and the single mobile population who have traditionally relied on the privately rented sector. Greater mobility and wider access to public sector housing would therefore have to accompany extensive municipalisation. Further, the transfer of management from a private to a public landlord can only be defended if local authority management is superior and fairer. While examples of bad relations between tenants and 'landlords' in the public sector abound, and there is a continuing need for improvement in management practices in local authorities, public sector management is, in general, superior or at least potentially so. Management is too often characterised by paternalistic attitudes, but there is no reason in principle why this cannot be reduced.

Finally, concern is often expressed at the possibility of local authorities having a monopoly of rented accommodation, and the potential problems that such a situation could cause. Such problems could be partially avoided by changes in management policy that improved the participation of tenants, and by the expansion of alternative forms of tenure such as housing associations and co-operatives. Indeed expansion of the activities of the voluntary housing movement has been widely suggested as a desirable policy in itself, as well as a way of preserving the availability of accommodation to let. In recent years, encouragement has been given to housing associations, in particular through the provisions of the 1974 Housing Act which expanded the role of the Housing Corporation. Nevertheless housing associations still play only a small role, accounting for less than 2 per cent of the total housing stock, though their contribution to relieving housing stress is not without significance.

These various constraints mean that the process of municipalisation is likely to be a very gradual one. While there is little case for, or likelihood of, halting the decline or stimulating new private lettings on any scale, except perhaps in the case of resident landlords who have surplus space, some transitional initiatives are needed to prevent the loss of needed rented accommodation and to deal with the continuing problem of lack of maintenance and improvement. Indeed, about 100,000 dwellings p.a. are currently being lost from the private sector, about four times the peak rate of acquisition of some 23,000 dwellings in 1974/5.

Existing policies towards the privately rented sector are inadequate. Policy to deal with obsolescence consists of improvement grants and the 'area approach' based on the declaration of housing action and general improvement areas in which grants are provided at a higher rate and local authorities have greater powers of compulsory improvement and the threat of compulsory purchase. These policies are proving to be ineffective. Landlords are insensitive to the use of improvement grants, even to the higher grants in action areas. This is partly because many landlords of unfurnished property are elderly people, often of limited incomes who cannot afford the costs of repairs and improvement, even with the aid of a grant. Company landlords, on the other hand, are in a better position to finance such expenditure. Housing action areas are being declared only gradually, the pace of work is slow, and compulsory improvement is ineffective. These policies are probably not even preventing further deterioration in the condition of privately rented dwellings. New initiatives are therefore needed (see Chapter 8). Improving the quality of the stock is a particularly important objective, not least because continuing disrepair will involve a heavy cost in public expenditure at the later date when the dwelling is municipalised.

In recognition of the weaknesses of existing policies, the government is now undertaking a separate *Review of the Rent Acts*, and a Consultative Document was issued in January 1977. Without altering the commitment to security of tenure for tenants and the need for restrictions on rent levels, there are a variety of measures that could be taken in any transitional period. To prevent the drying up of rented accommodation, changes could be made to speed up the process of obtaining possession which may currently act as a discouragement to letting by resident landlords. Wider use could also be made of flats over shops, which often remain empty, by, for example, placing them in the same category as resident landlords. To encourage improvement, the present system of improvement grants could be made more generous and flexible, and repair grants made more readily available. Another possibility is that tenants could be given more responsibility for main-tenance and improvement themselves in return for the foregoing by the landlord of his right to raise rents, or a share in the equity of the property. Alternatively, local authorities could undertake such work in return for a share in the equity, a form of 'partial municipalisation'.

Housing Associations, Co-operative and Co-ownership Schemes

Housing associations, like local authorities are non-profit making bodies. They build and improve housing for letting at subsidised rents, aided by public funds in the form of Exchequer grants. They therefore supplement and complement local authority housing programmes, letting accommodation to households in housing need, many of them nominated by local authorities. Alternatively known as the 'voluntary housing sector' or 'housing's third-arm', their roots go back to the nineteenth century. Until the 1974 Housing Act, however, they could not be described as an important force in housing provision. Although introduced by Labour, this Act was inherited from the outgoing Conservative Government, in the main enjoyed bipartisan support, and was aimed at encouraging the expansion of housing associations under public supervision.

Under the act, the Housing Corporation, which was originally set up in 1964 as a statutory overlord of housing association activity, had its size and functions greatly expanded with the role of promoting subsidised rentéd housing. To receive public grant, associations have to register with the Corporation, and there are currently over 2,500 registered associations, though many of these are small. In order to boost activity, the 1974 Act introduced a new once-and-for-all capital grant payable at the outset on each scheme, aimed to write off that proportion of debt that cannot be financed from expected rental income. Future annual loan charges on the remaining debt together with management and maintenance costs therefore have to be met from rents. On average, grant represents about 75 per cent of cost. In order to provide for associations who may incur a deficit on their annual revenue account, a discretionary Revenue Deficit Grant was also introduced to be payable to associations who cannot meet their expenditures. The method of financing association schemes contrasts with local authorities who receive annual subsidies and has been criticised on the grounds that it obliges governments to borrow 75 per cent of the cost immediately whereas a revenue-based subsidy would even out borrowing over time.[49]

In addition to this difference between the finance of local authorities and housing associations in the form of subsidy, housing association developments are financed on a scheme-by-scheme basis and there is no built-in provision for cross-subsidisation, unlike local authorities who pool all their costs in a single housing revenue account. Further, housing associations are not able to make rate fund contributions to housing costs. Rents are set at 'fair rent' levels under the provisions of the 1972 Housing Finance Act and are generally higher than similar local authority dwellings. Tenants lack legal security of tenure in the same way as council tenants.

The main objectives of the 1974 Act in respect of housing associations were that they would be able to fill some of the gap left by the diminishing private landlord, particularly in areas of a severe shortage of rented accommodation such as the stress areas of inner cities, and 'provide a third choice to prevent the tenure system polarising into the two monoliths of owner-occupation and council housing'.[50] In a Department of the Environment Circular issued after the act, the government saw housing associations playing a variety of roles in helping to meet housing need, especially in stress areas, including catering for particular categories of need such as the elderly and handicapped, in providing smaller-scale and less remote management than that provided by local authorities, in providing a base for co-operative management, and in experimenting with tenant participation. The circular also emphasised the importance of close co-operation between local authorities and housing associations in providing for local need.[51]

As a result of the greater financial viability provided by the 1974 Act, there has been a considerable expansion in housing association activity, 29,223 new dwellings being started and 13,867 renovations approved in Great Britain in 1976 compared with 11,137 starts and 5,055 renovations in 1973.[52] Housing associations now account for about 20 per cent of the public sector housing programme compared with about 5 per cent in 1973 and provide a not insignificant proportion of public sector housing. There are an enormous variety of associations, ranging from 'fair rent' associations offering conventional tenancies to co-ownership schemes, from associations specialising in particular needs such as the elderly to those that are more diverse, from large associations to very small.

There is every reason to expect the continuing expansion of housing association activity. The recent Green Paper supported their development, though the present financial arrangements are under consideration. As pointed out by the Green Paper,

The housing association grant system introduced by the Housing Act 1974 has been successful in stimulating housing associations' activities but it has serious defects. The calculation of once-for-all capital grant on completion of each project creates a great deal of work for all concerned, implies assumptions about the future course of rent levels and running costs which involve great uncertainty, and does not allow for recovery of excess grant if inflation subsequently reduces the real burden of loan charges to more manageable levels.[53]

The housing association grant is therefore likely to be replaced with a subsidy system analagous to that being proposed for local authorities. In addition, registered associations may be removed from the fair rent system, and some kind of pooling of costs within and between associations may be introduced. These would improve the financial arrangements for housing associations and enable greater parity with local authority rents.

Because of their great variety and range, some associations are inevitably poorer than others, especially in the quality of management and the degree of accountability. Nevertheless they have many benefits especially in the scope for innovation, and the flexibility of provision and management. If these financial changes are introduced and greater strides are made to improve their accountability, such organisations will continue to make a major contribution to improving the housing situation.

In addition to housing associations, other forms of tenure include co-operatives and co-ownership schemes. Housing co-operatives consist of management co-operatives in which tenants have collective responsibility for some or all management functions but do not own or lease the property, and non-equity co-operatives in which tenants also collectively own or lease the property but do not have an individual stake in the equity.

Encouragement to housing co-operatives was given in the Housing Rents and Subsidies Act of 1975 which improved the financial basis of such organisations by making them eligible for the full benefit of housing association subsidies. In January 1976, the final Report of the Working Party on Housing Co-operatives set up in December 1974 under the chairmanship of Harold Campbell, supported the encouragement of co-operatives, arguing that such housing represents 'a highly desirable departure from traditionally remote, depersonalised forms of housing management', promotes a sense of community, improves the efficiency of maintenance, creates greater involvement by tenants in their own environment and increases the choice of housing tenure. The government has given its backing to co-operatives by setting up the Co-operative Housing Agency under the aegis of the Housing Corporation, and by issuing a circular in January 1976 aimed at encouraging the setting up of co-operatives both on local authority estates and by housing associations. In consequence, a number of experimental projects are now being undertaken.

In contrast with the management and non-equity co-operatives discussed above, co-ownership schemes involve collective ownership, management and a share in the equity through a leasehold interest or an entitlement to some payment on leaving. In this way, tenants benefit directly from growth in the value of property. Co-ownerships were the main form of housing sponsored by the Housing Corporation after its formation in 1964, but have declined in recent years. In order to revive them, the Housing Corporation has been asked to implement a pilot scheme in which housing association grant is paid on part of the capital cost. This reduces the unsubsidised cost and therefore the mortgage repayments and the financial stake of members in the equity. Part of the equity therefore remains in 'social ownership'. Twenty such schemes were under way by January 1978, comprising 585 homes.

The encouragement of and experimentation with alternative forms of tenure stem from the concern of government about the effect of the continuing decline of the privately rented sector on housing choices. These tenures will offer an alternative to the polarisation of the housing system between owner-occupation and local authority renting, and prevent the local authority sector developing a near monopoly of rented accommodation. Housing associations and co-operatives have many special merits of their own that justify their encouragement, while they also offer a wider choice of housing tenure.

Notes

1. Department of the Environment, *Housing Policy Technical Volume I* (HMSO, 1977), tables II.1, II.2 and II.3.
2. Table 5.1, Ch. 5.
3. Department of the Environment, *Housing Policy Technical Volume I*, table II.14, p. 64.
4. The 10th percentile represents the level of income below which 10 per cent of households fall, the 50th percentile (or median) the income level below which 50 per cent of households fall and so on.
5. S. Lansley, *Tenure Patterns and the Distribution of Income* (National Institute of Economic and Social Research, unpublished paper, 1976).
6. All these results need to be modified to the extent that they do not allow for variations in household size and composition by income level and between tenures. Allowance for this factor, by, for example, deriving distributions of income *per capita* or per equivalent unit would be unlikely to contradict the conclusions reached or the trends observed. For methods of making such adjustments, see G.C. Fiegehen, P.S. Lansley and A.D. Smith, *Poverty and Progress in Britain,*

1957-73 (Cambridge, Cambridge University Press, 1977).

7. Department of the Environment, *Housing Policy Technical Volume I*, table II.33, p. 88.

8. Table 2.1, Ch. 2.

9. Peter Shore, Speech on Housing Tenure, Newcastle, 7 September 1976.

10. Department of the Environment, *Housing Policy, A Consultative Document* (HMSO, Cmnd 6851, 1977), para. 7.03.

11. Ibid., para. 7.16-7.32.

12. Stuart Weir, 'Red Line Districts', *Roof* (Shelter, July 1976).

13. See J. Wintour, 'Inner City Obstacle Course', *Roof* (Shelter, March 1978).

14. Political and Economic Planning, *The Facts of Racial Disadvantage* (1976).

15. Table 4.6, Ch. 4.

16. N. McIntosh, 'Mortgage Support Scheme Holds the Lending Lines', *Roof* (Shelter, March 1978).

17. House of Commons, *Hansard* (8 February 1978), col. 1431.

18. Department of the Environment, *Housing Policy, A Consultative Document*, para. 7.03.

19. See, for example, the responses to the housing policy review by Shelter, the Labour Party and the Housing Centre Trust.

20. Department of the Environment, *Housing Policy Technical Volume I*, table III.36.

21. The Building Societies Association, *Comments on 'Housing Policy, A Consultative Document'* (January 1978).

22. Department of the Environment, *Housing Policy, A Consultative Document*, para. 9.04.

23. Timothy Raison, Speech to the International Real Estate Federation, December 1975.

24. Ministry of Housing and Local Government, *Circular 54/70* (1970).

25. Department of the Environment, *Housing Policy, A Consultative Document*, para. 11.34-11.48.

26. National Economic Development Office, *Housing For All* (London, 1977), p. 41.

27. British Market Research Bureau, *Housing Consumer Survey* (National Economic Development Office, 1977).

28. Ibid.

29. Other comparisons, using different methods and assumptions, have been made by G. Hughes, *Inflation and Housing* (Housing Research Foundation, 1975); Department of the Environment, *Housing Policy Technical Volume I*, Ch. 4, appendix G. For a summary of the debate, see D. Webster, 'New Council and Private Housing: Can the Subsidy Costs Argument Be Settled?', in *Centre for Environmental Studies Review*, no. 3 (March 1978).

30. Tables 5.2 and 5.3, Ch. 5.

31. One survey of Birmingham showed that of the 88 per cent of the sample purchasing who were paying off a mortgage, 90 per cent had borrowed the money from a local authority: A. Murie, *The Sale of Council Houses* (Centre for Urban and Regional Studies, Birmingham University, 1976).

32. B. Kilroy, 'Jackpot from Council House Sales', *Roof* (Shelter, March 1977), and the replies to Kilroy's article in *Roof* (Shelter, July 1977), pp. 123-215.

33. B. Crofton, *Sales of Council Houses*, a discussion paper prepared for the Housing Strategy Committee of the Economic Development Committee for Building, 1976.

34. Murie, *The Sale of Council Houses.*

35. Frank Field, *Do We Need Council Houses?* (Catholic Housing Aid Society,

1975).

36. British Market Research Bureau, *Housing Consumer Survey*.

37. Department of the Environment, *Housing Policy, A Consultative Document*, paras 11.06-11.13.

38. S. Weir and B. Kilroy, 'Equity Sharing in Cheshunt', *Roof* (Shelter, November 1976).

39. House of Commons, *Hansard*, vol. 414 (1945/6), col. 1222.

40. Table 4.3, Ch. 4.

41. D.C. Stafford, 'The Final Economic Demise of the Private Landlord', *Social and Economic Administration*, vol. 10, no. 1 (Spring 1976).

42. Housing Centre Trust, *Evidence to the Review of Housing Finance* (1975), p. 54.

43. Fabian Society, *The End of the Private Landlord*, Fabian Research Series 312 (Fabian Society, 1973).

44. Ibid.

45. *Report of the Committee on Housing in Greater London*, Cmnd 2605 (HMSO, 1965).

46. A. Murie, P. Niner, C. Watson, *Housing Policy and the Housing System* (London, Allen and Unwin, 1976).

47. M. Wicks, *Rented Housing and Social Ownership*, Fabian Tract 521 (Fabian Society, 1973).

48. Table 4.6, Ch. 4.

49. B. Kilroy, 'Housing Associations', in *Housing Finance* (Institute for Fiscal Studies, no. 12, 1975).

50. M.E. Smith, *Guide to Housing* (Housing Centre Trust, 1977), p. 236.

51. Department of the Environment, *Circular 170/74* (December 1974).

52. Department of the Environment, *Housing Report for 1977*, Press Notice 74 (6 February 1976).

53. Department of the Environment, *Housing Policy, A Consultative Document*, para. 9.58.

7 THE HOUSING GREEN PAPER AND THE REFORM OF HOUSING FINANCE

This chapter looks in more detail at the proposals in the recent Green Paper on housing — *Housing Policy: A Consultative Document* — and alternative proposals for reform. The Green Paper was published in June 1977, some 2½ years after the review of housing finance was initiated by the late Anthony Crosland, Secretary of State for the Environment, in early 1975. The intention to hold the review was widely welcomed at the time, a reflection of the growing awareness of the need for a thorough analysis of existing arrangements and for major changes in policy. Whatever is felt about the precise proposals arising from that review, the Green Paper itself is to be welcomed as the first full, detailed and comprehensive analysis and statement about government housing policy, its merits, defects, intentions and likely development. The Green Paper puts the housing debate on a firmer foundation, and its technical appendices provide valuable analyses of a number of issues and new information.

The motivation for setting up the review was the lack of consistent and coherent objectives in government policy, and the inherent problems of the existing system of housing finance, problems which were widely recognised. Crosland himself, in a speech to the Housing Centre Trust in 1975, setting out the priorities for the review, was quite blunt about existing housing policy,

> for all this weight of law and money, *no* government in my view has ever had a consistent housing policy, and we still in 1975 have serious, indeed, often desperate, residual housing problems . . .
> We have a system of subsidies which distribute aid to housing in a whimsical manner and we have lurches in total investment in housing which, amongst other things, have seriously damaged the efficiency of our building industry. The fault lies in the tendency of successive governments to live from hand to mouth.[1]

The main elements and weaknesses of existing financial arrangements have been outlined in Chapters 4 and 5, where it was argued that existing provision is too often inefficient, indiscriminate and inequitable, and inadequate in helping those most in need. Housing finance has failed to provide a wide and fair access to and choice in housing.

Reforms of housing finance have to show that they would represent an improvement in existing policy, providing a more rational and redistributive system of subsidies. The objective of rationality and equity is in essence separate from the objective of redistribution and both can be aimed at independently. Aid to housing can be redirected in more equitable and efficient ways by modifications to existing tax concessions and by setting and regulating rents more fairly and consistently. Chapter 5 shows that a fair choice between tenures requires, for example, a reallocation of aid from owner-occupiers as a group towards tenants as a group (and among differing groups of tenants), and from established owners to recent buyers among owner-occupiers. Any scheme for reform of housing finance also needs to be progressively redistributive because of income inequalities.

The various proposals in the Green Paper need to be appraised in relation to the extent to which they contribute towards removing these weaknesses and meeting these objectives. Inevitably the detailed proposals have received a variable response. Some have commented favourably, some unfavourably, reflecting the variations in view about the nature of the reforms needed. Some proposals have received widespread support, while others have been more contentious, especially those more directly concerned with the structure of housing finance.

The major weakness of the Green Paper is that it contains no major recommendations for reform. It considers various proposals for change made in evidence presented to the review, but rejects most of them. In essence, and trimmed of its supporting evidence and minor recommendations, the Green Paper adds up to a defence of the *status quo* and support for the existing system of housing finance. The proposals for owner-occupation are very marginal. The recommendations in the case of the local authority sector are slightly more substantial, and contain both welcome and disturbing aspects. Few proposals for the privately rented sector are made, as the government is awaiting the current Review of the Rent Acts. Taken overall, the Green Paper can be seen as tilting the current balance even further in the direction of owner-occupation, a demonstration of the consensus that has emerged between the leadership of the two main political parties regarding the alleged benefits of home ownership. The recommendations for each sector are now considered in turn and compared with some of the alternative proposals made.

Owner-Occupation

In Chapter 5, it was argued that existing tax concessions to owner-occupiers are both inefficient and inequitable. Existing aid encourages the exchange process and higher housing and non-housing consumption and in the future there is good reason to believe that the growth of home ownership could under current arrangements inhibit industrial investment by absorbing too high a proportion of limited capital funds. At the very least, restrictions should be introduced to that portion of tax relief which assists existing owners changing houses at higher prices. Moreover since existing subsidies exacerbate rather than offset inequalities, there is also a case in equity for changes in existing arrangements.

Various proposals have been made for dealing with the inadequacies of the existing system of financial aid to owner-occupiers. The most radical and far reaching proposal would be for the re-introduction of Schedule A taxation, and the extension of capital gains taxation to cover owner-occupied dwellings. Such a policy has been advocated at various times by groups on the Left, including the Fabian Society, and on the Right, such as the Bow Group, for different reasons, and usually in the context of a more extensive package of reforms covering the other sectors as well. Such a move would represent a form of current value pricing in the owner-occupied sector based on the taxation of the notional income from occupation (para. 5.21).[2] The Green Paper's view about the introduction of such taxation is that it would present 'the gravest administrative difficulties' and 'be incompatible with the growth of home ownership' (para. 5.38). Further, whatever the merits of such a proposal on economic and social grounds, it would undoubtedly encounter severe political difficulties.

Changes in Tax Relief

Other, more modest, proposals have concentrated on the reform of the existing system of tax relief. Restrictions of some kind have been advocated by, among other, the Labour Party, the Fabian Society, the London Boroughs Association, Shelter and the Housing Centre Trust in their evidence to the review. In its evidence, the Building Societies Association, perhaps not surprisingly, rejected the case for such restrictions and even argued that 'there are no strong grounds for calling tax relief a subsidy.'

Most proposals have called for the phased reduction rather than the complete removal of tax relief. A widely canvassed proposal has been that tax relief should only be paid at the standard rate of income tax. One method of achieving this would be by replacing the present system of tax relief with a universal mortgage subsidy system in which interest is no longer allowable against tax but all mortgagors would pay the same subsidised rate of interest.[3] This would have the effect of limiting help to home buyers to that currently enjoyed by basic rate tax payers, as in the case of option mortgage subsidy. In 1976/7, about 1 million mortgagors qualified for £120m tax relief at higher rates (about 10 per cent of the total value of tax relief). Such a measure would go some way towards reducing the benefit of tax relief to higher income groups. In 1974/5 households with incomes over £6,000 received tax relief averaging £369 p.a. compared with only £59 p.a. in the case of households with incomes less than £1,000.[4] Restricting tax relief to the basic rate of income tax would reduce the average benefit to the higher income group to £275 p.a. As well as producing a less regressive distribution of subsidy, this measure would also restrict the extent of trading up that takes place in order to reduce the burden of taxation. A further advantage of the universal option mortgage is that it would automatically change the existing anomalous accounting practice whereby tax relief is not counted as public expenditure on housing while option mortgage subsidy and local authority subsidies are. This is a particularly serious anomaly because when a government provides additional subsidy to the local authority sector, as it has done in the last few years, the impression is given that the council tenant is being singled out for help, even though tax relief may be rising to a similar extent. Conversely when a government is in a position of wanting to restrain public spending, there is no mechanism under current arrangements for doing so in the case of the owner-occupier. Under a universal option mortgage subsidy, subsidy could be adjusted by small changes in the interest rate charged.

Other proposals have advocated further limitations. Some have argued for a reduction in the current £25,000 ceiling – with regional variations – above which mortgages are not eligible for tax relief, though the real value of this ceiling is now lower than when it was introduced by the Labour Government in 1974. The Green Paper says that this ceiling will be kept under review. Whatever the merits of this proposal, it would not of itself generate significant savings in tax relief. It has been estimated that, in 1976, a ceiling of £15,000 would save a mere £5m, and one of £10,000 would save £50m.[5]

The Housing Centre Trust, in its evidence, advocated a new type of compulsory mortgage, the single annuity mortgage. This would not affect the level of tax relief on a first mortgage, and so not alter the position of the first time buyer. Its effect would be to allow tax relief on a second or subsequent mortgage only on the notional interest which would have been due if a 25 year mortgage for the new higher amount had been taken out at the date of the original mortgage. For example, an owner moving after seven years from a house mortgaged for say £10,000 would be entitled to relief on the interest on his new mortgage, for say £15,000, only as if he had already held his higher mortgage for seven years. The proposal would not affect existing mortgagors who did not move, and those who did move would still enjoy higher tax relief if the sum mortgaged increased but not by as much as at present, and eligibility for subsidy for each owner would cease after 25 years. The effect of the scheme would be to phase out relief slightly more quickly by restricting the increase in tax relief that usually occurs on moving.

Others have proposed various kinds of index-linked mortgages. These would avoid the present system of front loading whereby inflation leads to a bunching of repayments in the early years of a mortgage, thereby restricting access to owner-occupation. Index linking would permit lower repayments in the early years in return for higher payments later, and in so doing provide greater scope for reductions in tax relief which would be less widely needed.[6] It would also permit investors' savings to (at least) maintain their purchasing power.

Restrictions in tax relief would have three types of effect: on the total level of investment in houses built for sale, on the mix of investment between houses of different size and quality and on the distribution of subsidies. Tax relief restrictions, whether on a limited or large scale, would tend to reduce the overall level of investment slightly and shift it away from the top end of the market towards a greater number of smaller, cheaper dwellings. This is desirable on the grounds that the top end of the market has absorbed too much investment in the past which has simply benefited those who have been, in the main, already well housed. Opponents might argue that this would interfere with the filtering system whereby the building of better-quality homes enables existing lower-quality housing to filter down to lower income groups, but as we have argued in Chapter 5, the filtering system is not of significant benefit to such groups. These policies would also discourage trading up and so the extent of under-occupation, by reducing the extent of additional tax relief on moving. Restrictions on tax relief would also mean that assistance is concentrated to a greater extent than at present where it is most needed, among lower income groups and first-time buyers. There is no case for continuing to subsidise those with high incomes so much more heavily than those with lower incomes.

They would also allow savings in public spending that could be channelled elsewhere. Such changes would be moves in the direction of greater social and economic justice and greater efficiency.

Despite the force of the case for such restrictions on tax relief, the Green Paper supports the continuance of mortgage tax relief and option mortgage subsidy. It intends to keep the present £25,000 limit admissible for relief under review, though this has been interpreted to imply in an upward rather than a downward direction (para. 5.38). It uses four arguments to reject such proposals (para. 5.37). First, it is maintained that the removal of tax relief on higher rates would hurt middle income groups on £8,000-£10,000 (from May 1978, the starting point of the first higher rate tax threshold is £8,000 for a single person), as well as higher income groups. This is equivalent to arguing that the tax system is too progressive at this income level, a strange stance for a Labour government; but even if the government feels that middle income groups cannot afford to lose tax relief, a more appropriate policy would be to reduce their tax burden directly by raising the tax threshold rather than provide generous indirect assistance in the form of a housing subsidy. The second argument is that a significant reduction in tax relief — whatever form it takes — would be damaging to those who have undertaken heavy financial commitments on the basis of existing arrangements. This, however, is recognised by the advocates of reform in their proposals for phased changes with suitable transitional arrangements. Few have argued for instantaneous changes.

It is also argued that such policies would disrupt the housing market by reducing demand in the upper end of the market and increasing demand at the lower end, thereby discouraging higher quality construction by reducing the demand for 'trading-up'. Provided that there are adequate phasing arrangements, it is most unlikely that serious disruption would occur. Further, it can equally well be argued that current arrangements have created their own distortions, in particular by artificially stimulating demand at the upper end, and so encouraging too much investment in too few dwellings at the top end of the market. These changes would then simply help to correct some of the current distortions imposed by existing financial arrangements. The market for housing is already subject to a variety of fluctuations and disturbances from a variety of sources. If anything, the tax relief proposals would create greater stability in the long run.

Finally, the single annuity proposal is rejected on the grounds of administrative difficulty and its discouragement to mobility. But this criticism represents a misunderstanding or a misrepresentation of the single annuity principle which would not actually reduce tax relief on moving with a higher mortgage, but simply involve a smaller increase than the increase that would be received under an ordinary annuity mortgage.[7]

Other Proposals

Other proposals in the Green Paper with respect to owner-occupation are of less importance, but not without significance. Recommendations include increasing the social responsibility of building societies by, for example, encouraging more low start and higher percentage mortgages, more loans for older property, greater co-operation between building societies and local authorities (paras 7.16-7.32) and ensuring greater stability in mortgage lending through stabilisation funds (7.49-7.64). While these proposals are welcome, it is doubtful whether they will go very far to improve the access of currently disadvantaged and discriminated groups, since building societies have proved largely unresponsive to such suggestions in the past. Others have argued for more direct control of the building societies rather than the exhortation of the Green Paper, and the expansion of local authority lending by requiring the building societies to make available a given proportion of their funds to local authorities for on lending. The proposal in the Green Paper for a new savings and interest free loan for first-time buyers (7.33-7.42) has been implemented with the introduction of the Home Purchase Assistance Bill in February 1978, which as we have argued in Chapter 6, must be criticised for its failure to help those in greatest need, particularly those in inner cities who cannot get loans from building societies and have to borrow from money lenders and fringe banks.[8]

The Local Authority Sector

While only minor changes have been recommended for the financial arrangements underlying owner-occupation, more substantial changes have been proposed for the public sector.

Housing Investment Programmes

First, a new system of capital spending allocation has been introduced whereby local authorities draw up four-year housing investment programmes (HIPs) covering all capital expenditure — clearance and demolition, renovation, conversion, home loans, improvement grants to private householders, acquisitions and new building (paras 9.06-9.10). These housing plans, based on a comprehensive assessment of the local housing situation, are to be used as a basis for capital spending allocations to each authority. The proposal to introduce this new block allocation system was first announced by Peter Shore in November 1976, confirmed in the Green Paper, introduced with interim arrangements in 1977/8 and operated in full in the financial year 1978/9. The basis of the scheme is a single block grant allocation for all local authority capital spending which replaces the existing system of separate provisions for new building, rehabilitation, municipalisation and home loans.

When fully introduced, each housing authority will produce an annual HIP covering all its housing activities. The HIP return is to consist of three parts: a 'strategy statement' which describes the housing problems in the area and the local authority's main policies for dealing with them; a 'housing strategy appraisal' giving a numerical statement of the number of households and dwellings in the area projected forward over the coming four years; and the 'bid' or request for capital grant allocation which contains a financial statement showing recent patterns of capital spending and spending proposals for the next four years.[9] Allocations are divided into three expenditure blocks covering new building, slum clearance, improvement of public sector dwellings and acquisitions; private sector improvement grants and home loans; and lending to housing associations. Authorities have complete flexibility to determine the mix of spending within each block, and there is limited transferability of funds between blocks ('virement') of up to 25 per cent, and between years ('tolerance') of up to 10 per cent.

In general, this new system has been welcomed as an improvement on previous arrangements which imposed cash limits on different spending sectors. It will allow greater flexibility in place of these arbitrary controls on particular kinds of investment. Local authorities will now have greater freedom to move resources between programmes. It will permit a move away from the setting of purely national targets to more locally based ones, and so provide, at least in principle, a better framework for deploying resources where they are most needed. As the Green Paper has argued, 'we can only establish precisely how much needs to be done, when and where, by local assessment' (para. 2.08).

Nevertheless, there are a number of reservations about the new system. While it is supposed to provide greater flexiblity in determining local housing programmes, the effect may simply be greater central government control. The effect of HIPs is that Whitehall will now determine both the size of the cake to be spent on housing investment and how it is to be distributed between authorities. HIPs therefore add another layer to the range of government controls over local authorities, controls which have already grown substantially in the last few years. Up to 1974/5 local authorities were largely free to decide how much they spent on housing, subject to Department of the Environment control on matters such as building standards, though these were concerned more with securing value-for-money than at controlling total expenditure. The role of central government was mainly limited to an enabling one – by adjusting the level of subsidy. Since then new controls of various kinds have been imposed, particularly as a result of government attempts to restrain public spending. Up to 1974/5, new building and improvement were controlled by the Department of the Environment accepting or rejecting individual schemes according to whether or not they met the yardsticks. Municipalisation and mortgage lending was controlled by requiring approval for purchases or loans outside of certain categories, specified in circulars, for which there was a general approval to spend. Since 1974/5, cash allocations have been imposed on local authority improvement expenditure in 1975/6, on mortgage lending in 1976/7 and on all capital expenditure in 1977/8. HIPs in fact represent an extension to all capital spending of the procedure for improvement expenditure introduced under section 105 of the 1974 Housing Act, of making a 'bid' and subsequently receiving an 'allocation'.

Any new flexibility provided under HIPs therefore needs to be seen in the context of the growth of controls in recent years, and HIPs ought to allow for the relaxation of some of these controls, especially the housing cost yardstick and loan sanction procedures. The Green Paper advocates the replacement of the cost yardstick with a new method of cost control based on a fixed level of costs per house eligible for subsidy (para. 9.11). These controls present a great number of hurdles for schemes to pass, and together with the burden of meeting excess costs under a cash limit system, have the effect of encouraging underspending. There is indeed continuing evidence that interference by the Department of the Environment in local authority housing programmes is causing delays in scheme approvals, making it difficult to plan expenditure and causing underspending.[10] There is a case for removing some of these controls and allowing greater flexibility to authorities within their allocation. Moreover, these controls are purely negative. Whitehall can restrict local spending plans, but not stimulate underspending authorities.

Finally, there is the question of determining the distribution of the total cake between authorities. The HIP approach is rightly designed to ensure allocation on the basis of need, but the assessment of such need is not an unambiguous exercise. A study of the stress and non-stress areas drawn up by the Department of the Environment for the new building controls introduced in July 1976, and which were based on indicators of overcrowding, lack of amenities and information from regional offices, has shown how difficult it is to identify a unique list of stress areas. Different criteria provide different sets of stress authorities.[11] The methods of assessing local needs recommended in the HIPs procedure are also far from unambiguous.[12]

The HIP system has not been in operation long enough to offer a conclusive assessment. Nevertheless, a disturbing aspect about the Government's overall investment intentions is that the Green Paper suggests that as the backlog of bad housing conditions are overcome, 'the overall level of public sector housing investment should decline in response to changing circumstances' (para. 6.16). In the Technical Volume, investment in public sector housing is projected to fall by around 30 per cent between 1976 and 1986,[13] though it is emphasised that this is a projection and not a target. Such a trend would be very worrying in view of the estimates of outstanding need presented in Chapter 3, and the continuing problems of access to decent housing by many groups, especially as the private rented sector continues to decline.

The New Subsidy System

In addition to these changes in investment allocation, the Green Paper has recommended a new housing subsidy system. The existing system is based on the 1975 Housing Rents and Subsidies Act. This repealed the 1972 Housing Finance Act and restored to local authorities the freedom to fix the rents of their dwellings and to determine the balance between rent income and general rate fund support, subject to the rule that in determining 'reasonable rents', local authorities should not budget for a surplus. The current subsidy system has three main elements, a 'basic element' consisting of the amount of subsidy payable in 1974/5 under the 1972 Act, fixed in cash terms for future years, a 'new capital cost element' equal to 66 per cent of annual loan charges arising from approved capital expenditure undertaken from 1975/6, and a 'supplementary financial element' representing 33 per cent of any increase in loan charges incurred on admissible capital expenditure undertaken before 1975/6. Because these subsidies alone would provide inadequate help for authorities with large building and improvement programmes in high cost areas, a 'high cost subsidy element' was also introduced payable from 1976/7 to authorities who after receiving the main elements of subsidy and increasing rents in line with national guidelines, still had a deficit.

The 1975 Act was intended to be an interim measure, pending the government's housing finance review, and does have certain acknowledged defects. Thus the subsidies take no account of the existing burden of debt on the authority nor the scope it may have for cross-subsidising by pooling. The 1975 system is also insufficiently flexible to deal with rapid changes in inflation and interest rates such as those experienced in recent years, and has produced unequal rent and rate fund changes between areas, with high cost and high investment authorities being at a particular disadvantage. Under the act, subsidies, apart from the high cost element, are related to specific aspects of cost and so are largely independent of an authority's need for subsidy as measured by the deficit it faces after a reasonable contribution from rents and rates. It has been argued that the system is over generous to authorities with small investment programmes where the burden of debt is falling in relation to tenants' incomes, while giving insufficient help to authorities in high cost areas of stress where bigger investment programmes are needed.

Another characteristic of the existing system is that some local authorities, and it is likely to be an increasing number are already in a position of surplus on their housing revenue accounts, and can therefore allow rents to fall in real terms. This applies particularly to those authorities whose need for additional investment is declining or has already come to an end, such that their costs are falling by comparison with the costs of authorities still undertaking investment. This situation may lead to a further widening in rent levels, since it is generally the case that those authorities with a surplus or near surplus are also those with relatively low current rents. The tendency towards surplus may be partially offset by improvements in management and maintenance, and by capital spending on amenities which will increase costs.[14] What is important to note is that there is a conflict here between the principle of the 'no profit' rule and of greater equity in inter-authority rent levels.

A fairer system of subsidies requires that aid should be distributed to authorities on the basis of need and ability to meet local housing need, in order to relieve the burden of that provision falling too heavily on local tenants or ratepayers. This means that local authorities needing large investment programmes and with rising costs should be helped with additional subsidy and not have to place additional burden on local sources, possibly even by reducing subsidy in areas where the need for it is declining because costs are falling.

The Green Paper proposes to replace the existing system with a single deficit subsidy which would operate in a similar way to the existing high cost element, and relate subsidy more closely to the varying needs of different authorities. The aim would be to meet remaining costs after a 'reasonable' contribution from local tenants and ratepayers, while leaving local authorities their present freedom to fix rents and make rate fund contributions (paras 9.34-9.50). The precise details of the proposed new subsidy system are not yet available. It is intended, however, that the system will take as its base each authority's existing subsidies as they stand in the year before the new system is introduced, and then relate additional subsidy to the difference between the authority's extra annual expenditure and assumed extra income.[15] Each year the government, after consultation with local authorities will determine an appropriate level of increase in the local contribution from rents and rates, and the subsidy will then meet the difference or a proportion of the difference between the increase in reckonable expenditure and this increased local contribution. The system therefore requires a guideline for local increases, the change in reckonable expenditure and the deficit proportion to be met. The rule suggested in the Green Paper for the local increases is that 'over a run of years rents should keep broadly in line with money incomes' (para 9.37). The local authority would then have a choice as to the relative contribution to the required increase from rents and rates. The system will also require the determination of expenditure that is admissible for subsidy and these allowed costs will be based on notional amounts rather than actual, especially in the case of management and maintenance.[16] Deficit subsidy systems require some method of expenditure control in this way.

The form of the new system will have important implications for the growth of rents, the size of the local rate fund contribution and variations in rent levels. Some have argued for a system that, while restraining rent increases to increases in earnings or prices, also permits reductions in the rate fund contributions in those areas where they are currently especially high, and a narrowing in rent variations between authorities. This could only be achieved, however, by allowing some redistribution of subsidies between authorities.

A particular concern about the new system is that it is unlikely to redistribute subsidies sufficiently to allow any major reduction in disparities in rent levels and rate fund contributions. One reason for this is that by relating future subsidies to current levels, current inequities in rent and subsidy levels would be built into the new system and currently high and low rented authorities would, respectively, continue to have high and low rents. Another is that though one effect of the new system would be to withdraw subsidy from authorities with small investment programmes, the resulting tendency for rents to rise will be checked by both the 'no profit' rule which is to be retained and the proposal in the Green Paper for the introduction of a 'minimum subsidy entitlement' or 'subsidy floor'. It is argued in the Green Paper that if such an entitlement were fixed to provide a minimum level of subsidy equal to say 34 per cent of the authority's interest charges (i.e., geared to the basic rate of income tax) this would foster some sense of fairness between owner-occupiers and local authority tenants. When this 'subsidy floor' is reached, subsidy would be held steady (paras 9.48-9.50). If introduced, this proposal would limit the scope of any pro-gressive withdrawal of subsidy from authorities with low investment programmes and low costs, such that they would move into surplus more quickly than otherwise. It would therefore have a capricious effect on the distribution of subsidy. The principle of the suggestion is far from clear, and it would appear to conflict with the objective of allocating subsidies on the basis of authorities' needs.

When the new system is introduced, there is every indication that its precise working will be left deliberately vague. The argument for flexibility is that it will enable funds to be channelled where they are needed and rapidly, both for investment purposes and to deal with economic instability. Such flexibility will be ensured by leaving open the rules governing the determination of the notional cost items, the level of subsidy, and the local contribution. This also means that ministers can intervene at short notice to change the basis of policy, and that they have to take decisions each year as to the rules to be applied.

One aspect of the proposed system over which there will be contro-versy concerns rent policy. The level of subsidy will depend on the government's view about the desirable level of rent increases. The Green Paper, as we have seen, has suggested that rents should move broadly in line with money incomes, and this is a departure from the situation of recent years when rents have kept pace with prices but not earnings. Some have argued that this policy is too severe, others that rents should be allowed to rise sufficiently to cover a higher proportion of costs in order to allow a reduction in the current level of subsidy. There are, however, a number of important constraints to allowing rents to rise at a faster rate than incomes. We have seen that 45 per cent of the poorest 10 per cent of households live in the council sector compared with 31 per cent of all households,[17] and that there has been a steady trend towards an increasing concentration of lower income groups in this sector.[18] Currently some 45 per cent of council tenants are in receipt of a rent rebate or a supplementary benefit rent addition, and since the take-up rate for these benefits is estimated at 75 to 80 per cent, this implies that around 55 per cent of tenants are currently eligible. Further increases in rents would increase the proportion of tenants requiring rebates to maintain their living standards. The availability of a range of means-tested benefits also means that a given increase in rents would lead to a less than proportionate increase in net revenue accruing to the Exchequer. Moreover, increasing rents without in any way altering the financial arrangements for owner-occupation would simply further increase the relative benefits of owner-occupation and accelerate the existing trend towards polarisation of households by income and tenure. The scope for increasing rents is therefore severely limited.

The effect of the new subsidy system on disparities in rent levels and rate fund contributions between authorities is as yet unknown, and it has been suggested that it will not go far enough in this direction. An alternative subsidy system which would assist in evening out such disparities, suggested by the Housing Centre Trust in its evidence to the review, is a system of 'national rent pooling'. This would operate by those local authorities with relatively low housing costs and hence low average rents, contributing towards the costs of those authorities with greater financial burdens.[19] In this way, the evening of costs which takes place within areas by local pooling would be extended onto a national basis. The advantage of such a scheme would be that rent increases could thereby be restrained for those boroughs with a continuing high level of investment, and rent disparities between areas be reduced, thereby producing a more equitable distribution of the rent burden. The major disadvantage of the proposal is that it would inevitably involve some authorities being obliged to charge higher rents (or rate fund contributions) than would otherwise be necessary to balance their accounts, and so the abolition of the no-profit rule. Unlike the provisions of the 1972 Housing Finance Act, however, these profits would be used to cross-subsidise the deficits of other local authorities and not be returned to Exchequer funds in order to reduce general taxation. The proposal has, however, been rejected by the Green Paper mainly on the grounds of its conflict with the no-surplus rule (para.

9.33).

Another consideration for reform, and one not mentioned in the Green Paper, is that of altering the structure and accounting arrangements underlying the housing revenue account. It is often pointed out that a number of items of local authority spending are charged directly to the housing revenue account, and therefore boost the costs which have to be met by tenants, but which should not be the responsibility of tenants alone. These include the provision of a comprehensive housing service, such as the administration of housing waiting lists, the running of housing advice centres and the provision of accommodation for the homeless, and the management costs of redevelopment and rehabilitation which should be borne directly by the community rather than tenants. It is also argued that the cost of sheltered housing, which is currently borne by the housing revenue account, is a responsibility undertaken by the public sector on behalf of the whole community. If changes such as this were made, alternative subsidy arrangements for these activities would be needed.

Other Public Sector Proposals

Other aspects of the Green Paper's proposals for local authority housing are less controversial and have been widely welcomed. These include the recommendations for changes in management, including proposals for extending the rights of tenants by, for example, the introduction of a Tenants' Charter (paras 11.05-11.18), and for improving allocation policies by embracing a wider range of needs, easing residential qualifications, improving mobility, and publishing allocation schemes (paras 9.16-9.22). There are also a number of recommendations in respect of the need and access of special groups including the needs of the homeless, which have been implemented in the Housing (Homeless Persons) Bill which became law in 1977, one parent families, battered women, the physically and mentally disabled, single people, the elderly, mobile workers and ethnic minorities (paras 12.11-12.59).

In addition to these recommendations for the public rented sector, a number of proposals were made regarding the voluntary housing sector and alternative forms of tenure. In particular it was argued that the role of registered housing associations should continue to grow and be integrated into local housing strategies (paras 9.24 and 9.25), encouragement should be given to the formation of housing co-operatives by the transfer of management responsibilities to tenants on estates and by helping private tenants to take over the control and ownership of their houses on a co-operative basis (paras 11.16 and 11.17), and to co-ownership housing and equity sharing schemes (paras 11.22-11.28). Few recommendations were made in regard to the private rented sector, since these will await the publication of the Review of the Rent Acts.

A number of proposals were also announced in connection with improvement policy. Improvement is going to remain a vital part of housing policy for many years to come. As the 1976 House Condition Survey showed, whilst the number of unfit and substandard dwellings has fallen since 1971, there has been a 50 per cent increase in the number of houses in serious disrepair over the five-year period. In 1971, an estimated 636,000 houses − including houses unfit and lacking amenities − required expenditure on repairs exceeding £1,000 (at 1971 prices), compared with 911,000 needing an equivalent amount of expenditure in 1976. Moreover, the 1976 Survey showed 1.1m houses that are neither unfit nor lacking amenities needed work costing over £1,000 at 1976 prices compared with some 500,000 in 1971. As the Green Paper observes, 'without effective measures, we shall see the growth of a new generation of slums' (para. 10.18). Nevertheless, the measures proposed hardly add up to what would appear to be a need for a major drive on improvement and rehabilitation. In the last five years, as Chapter 4 has indicated, the improvement programme has borne the brunt of public expenditure cuts. Recommendations in the Green Paper are concerned with minor adjustments in the existing system of improvement grants. Proposals include more flexible administration by local authorities, the extension of repair grants, the adjustment of cost and rateable value limits, the possibility of allowing private tenants, rather than landlords, to apply for grants, and the provision of grants to houses in multiple occupation. It is also intended that local authority powers of compulsory improvement should be made simpler and more effective (paras 10.22-10.33). Welcome as these proposals are, it is doubtful whether they will make a major difference to the standard of repair in the privately rented sector where there is a concentration of disrepair.

Fundamental Reforms

In addition to these basically piecemeal reforms discussed in the previous sections, some have advocated more thoroughgoing changes that would alter the basis of the housing finance system fundamentally. The Green Paper discussed four such proposals for major reform (para.

5.04). Each is discussed in the context of the existing system of aid in the form of tax relief and central government and rate fund contributions to housing revenue accounts, which is defined as 'general assistance'. One of the proposals 'that general assistance should be retained, but should be distributed more fairly and more effectively' essentially relates to the sort of piecemeal proposals discussed above, especially the proposals for the reform of tax relief and of subsidies to the public rented sector. As we have seen, the Green Paper rejected the case for even limited reforms.

The other three proposals are more fundamental:

(i) The elimination or reduction of general assistance together with the extension of the rent rebate and allowance scheme.

(ii) The introduction of new forms of pricing in which gross housing payments by households, both tenants and home owners, are related to the current value of housing rather than to its historic cost.

(iii) The replacement of general assistance with a scheme of universal housing allowances.

In general, proposals (i) and (ii) have the common objective of a substantial reduction in housing subsidies. They differ in their views about what constitutes the subsidy and would lead to different levels of subsidy reduction. Proposal (i) would involve the reduction of tax relief and Exchequer subsidy while (ii) is more far reaching in its impact, involving a more substantial fall in subsidy. As we have seen, housing payments are generally related to historic costs. In the public rented sector, the rents of individual tenants are based on the average pooled historic cost of provision of all the local housing stock. In the owner-occupied sector, no such pooling takes place, and the mortgage repayments of an individual buyer are related to the price of the house when initially purchased. In the privately rented sector, tenants pay rents that constitute a mixture of historic cost and current value. Current value pricing in the case of the owner-occupier would involve the taxing of notional income from occupation – the reintroduction of Schedule A – along with the retention of tax relief. In the public sector, current value pricing would involve the charging of 'market rents' to tenants.

Advocates of these schemes, generally those who favour a reduction in government intervention and a greater role for free market forces, argue that general assistance as currently cast meets housing costs without regard to a household's ability to pay and is therefore inefficient and wasteful. Moreover, it requires a very high level of taxation to finance. It is argued that removing general assistance would deal with some of these inefficiencies and enable a reduction in taxation. In addition, a move towards current value pricing would mean that housing payments are more closely related to the real current cost of provision and would therefore provide a more rational basis of choice for the individual in choosing between housing and other goods.

Some of these arguments are valid. The weaknesses of general assistance in its current form were discussed in Chapter 5. But sweeping reforms such as these would be unlikely to deal with these weaknesses, and would have a number of far reaching consequences. In the first place, they would have a substantial redistributional impact. A net gain would be enjoyed by those who receive more in tax cuts than they lose in additional housing payments. Others would be made worse off. Who lose and who gain would depend on the form and extent of changes in general assistance and the form that the tax cuts take. It is far from clear that such changes would be progressive in effect.

Further, as we have already seen, there is little scope for substantial increases in public sector rents. More than 50 per cent of tenants are currently entitled to rebates or supplementary benefit rent additions, and the public sector is increasingly housing lower income groups. Moreover, it is far from clear what would constitute a 'market rent' since in many areas there are too few houses let at market-related rents to provide a benchmark. Many recent first time purchasers would not be in a position to pay more for their housing, at least in the early years of the mortgage. Attempts to protect low income households by the extension of existing rent rebates and allowance schemes, and their extension to home buyers, would lead to a massive increase in means testing. Moreover, means tested housing benefits suffer from major disadvantages which make them a particularly ineffective means of assisting low income households. They increase the dependency of the poor for a decent standard of living on efficient and uninhibited form filling and declaration of income and need. They suffer from a depressingly low take up, and contribute to the problem of the poverty trap, whereby increases in earnings result in little or no increase in living standards because of the high rate of withdrawal of benefit. In addition, they encourage stigma, are socially divisive and complex to administer.

Further, as the Green Paper has pointed out, such reforms would lead to a complex set of changes in demand and supply, and an overall fall in demand. In consequence there would be a fall in the level of investment, especially in the public sector, where as argued in Chapter 5, cuts in public sector subsidies would lead to a cut in local authority investment. The effect on the supply of owner-occupied dwellings would depend on the type of change introduced. Such reforms would not ensure that subsidies were more fairly distributed, resources more effectively used and access of low income and disadvantaged groups improved, and were rejected by the Green Paper.

Universal Housing Allowances

An alternative proposal for reform is to replace existing subsidies with some kind of universal housing allowance (UHA). Again such a scheme was considered, though very briefly by the Green Paper but rejected. The main characteristic of a UHA scheme is that it would provide assistance on a non-means tested basis in order to avoid the disadvantages of income related benefits. Nevertheless, while the sum received in the initial instance would not depend on the household's level of income, the ultimate benefit of the scheme could be related to income on a progressive basis through the mechanism of the tax system. This could be secured by making the allowance taxable and subject to 'claw-back', i.e., a mechanism for withdrawing the value of the allowance systematically as income rises.

Such schemes can take a variety of forms. In their most comprehensive form allowances would be provided to all households. But full universality is not an essential feature of such schemes. More limited schemes have been proposed that see allowances, in essence, as an extension of existing social security provisions. With national insurance benefits and child endowment providing for other basic needs, the greater housing costs and space needed by families with dependents would be met through flat rate accommodation allowances paid as of right, irrespective of income and tenure, for each child and infirm, elderly or disabled dependant.[20] Since current entitlement to supplementary benefit usually arises in order to meet housing costs, such a scheme would have the strong attraction of relieving many households from the need to claim supplementary benefit, and providing assistance to those who, though entitled, do not claim. Such a scheme on its own, however, would not deal fully with the situation of wide variations in housing costs.

More comprehensive schemes would work by replacing all existing forms of aid with an allowance paid to all households as of right. The level of allowance received would depend initially on household need as measured by household size and composition and disability. The allowance could either be flat rate or vary with housing payments by having a variable element related to costs. The need for cost-related allowances would be the less, the more effective were policies aimed at rationalising and regulating housing payments. The main disadvantage of having a variable allowance is that records of housing costs would be required for the administration of the scheme.

Such schemes have powerful attractions. They would combine in one scheme the rationalisation and redirection of existing subsidies, and a potentially more progressive system of support, while avoiding the objections associated with means tested benefits. Nevertheless, they could not be introduced without overcoming various difficulties. Like other proposals for reform, there is the question of what subsidies should be replaced and hence whether housing payments before receipt of the allowance should be related to current or historic costs. This inevitably affects the level of net housing payments, the distribution of the benefit and the cost of the scheme. Secondly, again like other reforms, schemes designed to deal with major inequities in current arrangements would lead to major changes which could only be introduced gradually and with acceptable transitional arrangements. Housing allowance schemes have generally only been proposed as a long term possibility. There is also the practical question of determining eligibility in marginal cases, including, for example, outright owners.

Fourthly there is the problem that as rent rebates and allowances provide large assistance to those who receive them, housing allowances would have to ensure that low income families are not worse off after replacing rebates and allowances with housing allowances. This is a problem that is common to most universal benefit schemes. Means tested benefits can give substantial help to eligible households at relatively low cost precisely because of their limited coverage. The more generous a selective means tested scheme, the higher the universal benefits replacing them would have to be if they are not to make those receiving selective benefits worse off. This greatly increases the gross cost of the scheme and so the amount that has to be 'clawed back' from the better off through the tax system.

This raises the point that housing finance policies cannot be considered in isolation from wider social security and taxation policies. Reforms of housing finance need to deal with the misdirection of existing subsidies, but as these alone would not deal with the housing problems that derive from low income, they must also be seen in the light of wider policies of income redistribution. More effective redistributive policies would enable the less well off to consume a fairer share of housing resources and so reduce the level of housing allowance needed. Certainly a housing allowance scheme would be able to provide greater help for lower income families with a higher tax threshold and a more progressive tax system. Housing allowance schemes can only be considered as effective alternatives if contained within more effective income support policies on a wider basis.[21] Housing allowances have been rejected by the Green Paper because of the various difficulties discussed above. Nevertheless, many have argued that housing allowances in the long term offer the most effective way of achieving a rational and progressive system of housing support.

Summary and Conclusions

Solutions to the existing housing problems identified in earlier chapters depend in particular upon major changes in our current system of housing finance aimed at correcting the inefficiencies and inequalities contained within these arrangements. Within the owner-occupied sector, restrictions in tax relief are needed, with suitable phasing and transitional arrangements which would limit relief to that received at the standard rate of income tax, reduce the real value of the mortgage ceiling from its current £25,000, and introduce a mechanism for limiting the increase in tax relief that is presently gained on moving to a more expensive house − the single annuity mortgage. These reforms would help to improve the mix of housing investment, discourage unnecessary under-occupation and produce greater equity in the distribution of housing subsidies. Such changes should be accompanied by greater control over the lending policies of building societies, possibly by some kind of on-lending to local authorities, to increase the proportion of mortgages granted to lower income groups and on older properties. The Green Paper has rejected the case for such reforms.

In the public sector, changes are needed in the existing subsidy system which would lead to a closer relationship between subsidy and need, by reducing current disparities in rents and rate fund contributions between authorities arising from differences in costs, and prevent local authorities with high costs and large investment programmes having to meet the costs of such programmes through excessive increases in local rents and rates. The new subsidy system proposed in the Green Paper may lead to a fairer distribution of subsidies than under the present system, but is unlikely to lead to a significant reduction in existing and future disparities. Consideration should therefore be given to the scope for a scheme of national rent pooling, again an option rejected by the Green Paper.

Such policies are essential to put both sectors on a sounder financial footing and to provide greater equity of treatment among households within and between each sector. Finally, greater consideration should be given to the long term possibility of introducing a scheme of universal housing allowances which, if combined with other reforms in our wider system of income support and with changes in housing finance, could offer a more effective and fairer system of subsidising housing costs.

The failure of the Green Paper to accept the need for reforms along these lines is a reflection, not of the weakness of the case for such proposals, which are an essential requirement for improving the housing situation, but of the political impotency of governments to make changes that while socially and economically desirable, may have extensive short term political repercussions. For all the publicity gained during its 2½ year life and all the analysis presented in its 700 pages, the housing policy review is almost entirely a non-event in terms of its policy recommendations, and the housing situation in future years will suffer in consequence.

Notes

1. A. Crosland, 'The Finance of Housing', *Housing Review* (Sept.– Oct. 1975).
2. All bracketed references to paragraphs are to Department of the Environment, *Housing Policy, A Consultative Document* (HMSO, Cmnd 6851, 1977).
3. See, for example, the Labour Party,*Labour's Programme 1973* (1973), p. 47.
4. Table 5.6, Ch. 5.
5. B. Kilroy, *Housing Finance – Organic Reform* (LEFTA, 1978), p. 40.
6. See, for example, J.D. Whitley, 'Mortgages: The Case for Index-Linking', *National Institute Economic Review*, number 70 (November 1974).
7. See, for example, Housing Centre Trust, *Evidence to the Housing Finance Review* (November 1975), table 1, p. 29.
8. See the debate on the second reading of the Bill, *Hansard*, vol. 944, no. 63 (20 February 1978), cols 1024-96.
9. Department of the Environment Circular 63/77, *Housing Strategies and Investment Programmes: Arrangements for 1978/79* (HMSO, June 1977).
10. G. Stoker, 'Manchester Grapples with HIP Target', *Roof* (Shelter, May 1978), p. 76.
11. A. Harrison and R. Webber, 'Capital Spending on Housing: Control and Distribution', *Centre for Environmental Studies Review*, no. 1 (July 1977).
12. See, for example, S. Godfree, 'Housing Needs, Planning and HIPs', *Housing Review* (March-April, 1978).
13. Department of the Environment, *Housing Policy Technical Volume I*, table 111.30, p. 145.
14. See, for example, M. Smith and E. Howes, 'Current Trends in Local Authority Housing Finance', *Centre for Environmental Studies Review*, no. 3 (May 1978).
15. See J. Peeler, 'Public Sector Subsidies and Rents', *Housing Review*

(May-June 1978).

16. See 'The HPR Proposal', *Centre for Environmental Studies Review*, no. 2 (Dec. 1977), p. 88.

17. Table 6.7, Ch. 6.

18. Tables 6.5 and 6.6, Ch. 6.

19. See, for example, Kilroy, *Housing Finance – Organic Reform*, p. 42.

20. See, for example, F. Field and P. Townsend, *A Social Contract for Families*, Poverty Pamphlet 19 (London, Child Poverty Action Group, 1975).

21. For more details of such schemes, see Stewart Lansley, 'Housing Allowances for All?', *Roof* (Shelter, January 1976) and Stewart Lansley and Guy Fiegehen, *Housing Allowances and Inequality* (Fabian Society, December 1973).

8 INNER CITIES AND IMPROVEMENT POLICY

Recent years have seen a substantial growth in the attention focussed upon inner cities. Partly this is a response to the developing concern that inner cities were beginning to display the characteristics of decline and decay prevalent in the inner urban areas of the United States. In consequence, governments have introduced a number of measures, beginning in the late 1960s with the Urban Aid Programme, continuing in the early 1970s with a number of essentially research-based programmes of experimentation, and culminating in the publication of the White Paper, *Policy for the Inner Cities*, in June 1977.[1] While inner cities are by no means homogeneous in their problems, and are characterised by a variety and diversity of experience, they do tend to share a number of common difficulties. Typically they suffer disproportionately from a declining economic and industrial base, physical decay and adverse social conditions, a prevalence of poverty, a poor environment, poor housing conditions and employment prospects.

The Nature of the Problem

The roots of urban deprivation are generally less easy to identify than their characteristics. The heart of the problem is generally seen to lie in economic and industrial decline. Cities that developed very rapidly in the last century and were characterised by intensive concentrations of employment and housing had become highly congested by the Second World War, but since then have lost population as a result of both voluntary movement to existing and new towns and policies of planned dispersal. This migration has been unbalanced with the loss concentrated in skilled workers and young people, leaving the inner areas with a disproportionate number of unskilled and semi-skilled workers, the elderly, one-parent families and immigrants. This unbalanced loss of population has been accompanied by a rapid decline in jobs as a result of firms moving and contracting, and more important, the death of firms. Partly this has been the unintended effect of planning and housing polices — of comprehensive redevelopment schemes, uncertainty caused by planning blight, and the encouragement to relocate in development areas.

As a result of these processes, inner cities now suffer from a whole legacy of problems, an unbalanced population suffering a range of social disadvantages, a depressed industrial base, a population with below average incomes, and severe environmental problems. Housing decay is only one manifestation of the pervasive processes of urban change affecting these areas, and the concentration of poor housing conditions found in these areas is a situation therefore compounded by these wider social and economic circumstances. Typically these areas suffer from a variety of forms of housing stress, though with varying degrees — an ageing and deteriorating housing stock of low quality, and often lacking basic amenities, an unbalanced tenure structure, basic housing shortages and accompanying overcrowding and homelessness, and sometimes a large number of older council estates in poor condition that are becoming increasingly difficult to let.

The Spatial Concentration of Housing Stress

To justify an area-based approach to housing stress, it is necessary to show first, that particular small and compact areas suffer from a disproportionate share of problems, and secondly, that such areas contain a high proportion of all such problems. The most systematic evidence of spatial concentration is provided by Holtermann's study of urban deprivation using the 1971 Census.[2] While the census does not contain all the material that is relevant for identifying housing stress, and can therefore only provide a partial view, it does contain information on housing space, amenities and tenure type.

Holtermann attempted to identify those urban areas (Census Enumeration Districts — EDs[3]) in which there is a concentration of housing problems, using six indicators of housing stress: sharing or lack of hot water, lack of bath, lack of inside WC, living at a density of more than 1.5 persons per room, sharing a dwelling and lacking exclusive use of all basic amenities. The method used was to calculate the geographical distribution of the worst five per cent of EDs in Britain on the basis of each indicator of deprivation, and this showed a concentration of problems in conurbations on each indicator. While conurbations accounted for 49.2 per cent of all EDs, 69 per cent of the worst EDs on the basis of 'sharing or lack of hot water' were found in conurbations, 56.9 per cent of those that were worse on the basis of 'lacking a bath', 51.2 per cent of those 'lacking an inside WC', 77.9 per cent of those 'overcrowded', 79.8 per cent of those 'sharing dwellings' and 63.6 per cent of those 'lacking exclusive use of all basic amenities'.

Among the conurbations, Clydeside consistently had a very much higher than proportionate share of the worst five per cent of EDs on all indicators except 'sharing' which is a largely London phenomeon. This was especially so in the case of severe overcrowding, where Clydeside accounted for 37.7 per cent of the worst EDs on this basis, but only 4.3 per cent of all EDs. Inner London also had a more than proportionate share of the worst five per cent of all types of housing deprivation other than lacking an inside WC, though it was not as severely deprived as Clydeside. Tyneside and Merseyside both had more than their share of the worst five per cent on each of the amenity indicators. These figures all relate to deprivation on the basis of a single indicator. The study also showed a concentration of multiply deprived areas — EDs that are the worst five per cent on one indicator and on another — in contributions.

These figures do not of course indicate the distribution of deprived EDs *within* the conurbations which is more relevant to the question of whether the worst areas are predominantly in *inner* city areas. Evidence presented by Holtermann shows that there is a further spatial concentration of the worst five per cent of a conurbation's EDs within the 'core local authorities'. In Tyneside, for example, 63 per cent of the worst 5 per cent of EDs on the the basis of overcrowding were found in Newcastle upon Tyne and Gateshead compared with 41 per cent of all EDs in the conurbation. In Greater London, 81 per cent of the 5 per cent most overcrowded EDs and 94 per cent of those lacking exclusive use of all amenities were found in inner London compared with 47 per cent of all EDs.

In addition, these figures do not indicate the area distribution of all households in housing stress — whether a majority of households in poor housing live in the conurbations or inner cities. Some evidence on this question is again provided by Holtermann, and is important for determining the extent to which policies that discriminate in favour of particular areas will deal with a large proportion of the worst housing problems. Table 8.1 shows, for each indicator, the proportion of all households suffering that deprivation that fall in the worst 5 per cent and 15 per cent of EDs on that indicator. Thus 23 per cent of *all* households sharing or lacking hot water were found in the worst 5 per cent of all EDs on that indicator. While Table 8.1 provides evidence of significant local concentrations of substandard housing conditions, there is also a marked degree of dispersion. Poor housing conditions are not exclusively found in a few small areas. For example, 61 per cent of all households lacking a WC were found to be in 15 per cent of the worst EDs and 28 per cent in 5 per cent of the worst areas. This means that priority treatment to those 5 per cent or 15 per cent of worst areas would deal with only 28 per cent and 61 per cent respectively of all

Table 8.1: The Spatial Concentration of Poor Housing, Great Britain, 1971 (proportions)

Indicator	Proportion in Worst 5 per cent of EDs	Proportion in Worst 15 per cent of EDs
Share or lack hot water	23	53
Lacking bath	30	64
Lacking inside WC	28	61
Households overcrowded ($>$1.5 persons per room)	33	61
Shared dwelling	51	83
Lacking exclusive use of all basic amenities	18	47

Source: Holtermann, 'Areas of Urban Deprivation in Britain', table IV, p. 39.

households with this type of deprivation.

The Nature of the Inner City Housing Problem

This evidence shows that conurbations and inner cities do not have a monopoly of overcrowded and sharing households and dwellings lacking basic amenities, though they do have significantly more than their share. Overcrowding and lack of amenities, however, are not the only housing problems experienced within inner cities. Though it must be stressed again that every area has its own set of problems, and particular circumstances vary widely between areas, it is possible to identify certain features that are all too often found to be concentrated in such areas. The housing Green Paper, for example, has identified five main housing problems in inner cities: run-down housing and shabby neighbourhoods; bleak local authority estates; a limited choice of tenures; disproportionate numbers of people with special housing needs; and limited housing mobility.[4] Some of these problems derive from the special features of such areas. Some areas, for example, still suffer from a crude housing shortage, an excess of households over dwellings. The 1971 Census showed a crude shortage in three conurbations, Greater London, West Midlands and Merseyside. Within these conurbations, there are more localised shortages. Some housing problems, especially sharing and overcrowding, problems that are especially characteristic of London, are associated with housing shortages.

A prevalence of substandard and run-down housing is partly a result of the age of the housing stock, and partly the tenure structure. Inner cities generally contain a disproportionate number of older dwellings built before the First World War, and which are now in need of demolition, improvement or rehabilitation. They also often contain a relatively high proportion of privately rented dwellings, which because of their age, the lack of incentive to improve, and sometimes the inability of the owner to be able to afford to make improvements, have a relatively high chance of being in a poor state of repair. In 1976, for example, 22½ per cent of the Greater London housing stock was 'privately rented or other tenure' compared with 15 per cent for Britain as a whole, and the figure for inner London would be higher still.

Some areas are also characterised by a prevalence of low quality local authority estates. This is particularly a problem of age, since pre-1939 estates are often characterised by poor design, a lack of amenities and social facilities, obsolescence, high densities, a bleak and unattractive environment and sometimes a lack of adequate maintenance. The level of tenant dissatisfaction on such estates is often high. But there are also problems with some newer estates built to alleviate shortages, especially those with high rise blocks, and those very large low rise but monolithic high density estates situated in drab surroundings with inadequate social facilities. Such estates, even though they do not suffer from a lack of internal amenities, lack individuality and can be oppressive and anonymous, and are often the source of social problems. The need for large scale improvement in such areas is not therefore confined to dwellings, but also needs to deal with a poor environment, a lack of open space, vandalism, poor street lighting, a lack of trees, traffic noise and so on.

As well as the poor quality of the housing stock and the general environment, the population in inner cities is often handicapped by a relatively high level of immobility. Mobility is generally the more limited the larger the local shortage, the poorer the quality of the housing stock, the lower are average incomes and the more unbalanced the structure of the population, a combination of factors that are often found in inner city areas. Moreover, these housing problems are compounded by the other problems of inner cities, lack of jobs, unbalanced populations, low incomes and a deteriorating environment.

Of course, not all areas suffer from all problems and to the same degree. Some areas, however, are severely handicapped. To take one example, the London Borough of Lambeth, an area chosen for one of the government's special inner area studies and which has recently been made one of the new inner city partnership areas, is characterised by all of the deprivations apparent in inner cities. Lambeth has a severe and persistent housing shortage with, in 1976, an estimated 115,000 households in 93,000 occupied dwellings and 7,000 dwellings vacant. This current shortage of 15,000 dwellings is only expected to fall to 13,000

by 1981.[5] In a house condition survey conducted in 1973, 43 per cent
of dwellings were found to be structurally in poor condition, of
which about 60 per cent were privately rented. Six per cent of the total
stock was found to have an estimated life of less than seven years, and
a further 14 per cent from 7 to 15 years. In its housing investment
programme submission for 1978/9, Lambeth estimated that in
addition to 2,000 unfit dwellings, 21 per cent lacked one or more basic
amenities, many of which were also in substantial disrepair, and a
further 8,000 would decline into severe disrepair in the next four years
if no improvement were carried out. In consequence there is a need for
renewal and upgrading on a massive scale. Lambeth also contains a
number of older estates, and some more modern estates, on which there
is a high level of tenant dissatisfaction. Nearly 20 per cent of tenants are
on the transfer list. There is also widespread dissatisfaction with the
environment. Poor housing conditions are also exacerbated by high
residential densities. Lambeth's social structure compared with the
national or London average shows a disproportionate and increasing
number of the elderly and the unskilled, a high concentration of
ethnic minorities, a low level of owner-occupation and high level of
private renting.

Such a concentration of problems is, of course, not repeated
throughout every inner London Borough, though many others
experience similar problems, and it is not necessarily typical of the
inner areas of other conurbations. London has tended to be the
focus of many studies of housing stress and, as is often pointed out,
national policies have perhaps too frequently been framed on the basis
of the London situation, which is by no means relevant to other areas.
London's problems, for example, are associated with absolute shortages,
a problem compounded by lack of land, to a greater extent than in
other conurbations where poor physical and environmental quality is
often more important.

A further factor that has intensified the housing problems of inner
cities has been the nature and the speed of the decline of the privately
rented sector. In general, the privately rented sector has provided low
cost accommodation, albeit often of a low quality as well, to low
income households. Low income families have become concentrated
in the private rented sector because they have little other choice, they
cannot afford to buy their own homes and there has not been sufficient
council accommodation. Poor families have also had to compete with a
steadily increasing demand from those wanting second homes, from
students and other single people moving into city centres and the

growth of tourism. The disruption caused by slum clearance and redevelopment schemes has particularly affected these groups and limited
the availability of low cost housing. More recently, the property boom
in the early 1970s caused further disruption, though the problems
associated with the boom may have been predominantly a London
phenomenon. There is widespread evidence that the boom led to an
acceleration in the decline of privately rented accommodation by
increasing the incentive of landlords to obtain vacant possession and
sell their properties or convert them into flats for sale, sometimes with
the aid of improvement grants. There is certainly evidence of increased
harassment and pressure by landlords to obtain possession during this
period.[6] There was also an acceleration in the rate of 'gentrification'
during this period whereby higher income groups moved into areas
previously occupied by working class families. This process has added
to the difficulties of lower income and mobile groups finding
accommodation in inner city areas by increasing house prices,
encouraging the transfer of housing stock from renting to owner-
occupation, and reducing occupancy rates.

The Policy Response

The main housing problems of inner cities are therefore the concentration of unfit, substandard and poor quality dwellings; the poor quality
of the general environment, including the high residential density of
many areas; the lack of gardens, open space and general social amenities;
and the persistence of housing shortages. Here we examine the policies
that have been used, their effectiveness and some policy alternatives. To
deal with these problems, successive governments have adopted a
mixture of general and specifically area-based policies. As we have
seen, while housing problems are concentrated in inner cities, they do
not have a monopoly of such problems, and area-based policies alone
can therefore only deal with a proportion of them. In addition, because
housing problems are closely linked with other problems including
unemployment and low income, these problems will not be solved by
housing action alone. Indeed, doubts have been expressed by a number
of authors about the efficacy of area-based policies on the grounds
that the majority of the deprived live outside such areas and that the
deprived are more effectively helped by national policies aimed at
individuals.[7]

The scale of the need for improvement in the condition of the
housing stock can be gauged from the 1976 House Condition Survey,
which found an estimated 894,000 unfit houses in England and Wales

or 5 per cent of the housing stock, and a further 984,000 fit but lacking one or more basic amenities. In addition, the survey found a further 580,000 dwellings, not unfit, but in disrepair requiring an expenditure on repairs of more than £2,000.[8] Table 8.2 shows the reduction in the number of unfit and substandard dwellings since 1967. The number of unfit dwellings has fallen by some 950,000. This fall is the net result of approximately 630,000 unfit dwellings being demolished, 990,000 being made fit, and a further 720,000 becoming unfit. Again, the fall in the number of houses lacking amenities is the result of a combination of factors. The number of dwellings in disrepair, in contrast, has risen sharply since 1971. These dwellings are not, of course, uniquely found in urban areas.

Table 8.2: Houses Unfit, and Fit but Lacking Basic Amenities, England and Wales (Thousands; percentages of total stock in brackets)

	Unfit	Fit but Lacking One or More Basic Amenities	Total
1967	1,836 (11.7)	2,371 (17.0)	4,207 (28.7)
1971	1,244 (7.3)	1,872 (11.8)	3,116 (19.1)
1976	894 (5.0)	984 (6.0)	1,878 (11.0)

Source: Department of the Environment, *Housing Policy Technical Volume I*, table B.1, p. 159.

Slum Clearance and Redevelopment

Until the late 1960s, the major element of policy to deal with the poor quality of housing was slum clearance and their replacement with new and theoretically better housing, a process also aimed at achieving housing gain in order to alleviate local shortages of housing. Between 1945 and 1954 the average annual rate of demolition was low at about 9,000 per annum, but this figure rose rapidly from 1954 to average 42,000 between 1955 and 1959, about 90,000 between 1960 and 1970, but has fallen steadily since then to below 50,000 since 1974. While these policies have made a major contribution to improving the quality of the housing stock, they have not been without undesirable consequences. It has been claimed that wholesale redevelopment schemes were pursued with too much vigour especially in the 1960s, resulting in widespread disruption of community life and loss of jobs. Since 1955, 1½m houses have been demolished in Britain. In the early 1970s, some of the largest cities were demolishing more houses than were being built. These programmes have had widespread ramifications on the local housing market, on the role of the public sector, on the cost of housing, on the appearance of our cities and on the communities affected, effects that were rarely accounted or planned for.[9] Critics have argued that such schemes were often unduly expensive and socially disruptive, that many of the houses cleared were of sufficiently good standard to have been retained and improved, and that greater emphasis should have been placed on rehabilitation. Moreover the new large scale estates built to accommodate families displaced by redevelopment have often created their own problems, and are sometimes characterised by higher levels of social deprivation than were evident in the areas from which the families came. In some cases, too great an emphasis on large scale slum clearance may therefore have intensified inner city housing problems.

The Emphasis on Improvement

Partly as a result of the findings of the 1967 House Condition Survey, which revealed more unfitness and disrepair than expected, and the developing criticisms of the effects of wholesale clearance, the emphasis of policy gradually shifted from the late 1960s towards renovation and gradual renewal. In 1968, the government published the White Paper, *Old Houses into New Homes*[10] which led to the 1969 Housing Act. This Act widened the scope of improvement grants, first introduced in the 1949 Housing Act, increased their value, and gave local authorities new but discretionary power to declare general improvement areas (GIAs). Within GIAs, grants cover 60 per cent of eligible expenses, compared with 50 per cent elsewhere, cost limits are higher, there are specific grants for environmental improvement of £200 per dwelling, and local authorities have slightly wider powers to assist and persuade owners to improve houses, and to buy land and houses needed for the improvement of whole areas. This reflected the new emphasis on rehabilitation compared with clearance and new building.

The effect of these new policies was a massive increase in the take-up of improvement grants which rose more than threefold between 1969 and 1973, though some of the increase is also a result of the house price boom of the early 1970s.[11] Since 1973, there has been a significant fall in the take-up of improvement grants, partly as a result of the new restrictive conditions on the availability of grants introduced in the 1974 Housing Act in order to prevent the misuse of the grant system that had become apparent during the property boom. Some landlords were evicting tenants, improving their property with the aid of a grant and selling to owner-occupiers. In addition, there is some evidence that the wider availability of improvement grants encouraged the process of gentrification. Another disturbing feature of the boost in improvement grant activity was the low propensity for privately rented property to be improved. Landlords have proved reluctant to make use of improvement grants, except when they have been able to first obtain vacant possession. Grants have not therefore been used to help those in greatest need and improve houses most in need of improvement, for poor housing conditions are concentrated in the privately rented sector. In summary, it is apparent that the improvement in housing conditions that took place in the years following the 1969 Act did not benefit private tenants to any significant extent and in some cases intensified housing stress and added to the shortage of housing to rent, since it was rarely existing tenants or other low income tenants who rented high cost accommodation or purchased property put on sale. The Housing Act of 1974 therefore introduced the rule whereby owner-occupiers must give an understanding on receipt of grant that property will be retained for five years for exclusive use of the family, and a landlord is required to keep the property available for letting for at least five years (seven in housing action areas and general improvement areas), in order to direct resources more positively to those in worst housing conditions, and keep improved rented accommodation in the rented sector.

The introduction of GIAs was the first main attempt at an area-based renewal strategy, aimed at concentrating improvement in areas consisting mainly of owner-occupiers and fundamentally sound housing, capable of providing good living accommodation for many years to come. The emphasis in these areas is on environmental improvement as well as house improvement and is based on a concept of voluntary improvement and persuasion. At May 1977, a total of 977 GIAs were operating containing some 289,000 houses. Of these GIAs, 88 are in Greater London, 363 in metropolitan counties and 526 in 'shire' counties. Such evidence as exists suggests that GIAs have stimulated grant aided improvement, and have at least halted a decline into decay and a need for inevitable clearance.[12] Nevertheless, GIAs are of limited significance and have had some undesirable consequences. Since 1969, only 5 per cent of all improvement grants have been in GIAs, and many grants in GIAs have gone to local authority property. GIAs also exclude areas with a high proportion of rented dwellings subject to blight and housing stress. As well as being inadequate for coping with stress, they have sometimes added to such stress, particularly in London, where they have contributed towards the gentrification of some areas, the displacement of existing occupants by the better off buying previously rented property for owner-occupation or paying higher rents.

Housing Action Areas

In view of these weaknesses, the 1974 Housing Act introduced a new concept of housing action areas (HAAs) designed to give priority to the improvement of areas for which GIAs are not relevant, where poor physical condition of housing combines with social stress and deprivation. In selecting suitable areas, the criteria used are the proportion of households sharing facilities, the proportion of overcrowded households, the extent of private renting and the concentration of households with special problems such as the elderly, single-parent families, the unemployed and the low paid.

HAAs were aimed at improving the moderate rate of improvement activity in GIAs while avoiding gentrification by giving local authorities new compulsory powers to acquire properties and enforce improvement. In addition to these new powers, households in HAAs are entitled to receive grants, including repair grants, at the higher rate of 75 per cent rising to 90 per cent in hardship cases. There is also a small environmental works grant of £50 available to improve the external appearance and grounds of a dwelling. The main objectives of HAAs are to secure an improvement in living conditions within houses themselves during the five year life of an HAA, while keeping the local community together and ensuring the well-being of those residing in the area.

This policy represents a clear break with the earlier approach to urban renewal based on demolition and redevelopment, and a continuation of the area approach, a response to the limitations of policies of extensive redevelopment, and the growing evidence of a concentration of housing problems in small areas. It also represented a move towards a social approach to urban renewal, in which HAAs are one element of a more general policy of gradual renewal. Indeed, HAAs and the other provisions of the 1974 Housing Act were introduced in combination with a number of policies at the time designed to complement each other in a more integrated and comprehensive housing programme. These policies included the granting of security of tenure to furnished tenants in the 1974 Rent Act, a new boost to municipalisation and local authority mortgage lending, and encouragement to housing association activity in the 1974 Housing Act through, among other measures, the strengthening of the Housing Corporation.

To what extent has this new policy approach been successful? In

England up to 31 May 1977, 194 HAAs were in operation containing some 70,000 dwellings. Of these, 44 are in Greater London, 112 in the metropolitan counties and 38 in the 'shire' counties, a contrast with GIAs which are concentrated in the shire counties. This of itself is slow progress, the number of declarations being small in relation to the potential number of HAAs. A recent joint Greater London Council, London Boroughs Association report, for example, identified 130 to 200 possible HAAs in London, heavily concentrated in inner London. The main reason for the slow rate of declaration is that local authorities have insufficient resources to declare all the HAAs that can be identified. The combined physical and social approach required in such areas is extremely resource intensive and demanding of specialist staff input and co-ordination between local authority departments, and this has acted as a major constraint. The improvement policy embodied in the 1974 Act has never been backed with adequate resources and unless the Government is prepared to make more funds available, declarations will continue to be slow.

Within those HAAs declared, progress has also been slow and slower than expected. One reason for this is that while one of the innovations of HAAs is the use of compulsory improvement powers, considerable reliance is still placed on voluntary improvement, but the rate of such improvement has been low. Private landlords have proved especially resistant to the use of grants, perhaps not surprisingly since they require adequate financial incentive to do so, and the return on investment is rarely justified by the expenditure incurred. This is an especially important factor since HAAs are meant to be areas with a high proportion of private renting. The take-up rate is also low among owner-occupiers. Take-up depends to a large extent upon the financial attractiveness of improvement, and particularly the relationship between the level of grant and the costs actually incurred, and hence the total costs of improvement, the amount considered eligible for grant, and the rate of grant. The costs to be met by the owner include those above the eligible costs, those above the grant ceiling, and 25 per cent of eligible costs (or 10 per cent in the case of special hardship), and these can sometimes be considerable. It has been estimated that, taking all grants, not just in HAAs, the average amount per dwelling contributed by the owner has risen from £1,520 in 1975 to £2,270 in March 1977, about 64 per cent of total costs.[13] Households that have little capital of their own, or that are not able to use it for the improvement of their home, are not therefore in a position to benefit from grants, and there is considerable evidence of the inability of owners to meet their share of the cost, which can be upwards of £1,000 for even modest improvements. One problem has been the failure to raise the ceiling eligible for grant in line with inflation, though this was increased in August 1977 from £3,200 to £5,000, such that the maximum grant payable in HAAs is now £3,750 (or £4,500 in the case of a 90 per cent grant). It remains to be seen whether this increase will promote additional take-up.

A contributory factor to the low rate of improvement has been the problem of lack of confidence by owners that the area in which they live will improve. Individual owners are unlikely to undertake extensive improvement if they think that so few others in the neighbourhood will also do so that property values will not increase sufficiently to compensate them for the expenditure incurred. Each owner is therefore heavily influenced by what he thinks other owners will do. Improvement is less likely to occur the less confident individual owners are of widespread neighbourhood improvement. One of the main objects of HAAs is to overcome these problems of interdependence and uncertainty that act as a disincentive to individual improvement and an encouragement to neglect and blight, by promoting co-operation and a concentration of improvement in order to raise the physical and environmental quality of the area. The success of the policy must depend to a large degree on the confidence with which local residents view its likely outcome, and this has to face the problem of many years of neglect, decay and uncertainty in these areas.

A further question about the nature of improvement policy and in particular the role of grant-aided improvement relates to the beneficiaries of such aid. While there is little evidence as to how grants to private owners are divided between landlords and owner-occupiers the lack of any economic reason for private landlords to use such grants implies that the majority of grants have gone to existing owner-occupiers, and among them, for the reasons given above, to better-off households. Since the new emphasis on improvement since 1969, it is almost certainly the case that financial assistance has been of disproportionate benefit to those with above average incomes. As Christine Whitehead has argued, policy changes

> have worked to bring about a different distribution of housing
> services than that which would have prevailed under the policies of
> the 1960s. In particular, more of the gain has gone to better quality
> dwellings and to existing owner-occupiers and local authority
> tenants, while less has been available to help those in the private
> rental sector.[14]

A second reason for the slow rate of improvement within HAAs has been the inadequacy of the compulsory powers provided to overcome the reluctance to improve. Within HAAs, local authorities have powers to serve provisional improvement notices on landlords who are unwilling voluntarily to improve their properties, and if they still do not carry out the improvement, this can be followed up with compulsory improvement notices. They also have wider powers to serve compulsory purchase orders

> when a house was in disrepair or lacking in standard amenities, and where those responsible were unable or unwilling to rehabilitate it; where multiple-ownership prejudiced the improvement of groups of dwellings; where tenants had been subjected to harassment; where a house in multiple-occupation was unsatisfactorily managed; or where housing was unreasonably being kept empty or unoccupied.[15]

According to one commentator, the main problem with these powers are that they are 'ponderous and slow and can only be used to enforce improvement up to minimum standards'.[16] It has been argued that well-informed owners can delay enforcement for over two years from being served with the first provisional notice, a major area of delay being the lag with which the Department of the Environment sometimes confirms the CPO. Others have argued, however, that 'powers do exist to carry through ambitious and imaginative schemes for revitalising rundown neighbourhoods of older houses' if only the powers are effectively used.[17] Another problem is that local authorities have themselves sometimes been slow to improve their own properties in such areas, yet this is a vital element in encouraging confidence in the future of the neighbourhood.

Another important factor in the success of urban renewal is the range of other policies available to local authorities. The ability of local authorities to promote improvement in areas of housing and social stress has been handicapped by successive cuts in public spending since 1975 which have restricted the rate of municipalisation, the rate of improvement of local authority dwellings, the availability of local authority mortgages and the level of housing association activity. Indeed, between 1973/4 and 1977/8, there was a 37 per cent decline in the volume of public sector improvement, a 40 per cent decline in local authority acquisitions, and a 70 per cent decline in private sector grant-aided improvement activity.[18] This has inevitably undermined the effectiveness of the new policy emphasis on improvement and rehabilitation. These are all elements needed to reinforce and complement action in HAAs and GIAs, and their restriction has presented an important constraint on local authority activity. These policy reversals have severely undermined the integrated and comprehensive approach to housing renewal embodied in the programmes introduced by the Labour Government in 1974.

Apart from the poor record of achievement to date, there are a number of more fundamental questions surrounding HAAs. In the first place, they do not deal with the basic causes of housing and social stress. To the extent that some of these causes are not area-based, but are related to wider factors, area-based policies alone will be ineffective. Of particular importance here is the effect of low income and poor access to decent accommodation, problems that can only be solved by more effective income maintenance policies and wider reforms of housing policy.

Another contributory factor to urban blight and decay that remains unaffected by HAA policy is the well-documented reluctance of building societies to lend in such areas.[19] Indeed, there is evidence that some building societies are not lending in HAAs at all. The difficulty faced by lower income households and other would-be buyers of older housing in inner urban areas represents a severe handicap to the regeneration of these areas. In addition to their reluctance to lend on older property, building society bias against manual and lower income groups discriminate against households that are often prepared to buy homes in these areas. Evidence shows that the great majority of buyers of older property in inner cities have borrowed from banks and finance companies rather than building societies, and because of the small proportion of the purchase price covered by loans, many buyers are forced to take out additional loans. A study of inner Birmingham between 1972 and 1974 found that only 27 per cent of buyers had conventional building society mortgages, and of the other buyers, 28 per cent had taken out additional loans, evidence confirmed by studies of other cities.[20] The marginal buyer in the inner city is typically paying much more for worse property with little chance of the capital appreciation necessary to improve their housing condition.

While the volume of local authority lending was increased in 1974/5, it has since been drastically reduced. As we have seen in Chapter 6, the support lending scheme set up by the government in 1976/7 to compensate for the cut in council lending has a number of serious flaws, in particular that building societies are still failing to lend to applicants and on houses that the scheme is intended to help, especially properties in need of repair and improvement. Buyers of older property are still forced to go to banks and finance houses, obtaining loans at much higher rates of interest and for much shorter periods. In addition, the option mortgage subsidy designed to help those with incomes too low to pay tax, is only available on building society and local authority mortgages, such that these borrowers may not even benefit from government subsidy. Existing arrangements are therefore heavily loaded against low income owner-occupiers and would-be buyers in inner cities, a factor contributing towards urban decay and frustrating improvement policies. Nevertheless the government has failed to take other action, and in its Green Paper, while claiming a concern for the revival of inner cities, makes no proposals for changes in policy.

Another weakness of the HAA approach is that within HAAs, the major emphasis is on the improvement of housing conditions rather than on the general environment, and the environmental grant of £50 per house is minimal. The intention of the legislation is that environmental improvement should await the subsequent declaration of a GIA. This approach ignores the fact that the quality of life is dependent on the feature of the locality as well as that of the dwelling, and that improvement to the area in terms of open space, social facilities and general attractiveness, should go hand in hand with housing improvements. This is particularly important if sufficient confidence is to be restored to encourage voluntary improvement. There is therefore a need for changes in existing arrangements in order to provide larger environmental grants for owners and for government subsidy for environmental works. It is not possible for local authorities to fund all such works from local resources.

A further qualification is that area based policies do not help those households living in poor houses outside GIAs and HAAs. We have already seen that poor housing conditions are not exclusively found in inner city areas, and in small areas within inner cities, and it is here that HAAs appear to be concentrated, though not GIAs. The fact that the declaration of HAAs is proceeding at a very slow pace means that the benefits of these areas will apply to only a small proportion of the total housing stock in poor condition, leaving the remainder to be tackled in other ways.

A final consideration relates to the old question of whether rehabilitation is a preferable alternative to clearance and redevelopment. We have seen how the emphasis on redevelopment has gradually shifted towards rehabilitation over the period since the early 1970s, until it was given full legislative endorsement in the 1974 Housing Act. Some have now argued that the pendulum may have swung too far in favour of modernisation, and that we may simply be storing up long term structural problems of obsolescence and decay by preserving older houses which must inevitably have a limited life. While clearance can be undertaken in HAAs, for example, it is rarely used.

The relevant factors have, of course, not changed, the appropriate policy depending on an assessment of the relative costs and benefits of renovation and redevelopment, taking into account both economic and social considerations. The main economic factors are that while rehabilitation is generally initially cheaper, because it involves fewer structural changes, the maintenance costs of renovated houses over their remaining lives are likely to be greater than in the case of new houses *and* modernised houses have a shorter physical life and need replacement much sooner. The benefits of the lower initial costs of rehabilitation therefore have to be compared with the net present value of the cost of rebuilding some time in the future *plus* the net present value of the extra maintenance costs over the life of the modernised dwellings. The calculation in the case of economic factors therefore depends crucially on the discount rate used, the life of the modernisation scheme and the difference in running costs. The less the initial cost of rehabilitation, the higher the discount rate, the longer the life of the rehabilitation scheme and the smaller the difference in running costs, the greater the economic advantage of modernisation.[21]

Economic factors have to be weighed against social considerations. It is generally argued that renovation creates less upheaval, less uncertainty, and avoids the breaking up of established neighbourhoods and social ties. This is of course true to a degree. Its force depends upon both the strength and durability of existing communities and on the quality of the new environment and accommodation that would be provided by redevelopment. Too often in the past, as we have argued, the alternatives provided have been little better than what has been replaced. The more attractive and inviting the new development the less serious the problem of disruption caused. Another social argument in favour of rehabilitation is that renovation is quicker and therefore causes less blight. This is so in the case of the installation of amenities and other minor improvements, but may not be so in the case of a large-scale rehabilitation of a run-down area. The question of rehabilitation or redevelopment therefore remains a complex issue that allows for no simple rule; the appropriate action can only be determined in the context of the local situation.

Inner City Initiatives

GIAs and HAAs are not the only policies used to alleviate housing problems in inner city areas. A number of aspects of current and intended national housing policy are of benefit to urban areas. These include, for example, the generally greater emphasis on gradual renewal and rehabilitation; the proposals for a Tenants' Charter to strengthen tenants' rights and increase their involvement in the management of estates which should help to increase the status of tenants and relieve the sense of frustration and alienation that is widespread on many estates in the inner city; the encouragement of other forms of tenure which may help to prevent the loss of skilled workers from inner cities; the new housing investment programme which is claimed will give greater priority to urban areas in the allocation of loan sanction.

In addition, the increasing realisation of the spatial concentration of problems has led, in the last decade, to a number of specifically area-based policies aimed particularly at the inner cities. While these policies have been directed at the whole range of urban problems, not just housing, any success at dealing with these wider problems of industrial decline, environmental decay, population imbalance and low incomes will contribute towards the relief of housing problems. The Urban Aid Programme was introduced in 1968 designed to help certain communities in areas of special need by providing special grants for local authorities to finance locally based projects such as play schemes, nursery schools, advice centres, language classes for immigrants, etc. The scheme is still functioning and its grant has been increased from an annual level of £4m to £30m in 1977/8 and to £125m in 1979/80, and it has been extended to cover industrial, environmental and recreational provision as well as social projects. In 1969, the Home Office set up the National Community Development Project, a neighbourhood based action research experiment, carried out in 12 selected urban localities, aimed at finding new ways of meeting the needs of people living in areas of high social deprivation, by, for example, improving the co-ordination of existing services and involvement of local people and groups. In 1973, the Inner Area Studies were set up to be carried out by consultants in Small Heath in Birmingham, Central Lambeth in London and Liverpool 8, with the object of identifying in some detail the problems of the areas and finding ways in which they might be improved. In 1974, Comprehensive Community Programmes were introduced as a way of dealing with areas of intense urban deprivation, and are now under way in Motherwell and

Gateshead.

Following the White Paper *Policy for the Inner Cities* published in June 1977, and growing largely out of the three inner areas studies, the government in 1978 has designated seven partnership areas in which schemes to revitalise the inner city are to be developed and co-ordinated through joint action by the local authority, the government, the education and health authorities and voluntary and community groups. The seven partnership areas are: Birmingham, Liverpool, Manchester/ Salford, Newcastle/Gateshead, and in London, Lambeth, Hackney/ Islington and Docklands, and are to receive priority under the new enhanced urban programme which has been transferred from the Home Office to the Department of the Environment and had its fund increased from its present level of less than £30m to £125m in 1979/80. In addition, the government has asked 15 other local authorities to prepare city programmes. The partnership areas are to receive £70m of the £125m urban programme, and the programme authorities £25m, leaving only £30m for the rest of England and Wales. Each partnership is intended to last for ten years and will receive in the order of an additional £5m a year from 1978/9 over the ten years, from the urban programme towards the funding of local projects. In addition, the government has allocated £57m for construction works for partnership areas out of £87m announced by the Chancellor in his budget statement of 29 March 1977. The government has also been using the rate support grant to increase the level of resources going to inner cities, by increasing the share of the total grant received by inner cities, especially London, and reducing the share going to the shire counties.[22] The White Paper also gave a commitment to review existing legislation in the light of the problems of inner cities.

Until the publication of the White Paper, these specifically inner city initiatives were at the best only modest in intention and effect. The emphasis had been on research and experiment in order to identify what should and can be done. Very few additional resources had been provided, and the measures taken had only been cosmetic.

It is too early to comment on the effectiveness of the new partner- ship and other measures introduced as a result of the White Paper. There are signs of a greater commitment to inner cities as a result of the increased funding for the urban programme and the redistribution of the rate support grant to the conurbations. Nevertheless, a number of reservations can be made about the current programme. Firstly, doubts have been raised about the objectivity of the criteria used to select the seven partnership and 15 programme areas. Secondly, the concentration of the urban programme funds, nearly 60 per cent of it, in the partnership areas leaves little for the other stress areas. Thirdly, despite the extra funds, the annual increases remain minuscule in relation to the extent of the problems they are designed to alleviate, and the current revenue and capital expenditure of the local authorities benefitting. Fourthly, it appears that the partnership schemes are resulting in new and complex bureaucratic structures designed to co-ordinate the various participating agencies in determining the local programme, and will tie up considerable manpower resources, and skilled manpower at that, for what appears may be a marginal return. Finally, in relation to housing specifically, and this is not a criticism, the emphasis in these designated areas is on industrial regeneration and job creation, as reflected in the Inner Urban Areas Bill which is designed to enable local authorities to give financial assistance to industry and provide them with stronger powers to promote industrial activity. The benefit to housing will depend largely on the proportion of the additional funds used for housing projects, which it is intended should be small, the use of the housing investment programme procedure and the rate support grant to concentrate help in inner cities, any changes in existing legislation that may benefit inner cities, and the impact of the proposed new subsidy system in the national allocation of housing subsidies.

Summary and Conclusions

There is evidence that certain housing problems are concentrated in certain inner city areas, though it must be emphasied that a majority of such problems are not found in these areas and a majority of households in such areas are not generally suffering from housing stress. Area-based policies that concentrate action in selected areas of our inner cities and in selected cities therefore have an important role to play, but only as part of wider nationally based policies. Inner city deprivation and housing stress are the result of a wide range of social, economic and political forces, and locally based housing programmes alone cannot deal with the underlying causes of inner city decline. Policies which treat the symptoms of such decline must go hand in hand with national measures which deal with the basic causes of structural change, economic decline and income inequality.

A number of special national and area-based policies have been employed and have had some success in dealing with housing stress. The House Condition Surveys, for example, have shown that between 1967 and 1976, the proportion of houses unfit or fit but lacking a basic amenity fell from 28.7 per cent to 11 per cent of the total stock. In recent years, the emphasis of policy has shifted from redevelopment to gradual renewal, a process which culminated in the introduction of housing action areas in the 1974 Housing Act. These have had limited impact to date. Indeed, little progress seems to have been made since 1974 in dealing with the backlog of bad housing conditions; the rate at which houses have deteriorated into fitness and disrepair may only just have been equalled by the rate of improvement. With some changes and above all more resources, however, existing policies can be made more effective in relieving housing and social stress. To improve the take-up of grants, especially in the privately rented sector, more flexibility in the conditions, more 90 per cent grants, and more repair grants are needed. Repair grants should be introduced outside HAAs and GIAs. More emphasis should also be given to environmental improvement by, for example, giving higher environmental grants, and allowing local authorities subsidies for environmental works. Local authority improvement powers in such areas need to be simplified and strengthened, and delays by central government reduced. The new wider approach introduced in the partnership areas are potentially of value, but the basic key to success is the provision of more resources for improvement and municipalisation.

Notes

1. *Policy for the Inner City* (London, HMSO, Cmnd 6845, June 1977).
2. S. Holtermann, 'Areas of Urban Deprivation in Great Britain: An Analysis of 1971 Census Data', *Social Trends*, vol. 6 (London, HMSO, 1975), pp. 33-47.
3. The EDs included in the study were urban EDs and covered 87,578 Districts compared with 120,00 in GB as a whole. These contained an average of 163 households (470 persons).
4. Department of the Environment, *Housing Policy, A Consultative Document* (London, HMSO, Cmnd 6851, 1977), para. 13.12.
5. London Borough of Lambeth, *Lambeth Community Plan, 1978* (London, April 1978), vol. 3.
6. See. S. Lansley and G. Fiegehen, *One Nation? Housing and Conservative Policy*, Fabian Tract 432 (London, Fabian Society, 1974), ch. 5.
7. See D. Donnison, 'Policies for Priority Areas', *Journal of Social Policy*, vol. 3, no. 2 (1974), pp. 127-35; P. Townsend,' Area Deprivation Policies', *New Statesman* (6 August 1976), pp. 168-71. For an alternative view, see S. Holtermann, 'The Welfare Economics of Priority Area Policies', *Journal of Social Policy*, vol. 7, no. 1 (1978), pp. 23-40.
8. Department of the Environment, *Housing Policy Technical Volume III* (London, HMSO, 1977), table B.7, p. 151. Some of these may also have been substandard.
9. See J.B. Cullingworth, *Problems of an Urban Society*, vol. II (London, Allen and Unwin, 1972), ch. 3.

10. *Old House into New Homes* (HMSO, Cmnd 3602, 1968).

11. Table 1.1, ch.1.

12. See Department of the Environment, *Housing Policy Technical Volume III*, ch. 10, para. 88.

13. G. Lomas and E. Howes, 'Private Sector Improvement Since the 1975 Act', *Centre for Environmental Studies Review*, no. 2 (London, December 1977).

14. C. Whitehead, 'Where Have All the Dwellings Gone?', *Centre for Environmental Studies Review*, no. 1 (London, July 1977), p. 46.

15. Department of the Environment, *Circular 14/75* (January 1975), para. 48.

16. Chris Paris, 'Housing Action Areas', *Roof* (London, Shelter, January 1977), p. 12.

17. Chris Holmes, 'Islington's Tough Approach Works', *Roof* (London, Shelter, May 1977), p. 81.

18. See ch. 4, Table 4.6

19. Stuart Weir, 'Red Line Districts', *Roof* (London, Shelter, July 1976), p. 109.

20. Valarie Karn, 'Housing Policies Which Handicap Inner Cities', *New Society* (London, 11 May 1978), p. 301.

21. See L. Needleman, *The Economics of Housing* (London, Staples Press, 1965); E.M.Sigsworth and R.K. Wilkinson,'Rebuilding or Renovation?', *Urban Studies*, vol. 4, no. 2 (June 1967), pp. 109-21; L. Needleman, 'Rebuild or Renovation? A Reply', *Urban Studies*, vol. 5, no. 1 (February 1968), pp. 86-90; L. Needleman, 'The Comparative Economics of Improvement and New Building', *Urban Studies*, vol. 6, no. 2 (June 1969), pp. 196-209.

22. See R. Jackman and M. Sellers, 'The Distribution of RSG', *Centre for Environmental Studies Review*, no. 1. (London, July 1977), pp. 19-30.

INDEX